Copyright in Historical Perspective

Lyman Ray Patterson

Vanderbilt University Press

Nashville :

04 03 02 01 00   5 4 3 2 1

Library of Congress Catalogue
Card Number 68-22415
ISBN 0-8265-1373-5 (paper)

Preface

THE STUDY of the history of copyright has been left largely to bibliographical scholars and, the excellence of their endeavors indicates, justifiably so. But for the work of these dedicated men, this book could not have been written, and the fact that it relies so heavily on their superb efforts indicates the obvious. This study is intended to serve a different purpose—to view copyright in a historical perspective from a legal standpoint.

Lawyers and judges have, generally, ignored the history of copyright in litigation, and when they have resorted to history, they have more often than not been mistaken. The blame, however, does not rest heavily on their shoulders. Lawyers are concerned with winning cases, judges with deciding them, and the opportunity of delving into the complicated history of copyright has not been available to them.

Still, to view copyright in its historical perspective may be of some use to men of law, for a historical perspective may reveal aspects of law which logical analysis does not bring into focus. With the increasing importance of industrial or intellectual property, of which copyright is a part, the "logic of experience", to use Professor Willard Hurst's perceptive phrase, may well be of aid in analyzing many troublesome problems in this field. Thus, the "logic of experience" that the history of copyright reveals suggests that the approach most likely to yield profitable results in the future is to separate the creative interest and the economic interest of the author, which have been combined under copyright. Such an approach would leave the way open for the development of a federal common law of literary property, consonant with the statutory copyright, and provide a sounder basis from which to deal with copyright problems than has been used in the past. At the least, a historical perspective provides a new way of looking at old problems.

The most pleasant part of concluding my work on this book is the opportunity to give public expression to the gratitude I feel to those who have so graciously helped me and prevented many errors of judgment, and otherwise. Not all of them can be acknowledged, and their success in preventing my mistakes may be less than they would have wished. For that only I am to blame.

To Dean James C. Quarles of the Walter F. George School of Law, Mercer University, my thanks for his aid and cooperation in the beginning of this endeavor. To Dean John W. Wade of the School of Law, Vanderbilt University, my thanks for his aid and cooperation as my efforts continued. To Professor Robert N. Covington of the Vanderbilt Law Faculty, my thanks for his willingness to read and criticize, always with insight and understanding.

And, finally, to Professor Elliott E. Cheatham of the Vanderbilt Law Faculty, for his unfailing kindness, his continued encouragement, and his ever ready willingness to make me a beneficiary of his experience and wisdom, I must say: "Thanks, thanks, and ever thanks."

Lyman Ray Patterson

Nashville, Tennessee
March 1968

Table of Contents

Copyright in Historical Perspective

1

Overview

"WHAT IS its history—its judicial history? It is wrapt in obscurity and uncertainty." Common-law copyright was the subject of inquiry. The question, asked in the landmark case of American copyright law, *Wheaton v. Peters*, was posed by Circuit Judge Joseph Hopkinson in the lower court opinion.[1] The obscurity and uncertainty of which he spoke extended back into sixteenth-century English history. It was manifest in the first major English decision on copyright, *Millar v. Taylor*,[2] in 1769, sixty years after the enactment of the Statute of Anne, the English copyright act of 1709.[3]

The Statute of Anne, a successor to sixteenth- and seventeenth-century legislation in England, served as a model both for the early American states' copyright acts and for their successor, this country's first federal copyright act in 1790.[4] Construing the federal act in 1834, the U.S. Supreme Court in the *Wheaton* case followed the second major English decision on copyright, *Donaldson v. Beckett*,[5] rendered in the House of Lords sixty years earlier, in 1774. The English line of descent for American copyright law was thus confirmed.

1. 29 Fed. Cas. 862, 871 (No. 17 486) (C.C.E.D. Pa. 1832). The opinion is also reprinted in 33 U.S. (8 Pet.) 725, Appendix II. (Brightly's 3rd ed.)

2. 4 Burr. 2303, 98 Eng. Rep. 201.

3. 8 Anne, c. 19. The statute was enacted in the calendar year 1709 and became effective in April 1710. At this time, however, the beginning of the year in England was March 25. It was not until 1752 that January 1st was designated as the beginning of the year in England by the Calendar Act of 1750. 24 Geo. II, c. 23. By modern reckoning, the statute was both enacted and became effective in 1710.

4. 1 Stat. 124.

5. 4 Burr. 2408, 98 Eng. Rep. 257, 2 Bro. P.C. 129, 1 Eng. Rep. 837; 17 COBBETT'S PARL. HIST. 953–1003 (1813).

3

While modern American copyright law is descended directly from the Statute of Anne, it is the earlier period of English copyright, so little understood in the *Millar* and *Donaldson* cases, that is of primary interest here. A convenient beginning date for a study of this earlier period is 1557, the date the members of the book trade received a royal charter and became the Company of Stationers of London. The events of the hundred-and-fifty-year period from the incorporation of the Stationers' Company to the enactment of the Statute of Anne were a prelude to the decisive events from 1709 to 1774, which determined the course of modern Anglo-American copyright. The line of historical development prior to the Statute of Anne has three principal features: the stationer's copyright, the printing patent, and government press control.

The inevitability of a need for protecting published works after Caxton introduced the printing press into England in 1476 makes it almost certain that, in a manner not entirely clear, members of the book trade had developed some form of copyright prior to receiving their charter of incorporation in 1557. The grant of a royal charter, however, gave added dignity and powers which the company used in giving definitive form to its copyright.

The term "copy right," however, was not used in the Stationers' Company records until 1701, and then only twice.[6] In the early days of printing, the term "copy" was used by the stationers to mean what today is called "copyright," and it was also used as signifying the manuscript in much the same way the term "copy" is used today.[7] The term "stationer's copyright" identifies the "right to copy" issued and regulated by the stationers, and is to be distinguished from the later statutory copyright provided by the Statute of Anne. The term "common-law copyright"—that is, a copyright recognized by the common-law courts—distinguishes that concept from the statutory copyright and the stationer's copyright. One of the major contro-

---

6. III EYRE & RIVINGTON, A TRANSCRIPT OF THE REGISTERS OF THE WORSHIPFUL COMPANY OF STATIONERS, 1640–1708 A.D. 494, 496 (1914), hereafter referred to as EYRE & RIVINGTON.

7. " . . . entred by commaundment from master warden newbery vnder his own handwryting on ye backside of ye wrytten copie." I EDWARD ARBER, A TRANSCRIPT OF THE REGISTERS OF THE COMPANY OF STATIONERS, 1554–1610 A.D. 440 (1875), hereafter referred to as ARBER.

versies in copyright history centered on the meaning and existence of the common-law copyright, which the House of Lords defined as the right of first publication in the *Donaldson* case.

The name "stationer's copyright" comes from its progenitor, the Stationers' Company, and it was a private affair of the company. The common-law courts had no part in its development, for it was strictly regulated by company ordinances. The Stationers' Company granted the copyright, and since it was developed by and limited to company members, it functioned in accordance with their self-interest. This early copyright was deemed to exist in perpetuity, and the owner could publish the protected work, or assign, sell or bequeath the copyright, but only in accordance with company regulations. The primary purpose of the stationer's copyright was to provide order within the company, which in effect meant within the book trade, since all members of the trade—bookbinders, printers, and booksellers (in modern terms, publishers)—belonged to the Stationers' Company. Authors, not being members of the company, were not eligible to hold copyright, so that the monopoly of the stationers meant that their copyright was, in practice and in theory, a right of the publisher only. Not until after the Statute of Anne did the modern idea of copyright as a right of the author develop.

The basis of the printing patent, an exclusive right granted by the sovereign to publish a work, was the royal prerogative. Except for its source and the fact that it was limited in time, the printing patent was a copyright very similar to the stationer's copyright. Indeed, it may have served as the model for that copyright, which it apparently preceded. The printing patent, too, protected the right of exclusive publication, and in the early days of the Stationers' Company, it was more desirable than the company's copyright: as a grant of the sovereign, the printing patent contained its own sanctions and the patents covered the most profitable works to be printed—bibles, prayer books, and school books, most notably the *ABC*, the first reading book placed in the hands of Elizabethan children and probably the most profitable book on the market.[8] Although printing patents were not limited to

8. For a history of the printing of this book, see Anders, *The Elizabethan ABC with the Catechism*, XVI THE LIBRARY, 4th ser., 32 (1935).

members of the company, stationers were the most frequent grantees, and the company itself was the grantee of valuable printing patents from James I in 1603 and 1616. Thus, the value of the printing patent to the stationers during the early years of the period here involved, when the royal prerogative was at its height, was great indeed. Gradually, however, as the prerogative was circumscribed and as English writers increasingly produced enduring works, the stationer's copyright, unlimited in time, surpassed the printing patent in importance, until, by the end of the period, the latter was of little significance.

The efficacy of the stationer's copyright depended upon the power of the company to control printing and publishing, which helps to explain the role of censorship and press control in the early development of copyright. During almost the whole of the period from 1557 to 1709, a time of continuous religious struggle, censorship was a major policy of the English government. This policy made it convenient for the government to give the stationers large powers, which it did in increasing measure, in order to have them serve as policemen of the press. The stationers were eager to receive these powers—indeed, actively sought them—for they meant a more effective control of the book trade and thus stronger support for their copyrights.

Prior to the Licensing Act of 1662,[9] the government's acts of censorship were the Star Chamber Decrees of 1566, 1586, and 1637, in addition to three acts in the 1640s during the Interregnum. These acts of censorship, sustaining the Stationers' Company's copyrights, became the main support of the company's monopoly; and the final lapse in 1694 of the Licensing Act of 1662, the last of the censorship acts, meant more than the end of censorship: it meant also the end of legal sanctions for the stationer's copyright. The Licensing Act, based on the Star Chamber Decree of 1637, was a comprehensive statute, and in addition to the censor's license, it required the stationer's copyright for published works. Without this latter requirement, there was no law to prevent one from printing published works at will. The Stationers' Company, in anticipation of the end of censorship, had strengthened its ordinances concerning copyright several years earlier,

9. 13 & 14 Car. II, c. 33.

but the demise of the parliamentary statute created uncertainty as to the rights of copyright owners. Even so, fifteen years passed before those most affected by the absence of a copyright law, the booksellers, succeeded in securing new legislation from Parliament—the Statute of Anne—to protect published works.

Popular resentment against their monopoly, not lack of effort, explains the delay, for notwithstanding the end of the Licensing Act, the booksellers adhered to their trade customs. The strength of their monopoly, based on the perpetual nature of the stationer's copyright and its limitation to stationers, and their control of the trade were such that the absence of an effective copyright law was more of an irritation than a threat to their position.

Even after the Statute of Anne made copyright immediately available to anyone, it was over sixty years before the issue of the booksellers' monopoly was finally resolved. Part of the delay there was because the new legislation gave renewed protection for the old copyrights, as the stationer's copyrights were then called, for a period of twenty-one years from the effective date of the act, 1710. Thus, the Statute of Anne protected the monopoly of the booksellers until 1731, when they began extensive efforts to gain new protection, continuing all the while to exercise their monopoly. The result was the "Battle of the Booksellers," a battle the monopolists finally lost in 1774 in *Donaldson v. Beckett*, which limited the protection of published works to the statutory copyright.

Since this country's first federal copyright in 1790 was modelled after the Statute of Anne, the U.S. Supreme Court in *Wheaton v. Peters*[10] naturally followed the *Donaldson* case as precedent, and American copyright descends directly from the stationer's copyright through the Statute of Anne.

The obscurity and uncertainty of the history of common-law copyright which plagued Judge Hopkinson in 1834 have remained. The Supreme Court, in following the *Donaldson* case, effectively blunted efforts to gain recognition in this country for a common-law copyright of published works and limited the protection of works after publi-

10. 33 U.S. (8 Pet.) 591 (1834).

cation to statutory copyright, as in England. It is not surprising, then, that subsequently little inquiry has been made into the origin of rights the Supreme Court had held not to exist. Even so, such an inquiry might have been helpful, for it would have shed light on the nature of copyright.

The modern concept of copyright is difficult, complex, and on the whole, unsatisfactory. In 1961, the Register of Copyrights, in connection with the fourth general revision of the copyright law in some one hundred and fifty years, defined copyright as "a legal device to give authors the exclusive right to exploit the market for their works. It has certain features of property rights, personal rights, and monopolies. The principles . . . [of which] are not always appropriate for copyright."[11] This statement points up the basic and continuing weakness of copyright law in this country, the absence of fundamental principles for copyright. As it implies, "No workable, unifying concept of copyright has yet been formulated."[12]

The failure to formulate a workable, unifying concept of copyright can be traced to the events in England during the eighteenth century, when the major development in copyright history occurred. This development was the change of copyright from a right of the publisher to a right of the author. The change is not often perceived, for the history of modern copyright begins with the Statute of Anne, and the earlier developments are generally ignored. Moreover, the idea of copyright as an author's right is now so firmly fixed in Anglo-American jurisprudence that superficially it may appear always to have been this way. But as history shows us, copyright began as a publisher's right, a right which functioned in the interest of the publisher, with no concern for the author. Indeed, it existed as such for over a hundred and fifty years before it was changed into an author's right, a right deemed to function primarily in the interest of the author. To appreciate the significance of the change, it is necessary to understand the nature of the stationer's copyright, the statutory copyright pro-

---

11. Staff of House Comm. on the Judiciary, 87th Cong. 1st Sess., Report of the Register of Copyrights on the General Revision of the U.S. Copyright Law 6 (Comm. Print 1961).

12. Morris Ebenstein, *Introduction* to Stanley Rothenberg, Copyright Law xix–xx (1956).

vided for by the Statute of Anne, and the reasons for and the consequences of the change.

Any attempt to state the precise nature of the stationer's copyright calls for a word of caution. Since businessmen developed and shaped it to their own ends, there was little or no regard for underlying principles or a sound theoretical basis for copyright. The records of the company on which one must rely are incomplete, and even if they were complete, one could not expect to find a statement of the concept of copyright articulated with satisfying precision. Moreover, the stationer's copyright existed for over a hundred and fifty years regulated not only by the common law, but by guild ordinances and acts of censorship. And, during this time, growth and change, resulting from events and forces directed by persons concerned with copyright only as a means to an end for themselves, were inevitable. Still, there is sufficient information upon which to base dependable conclusions.

Of certain facts about the stationer's copyright we can be relatively certain. As it was granted by the company, limited to members and regulated by company ordinances, a record of it was maintained only in the company registers. Copyrights were often owned jointly, were frequently pledged as security, and disputes over the ownership of copyright were determined by the governing body of the Stationers' Company, the Court of Assistants. Works subject to copyright included not only writings, but also maps, portraits, official forms, and even statutes. Meager as these facts are, when considered in context, they reveal much.

The stationer's copyright was strictly a right of the publisher and, unlike today's copyright, was almost certainly limited in scope. At one time during the period of its greatest use, there was an analogous printer's right, a right of the printer as copyright was a right of the publisher. The obviously limited scope of the printer's right, merely a right to print a work, gives a clue to the limited scope of copyright, after which it was almost certainly patterned. The scope of copyright was the right to publish a work, and no more, for the stationer's copyright was literally a right to copy. The copyright owner did not own the subject work as such and was not free to alter it any more than the grantee of a printing patent was free to alter the work he was privileged by the sovereign to publish. The stationer's copyright, then, was a right to which a given work was subject rather than the ownership of the work itself as it is today, a point which bears further explanation.

Ownership consists of a series of rights of control over the subject of ownership: the right to use it, to alter it, to give it away, to sell it, to destroy it, and to prevent anyone else from doing likewise. It follows, then, that the fewer the rights, the more limited the ownership. A lease of a building, for example, gives one certain rights, but we do not usually think of these rights as constituting ownership, because they are limited. Even so, a perpetual lease would probably create such rights in the lessee as to make them a form of ownership, although ownership of another kind remained in the lessor.

The stationer's copyright can be analogized to a perpetual lease of personal property, a manuscript or copy, as it was called, for one specific purpose, that of publishing.

The right of publishing, however, did not vest the ownership of a work itself in the ordinary sense, for this would have given the holder of the right of publishing other rights incident to ownership. Since these other rights did not exist, not having been recognized by the law, the stationers owned only the right to publish, not the work itself. Thus, copyright itself was subject to ownership, but it was only a right to which the copyrighted work was subject. This, of course, left the ownership of the work itself in abeyance, a consequence of the fact that copyright was a concept created not by the common law, but by a special group for a special purpose, under special conditions. Rights of ownership must be defined and recognized by law, and there was no occasion for the law either to recognize or define other rights that would have constituted complete ownership of the copyrighted work.

It is not likely that the stationers gave this point much thought, for from their standpoint, there was no need to. To them, copyright was an economic property, a right which protected their investment from competitors. As businessmen, they would not feel any need to claim an ownership which gave them the right to alter a copyrighted work or change it in any way. The limited use to which they could put a copyrighted work, the variety of works subject to copyright which

they could not change if they wanted to, the joint ownership of copyrights, and the practice of pledging copyright as security all point to
one basic fact: the integrity of copyright as only a right to publish a
work was of paramount importance to stationers. To have recognized
the right of a copyright owner to change the copyrighted work and
acquire a new copyright would have endangered this integrity. It
would have established the basis for a dangerous precedent, facili-
tating a practice whereby rival stationers could more easily, by changing a work, acquire a competing copyright, as occasionally happened.
Moreover, the laws of censorship were an inhibiting factor in this
regard, for the stationer's copyright was essentially a trade-regulation
device which functioned not only in the interest of the publisher, but
also in the interest of the government.

To say that the stationer's copyright was a right of limited scope,
a right to which a given work was subject rather than the ownership
of the work itself, is not very satisfying from a legal standpoint. It
implies a continuing inchoate property, a type of property upon which
the common law did not look with favor. But the stationer's copyright was not a common-law concept at all; and to the stationers, the
limited scope of their copyright was sufficient. It is when that copyright is compared with the modern copyright that the limited scope of
the stationer's copyright is significant. Present day copyright, as an
author's right, embraces the entire property interest in a work. It gives
the copyright owner, theoretically the author, the right to publish the
work, to alter it, to change it in any way he chooses, to prepare derivative works, and to prevent others from doing likewise. Thus, the
limited scope of the stationer's copyright suggests the question of the
nature of the author's right in the period when the stationer's copyright flourished.

The nature of the author's rights recognized by the stationers is
even more difficult to ascertain than the nature of the copyright itself.
Superficially, the author gave up his rights in his works when he
sold the manuscript to the stationer. But the limited scope of the stationer's copyright implies that the stationers recognized that only the
author had a right to change or alter his work. Such a recognition
would have been consistent with the stationers' self-interest in maintaining the integrity of copyright, and it would have interfered not at

all with their monopoly. At the time, however, the problem of authors' rights was not sufficiently important to be a significant issue. Since only stationers were free to publish, the problem of monopoly existed only within the company itself, where the wealth of individual members would give them more power and the control of more copyrights than less fortunate members. And since the copyright owner was not free to alter or change the work, the author had no concern for protecting the integrity of his work, as there was nothing to do with it other than to print it. The problem of authors' rights thus did not become a significant issue until the eighteenth century, and then only because the booksellers made it so in an effort to perpetuate their monopoly after the Statute of Anne.

The Statute of Anne can be understood only when it is related to the history of events which preceded its enactment. That this has been done seldom, if at all, is indicated by the phrase which is often used to identify the statute: the first English copyright act.

The Statute of Anne was not the first English copyright act, for the earlier Star Chamber Decrees, the ordinances of censorship during the Interregnum, and the Licensing Act of 1662 were copyright as well as censorship acts.

The enactment of 1709 was the first *Parliamentary* English copyright act, except for the ordinances during the Interregnum; and it was the first copyright act without provisions for censorship. The relationship of the Statute of Anne to the acts of censorship is made clear by the fact that it is modelled after the copyright provisions of two of those acts, the Licensing Act of 1662 and the Star Chamber Decree of 1637, with modifications to deal with the problem of monopoly.

The importance of understanding this early eighteenth-century statute, long since superseded by other legislation, is that its provisions were the foundation upon which the concept of modern copyright was built. And notwithstanding the other forces and events which shaped copyright, it is impossible to study the Statute of Anne in the light of its historical perspective without feeling that it was never properly interpreted, and that had it been construed correctly, modern American copyright law would rest on much sounder principles than it does.

The central problem in analyzing the Statute of Anne is to determine the nature of the statutory copyright it provided for. From the perspective of today, one would almost certainly say that it provided for an author's copyright which embraced all of the author's rights in his work after publication. Yet, from the perspective of events preceding the enactment of the statute, such an interpretation is wholly untenable.

The statutory copyright, save in two respects, was intended to be no different from the stationer's copyright. At the time the Statute of Anne was enacted, there was only one concept of copyright known to the legislators—the stationer's copyright. Their problem was not to create a new copyright, but to limit the old, in order to destroy the monopoly of the book trade by the booksellers—who, incidentally, were the lobbyists for the legislation.

In such a context, it is not realistic to think that the legislators were intent on enlarging or changing the scope of copyright, and the provisions of the statute bear this out. The mechanics for obtaining the statutory copyright were substantially the same as for obtaining the stationer's copyright. There were only two major differences between the two copyrights, and both differences struck directly at the booksellers' monopoly: the statutory copyright was limited to a term of fourteen years, with a similar renewal term available only to the author; and statutory copyright was available to anyone, not to stationers only. Thus, the statutory copyright was not to be limited to the members of a guild, and it was not to exist in perpetuity.

It is these two provisions, however, that were to give color to the subsequent idea that the statutory copyright was an author's, rather than a publisher's right. They meant that only the author could have a renewal term, and that the author could, for the first time, own the copyright of his work himself. On the first point, the author was being used as an instrument against the monopolists, to prevent them from having the renewal term. On the second, the author could own the copyright only by virtue of the fact that anyone was now eligible to hold copyright. The steps an author took to obtain a copyright for his own work were no different from those required for anyone else.

Finally, it should be remembered that the Statute of Anne continued the existing copyrights, the stationer's copyrights, for a period of twenty-one years. This feature of the act was undoubtedly in re-

sponse to the booksellers' argument that without such continued protection they would suffer economic ruin—a questionable assumption,
but a valid argument. The booksellers were to use it again when they
sought new legislation.

The Statute of Anne was not primarily a copyright statute. Rather,
just as prior acts involving copyright were basically censorship acts,
the Statute of Anne was basically a trade-regulation statute. It was
designed to insure order in the book trade while at the same time preventing monopoly. In one respect, the statutory copyright was to
share a fate similar to that of the stationer's copyright: it was to be
shaped by events and forces directed by persons concerned with
copyright only as a means to an end for themselves and not for the
author. The irony is not that this should have been so, but that in the
process copyright should have come to be known as an author's right.

The purpose of the Statute of Anne, then, was to provide a copyright that would function primarily as a trade regulation device—acting in the interest of society by preventing monopoly, and in the
interest of the publisher by protecting published works from piracy,
as did the stationer's copyright. Yet, it was construed as providing for
an author's right.

There were several reasons for this. The precise nature of the stationer's copyright was never appreciated by the common-law courts,
which had no part in its development. Moreover, the Statute of Anne
was not given a definitive construction until some sixty-five years after
its enactment, when the House of Lords was concerned primarily with
making it an effective instrument in destroying the booksellers' monopoly. During this interval, the booksellers continually represented
copyright to the courts as an author's right—a tenable position, since
the statute was beneficial to authors, as almost any statute designed
to destroy the booksellers' monopoly was bound to be. More significantly, however, the stationers apparently never claimed the ownership of a work, as opposed to the ownership of copyright; and the
common-law courts readily assumed this ownership to exist in the
author as creator. The common-law judges thus easily equated copyright with this ownership, for they could not conceive of copyright
based on the nonownership of the subject work. Thus, by presenting
the copyright to the courts as an author's right, the booksellers so

effectively tied in the author with copyright that copyright became known exclusively as an author's right.

The story of how and why they did this is the story of the Battle of the Booksellers. After the expiration of the twenty-one-year period of grace provided for the stationer's copyright by the Statute of Anne, the booksellers sought to perpetuate their monopoly. First, they lobbied for new legislation from Parliament, and failing in this, they resorted to litigation. Their argument in the courts was simple and appealing—the author, they said, had a perpetual common-law copyright in his work, based on his natural rights, since he had created it. Having this common-law copyright, which existed independently of the statutory copyright, the author could assign it to the bookseller. This invariably he was alleged to have done, as it was booksellers and not authors who were litigating. Since the custom was for the author always to assign his rights to the bookseller, their strategy was obvious. Once the courts accepted the author's common-law copyright in perpetuity, the booksellers would have succeeded in reviving the stationer's copyright under a different name, and their monopoly would be safe, despite the limitations imposed by the Statute of Anne.

In spite of the transparency of their strategy, the booksellers almost succeeded. They successfully tied in their rights with the rights of authors, and once this was done, their arguments as to the natural rights of the author as creator of the work were appealing and difficult to refute. They did succeed, in 1769, in getting the Court of King's Bench in *Millar v. Taylor* to accept their argument by a vote of three justices to one. The outstanding opinion of the three justices was that of Lord Mansfield, who based his recognition of the author's common-law copyright wholly on the natural rights of the author, because, as he said, "It is just."

The *Millar* case was not appealed, and it was overturned by the House of Lords in the *Donaldson* case, five years later. The importance of the *Millar* case, however, is greater than its short existence as precedent indicates, for it was this case that firmly fixed the idea of copyright as an author's right. Even more significant is the fact that it recognized copyright under the common law as a natural right of the author.

Except for the *Millar* case, the idea of copyright as an author's right might have gone by the board, for the opinions in the *Donaldson* case carefully avoided the use of the term copy or copyright. The judges spoke instead of the right of "printing and publishing for sale." The choice of language may or may not have been fortuitous, but it was consistent with an effort to avoid the dilemma the judges faced. They were faced with the oppressive monopoly, which continued in flagrant disregard of the limitations imposed by the Statute of Anne; and with the idea, so firmly and clearly delineated in the *Millar* case, that an author as creator has natural rights in his works which should be recognized by the law. Their solution was simple: they acceded to the author's natural rights in his work until publication by acknowledging for the first time the so-called common-law copyright. They then limited his protection after publication to the statutory copyright.

Even after the *Donaldson* case, it would have been possible to concede, independently of statutory copyright, rights in the author based on the fact of his creation. Such a closely analyzed interpretation of the case, however, was not feasible without a clear understanding of the history of copyright, for after the *Donaldson* case, copyright itself was deemed to be a monopoly of a work, rather than the basis of the monopoly of the book trade. Here, too, the *Millar* case had its effect, for Justice Yates in his dissenting opinion had argued that while an author does have natural rights in his works, he voluntarily forfeits those rights to the world if he publishes the work without statutory copyright.

The ownership of the work itself, a matter held in abeyance under the stationer's copyright, was coming to be recognized as existing in the author. The fiction of voluntary forfeiture, however, provided a facile escape from the dilemma which emerged as copyright became an author's right: the idea that copyright was both a natural right of the author and a monopoly. It also obscured the basic points that the monopoly with which the lawmakers were concerned was not a monopoly of authors but of publishers, and that the monopoly of the book trade owed its existence as much to the monopoly of the Stationers' Company as to copyright.

Little, if any, consideration was given to the fact that recognition of rights in the author as creator of a work did not make it necessary to allow those same rights to the publisher or copyright owner. Here emerges what is probably a major consequence of the fact that the common-law courts had no role in the early development of copyright. That the common-law courts, given the opportunity, would have recognized such rights of the author is strongly indicated by the cases in the first three-quarters of the eighteenth century, showing that the English courts were genuinely sympathetic to the rights of authors. Indeed, the *Millar* case and the closeness of the *Donaldson* decision are prime examples. Unfortunately, however, by this time, copyright had been in existence well over a hundred and fifty years without the aid of the common law. When the opportunity arrived, it was too late. The courts no longer had time to work out in the careful, case-by-case method of the common law, the problem of distinguishing and defining the rights of an author as creator from those of the publisher as entrepreneur. The custom was for the author to convey all his rights to the publisher; the problem was the booksellers' monopoly. The custom was too strong, the problem was too pressing. And the idea of copyright as a monopoly of the work itself together with the idea that copyright is a natural right of the author remained to create the conceptual dilemma of modern copyright. This dilemma is the idea that an author has a natural right in his work, combined with the idea that after publication he possesses only a monopoly conferred by statute.

Subsequent lawmakers in the United States gave greater weight to the idea of copyright as a monopoly than to the idea of it as an author's natural right. But the idea that copyright is an author's right, in some vague measure based on his natural rights, continued to exist and had a subtle effect on the concept, for it enlarged the scope of copyright. While the publisher's right in a book has no basis other than contract, an author's right in his work, whatever form that right takes, is based on the fact of his creation. Lawmakers, both legislative and judicial, could say, as they did, that an author forfeited all rights in his work after publication if he did not obtain the statutory copyright. It would have been going too far, however, to say that the author's rights in his work as protected by copyright were limited to the exclusive right of publication. After copyright became an author's right, it was inevitable that it cease to be merely a right to which a given work was subject and that it come to embrace the author's entire interest in his work.

Copyright, however, was not limited to the author, and since the rights embraced in copyright were those of the copyright owner and not the author, the publisher benefited by the enlarged scope of copyright. The result was that copyright gave the copyright owner complete control of the copyrighted work. The problem of one type of monopoly was substituted for another.

The major consequence of the change of copyright from a publisher's right to an author's right, then, was this: instead of being a limited right in connection with a work for an unlimited period of time, it became an unlimited right for a limited period of time. Unfortunately, the lawmakers passed over the desirable alternative which the Statute of Anne might have been interpreted to provide—a limited right for a limited period of time.

Acceptance of this alternative would have had two results: it would have enabled the courts to deal directly with monopoly as a problem of publishers rather than authors; and it would have given the courts an opportunity, which they never had, to develop a body of law in the interest of the author as creator, to enable him to protect the integrity of his work. Such a body of law, which exists in civil-law countries under the name of moral right, is warranted on its own merits, for any creative endeavor is an extension of one's personality.

If a more practical justification is needed, however, it exists. A body of law recognizing the author's creative interest in his work would require a limitation of the scope of copyright, for it would require recognition of rights in the author independent of copyright. By limiting the scope of copyright, such a body of law would provide an effective weapon against the problem of monopoly, which has continually plagued copyright. Thus, a law recognizing the author's creative interest would be not only beneficial to the author; it would also be beneficial to society, for it would effectively limit the absolute control of a work which the copyright owner has today.

These points are discussed more fully in the final chapters, after the developments here sketched have been traced in detail. It may be appropriate, however, to answer now Judge Hopkinson's question, "What is its history—its judicial history?"

The answer is that there was no common-law copyright in the sense in which he spoke. Copyright was not a product of the common law. It was a product of censorship, guild monopoly, trade-regulation statutes, and misunderstanding. Judge Hopkinson's problem was that he did not ask the right question. If the following materials do not provide any answers, it is hoped that they will at least enable the reader to ask the right questions. The problem must be perceived before the solution can be provided.

2

Prelude: Early Government Press Control

WHEN WILLIAM CAXTON introduced the printing press into England in 1476, the creation of a new form of property, eventually to be called copyright, was inevitable. The new property concept developed over some two hundred years, and it was not until the eighteenth century that the copyright to be received in the United States finally evolved in England.

It is difficult to think of the early copyright as property, for the rights it entailed were limited to a special group. Moreover, the members of that group, primarily as a result of policies of censorship and press control, were allowed to impose their own sanctions to support those rights. But by the eighteenth century, when copyright was available to all, with sanctions imposed by statute, the effect of censorship and press control on the early development of the concept had been obscured.

Even so, the effect was of major and lasting significance, for these policies meant that copyright, a property concept vested with a large public interest, was created and existed without any interference from the courts or the legislature for some hundred and sixty years. In the context of the religious and political ferment that made censorship a major policy of government during this period, this consequence was perhaps inevitable, for censorship is invariably a function of the executive rather than the legislative and judicial branches of government. A less obvious consequence of the policy of press control, however, was the exclusion of any consideration of the author's right in his work in the early development of copyright.

It has been suggested that if Caxton, an exceptionally prolific literary producer with considerable influence at Court, had had a competitor possessed of sufficient capital to be a really formidable pirate, the recognition of an author's rights in his works would not have been so long delayed.[1] But there was no general pirating of Caxton's publications, and "the one English printer and man of letters who possessed the advantage of powerful friends at Court was never driven into a course of self-defence."[2] Thus, the concept of property rights in publishing was left to the printers and publishers, and their ignoring of the author points up the development of copyright as a by-product of the political and religious forces at conflict in England during almost the entire formative period of early copyright.

The separation of England from the Church of Rome, in the 1530s, occurred less than sixty years after the introduction of the printing press, and the ferment occasioned by the separation continued until the "Glorious Revolution" of 1688, only twenty-one years before the enactment of the Statute of Anne.

Although continual unrest in England during this time made censorship and press control perennial policies of the Tudor and Stuart sovereigns, copyright was not a product of censorship and press control, as has been sometimes assumed.

Censorship was a government policy unrelated to property concepts. The governing officials remained wholly indifferent to the ownership of copy, as copyright was then called, but their use of members of the book trade as policemen of the press gave the printers and publishers a national monopoly of printing and freedom to create rights involving ownership of copy which developed into copyright.

In short, copyright was not created because of censorship, nor would the absence of censorship have prevented its creation, but censorship did aid private persons, publishers and printers, in developing copyright in their own interest with no interference from the courts and little from the government. The early censorship regulations thus serve as a prelude to the development of copyright.

The introduction of the printing press into England meant for the government at first a new trade to be encouraged, and then an instrument to be controlled. In 1484, a statute regulating and restricting the

1. A. W. POLLARD, SHAKESPEARE'S FIGHT WITH THE PIRATES 1 (1920).
2. *Id.* at 2.

conditions under which foreigners might carry on trade in England excepted printing and bookselling.[3] There were only four presses in England at the time, owned by Caxton; the Oxford Printer; "the mysterious schoolmaster of St. Albans"; and John Lettou, who was the first printer in London, having set up his press in 1480.[4]

The government's special encouragement of foreign printers and booksellers, lasting for fifty years, did not find favor with native workers. One instance revealing the prejudice against alien workmen is *Pynson v. Squyer*, a Star Chamber action in 1500 by Richard Pynson, a Norman-born printer, against Henry Squyer and others for murderous attacks against himself and his servants: "Also the seid Harrye Squier, John Walker, John Viker & other of their malicious & euyl disposed sect haue made great othys and promisys that their shall nother frenshmen nor flemmying dewell nor abide wythyn the seid parish of seynt Clementes and thus dailye and contenuellye the seid Riottourz manass your seid Oratourz & their seruantz so that they nother their servauntz dare nott goo aboute their laufull besynez to the vtter vndoyng of your seid Oratourz."[5]

By 1500, the pinch of competition from the foreign craftsmen began to be felt severely[6] and the grievances against alien craftsmen in general culminated in the "Evil May Day" of 1517, when a mob of two thousand attacked the French and Flemish quarters and sacked the houses.[7] Subsequent statutes designed to protect domestic trade in 1523[8] and in 1529[9] did not except printing and bookselling.

And in 1533, the statute of 1484 was repealed. The later statute informs us that since the enactment of the earlier provision, when there were few books and printers in England, "many of this realm, being the King's natural subjects, have given them so diligently to learn and exercise the said craft of printing, that at this day there be

3. 1 Rich. III, c. 9.

4. MUMBY, PUBLISHING AND BOOKSELLING 49 (1931).

5. Pynson v. Squyer, 16 SELDEN SOCIETY PUBLICATIONS 114, 116 (1902).

6. Aldis, *The Book Trade, 1557–1625*, 4 CAMBRIDGE HISTORY OF ENGLISH LITERA-TURE 458 (1909).

7. MUMBY, *op. cit.*, 50–51.

8. 14 and 15 Hen. VIII, c. 2, (requiring aliens, including denizens, to hire only English-born apprentices, and limiting them to two foreign journeymen).

9. 21 Hen. VIII, c. 16, (prohibiting artificers not denizens from setting up shop in London).

within this realm a great number cunning and expert in the said science or craft of printing, as able to exercise the said craft in all points, as any stranger in any other realm or country."[10]

The 1533 statute further forbade the importation of books for re-selling and the purchase at retail of any books imported. It also contained a price-control provision. Although the economic reasons for the statute were no doubt bona fide, the change in policy was consistent with the revival of a policy of stringent censorship under Henry VIII.

Censorship, incidentally, had long preceded the arrival of the printing press in England. A proclamation of Mary in 1555 was based on a statute of Henry IV[11] concerning the repressing of heresies and providing punishment "not onely for the aucthors, makers, and wryters of bookes, conteynynge wycked doctryne . . . but also for suche as shall haue or kepe any suche bookes, or wrytinges . . . "[12]

But the advent of the press caused a change in the emphasis in the proclamations from the author to the printer. After the proclamation of Henry VII in 1486–87 for "suppressing of forged tydings and tales and seditious Rumors and for discouery of the authors thereof,"[13] the printer replaced the author as the key person in censorship regulations.

Henry VIII's first proclamation of censorship, "for resysting and withstandyng of most dampnable Heresyes / sowen within this realme / by the disciples of Luther and other Heretykes / perverters of Christes Relygion," included the first English list of specifically prohibited books,[14] and was issued in 1529, the year the Reformation Parliament began. This was followed in 1530 by a proclamation against erroneous religious books establishing the first secular licensing system,[15] another in January 1536 aimed at the writings of John Fisher, late Bishop of Rochester, who had been convicted of treason.[16]

On November 16, 1538, Henry VIII established by proclamation the first royal licensing system.[17] It provided that no English book printed abroad was to be brought into the country on pain of for-

10. 25 Hen. VIII, c. 15.
11. 2 Hen. IV, c. 15.
12. I ARBER 52.
13. I STEELE, TUDOR AND STUART PROCLAMATIONS, 1485–1714 (1910), Procl. No. 7.
14. STEELE, Procl. No. 114.
15. STEELE, Procl. No. 122.
16. STEELE, Procl. No. 155.
17. STEELE, Procl. No. 176.

feiture of all goods and of imprisonment; that no person was to print any English book except after examination by some of the Privy Council or other persons appointed; and that no printer was to publish any books of scripture in English until they were examined by the king, one of the Privy Council, or a bishop.

It is, of course, no accident that these proclamations were all directed to heresies, because they were merely incidents in the religious struggle then going on between Henry and Rome. From the standpoint of history, they are minor footnotes to the more significant events of the time. Henry, having decided to break with Rome, determined "to act by legal and constitutional methods, namely through Parliament and Convocation,"[18] and the press was just another instrument, and a relatively minor one, to be used for his purposes. While the proclamations all indicate that the press was only to be kept in line, it was also used affirmatively, particularly by Thomas Cromwell, Henry's Secretary of State (1533–36), who was charged with suppressing the monasteries. "To help the business to go off smoothly, Cromwell resorted to popular propaganda, sermons, pamphlets, and troupes of strolling actors, denouncing the iniquities of monks. . . . "[19]

Henry's proclamation of 1538 marked the beginning of a system of censorship in England that was to last until 1694, with varying degrees of success and some lapses, most notably between 1660 and 1694. It was a censorship always directed to various phases of the religious conflict, for regardless of what party was in power, "its principal concern as regards printing was to suppress what it stigmatized as heretical and seditious opinion."[20]

The relationship of religion and censorship is well illustrated by "An Act for the Advancement of true Religion, and for the abolishing of all false Doctrines," passed in 1542–43, prohibiting English versions of the scriptures.[21]

The 1538 proclamation was followed on May 18, 1544, by one for the "calling in and prohibiting of certain bookes printed of Newes of the Prosperous successe of the Kings Maiesties Armie in Scotland

---

18. CROSSE, A SHORT HISTORY OF THE ENGLISH REFORMATION 29–30 (1950).
19. CROSSE, op. cit., 40.
20. GREG, LONDON PUBLISHING BETWEEN 1550 AND 1650 1–2 (1956).
21. 34 & 35 Hen. VIII, c. 1.

to be brought in and burned within 24 houres after proclamation made on paine of ymprisonment,"[22] and on May 6, 1545, by a proclamation authorising and establishing a new primer.[23] Henry's last proclamation of press control was issued on July 8, 1546.[24] It was "to auoide and abolish suche englishe bookes, as conteine pernicious and detestable errours, and heresies," and it forbade any version of the New Testament except in accordance with the statute of 34 & 35 Henry VIII, c. 1, and any works by certain named authors, most notably Wycliff, Tyndale, and Coverdale. More significantly, it set up a new scheme of press control, providing that "no printer do print any maner of englishe boke, balet or playe, but he put in his name to the same, with the name of thautour, and daye of the printe, and shall presente the fyrst copye to the mayre of the towne where he dwelleth, and not to suffer any of the copies to go out of his handes within two dayes next following."[25]

It is not likely that the scheme set forth in 1546 was intended to supersede that of 1538; in fact the later proclamation is not inconsistent with the earlier, since the mayors could be deemed appointed by the king for licensing in accordance with the earlier proclamation. The new scheme, however, does show that the first one was ineffective and indicated the need of the government for a group of ready-made agents for the purposes of censorship. In this respect, the plan presages the use of the Stationers' Company for this very purpose a few years later.

Henry died shortly after this last proclamation, and presumably his proclamations would have ceased to have any legal effect. "After the distinction between Statutes and Ordinances was clearly marked in the reign of Edward III, a theory grew up that the validity of proclamations was limited to the lifetime of the king by whom they were issued. This theory was fully recognized in Stuart times by the re-issue of proclamations on the accession of a new monarch."[26]

Parliament, however, had passed a statute giving the proclamations of Henry VIII the force and effect of an act of Parliament;[27] but the

22. STEELE, Procl. No. 253.
23. STEELE, Procl. No. 271.
24. STEELE, Procl. No. 295.
25. A. W. POLLARD, op. cit., 7.
26. I STEELE, op. cit., xxxii (1910).
27. 31 Hen. VIII, c. 8.

problem was shortly resolved, for the statute was repealed in an act repealing "All Acts of Parliament and Statutes touching, mentioning or in any wise concerning Religion or Opinions"[28] soon after Edward VI came to the throne. The purpose was not to end Henry's work, but to complete it, because Henry's religion was Catholicism without the Pope, and under Edward VI the Protestant reformers took over. The Act of Repeal meant that "every legal restraint on religious propaganda was swept away at a stroke, every one was free to preach or teach what he liked."[29] Thus, the press in England was free, in theory at least, for a few years, but it was a short-lived freedom.

Edward VI returned to censorship by a proclamation of April 28, 1551.[30] The proclamation is not phrased in terms of religion, but was issued because "diuers Printers, Bokeselers, and Plaiers of Enterludes, without consideracion or regarde to the quiet of the realme, do print, sel, and play whatsoeuer any light and phantastical hed listeth to inuent and deuise" resulting in "many inconueniencies" to the king's subjects. It required that no books in the English language were to be printed or sold "onles thesame be firste allowed by his maiestie, or his priuie counsayl in writing signed with his maiesties most gratious hand or the handes of sixe of his sayd pruiuie counsayl, vpon payne of Imprisonment, without bayle or mayneprice, and further fine at his maiesties pleasor."[31]

The accession of the Catholic Mary occasioned yet another turn in religious matters, and she, of course, resorted immediately to censorship. In a proclamation of August 18, 1553,[32] Mary sought to reassure her subjects on the question of religion, saying that while she would retain her religion, she did not intend at present to force any subjects to conform to it. After condemning "the pryntynge of false fonde bookes, ballettes, rymes, and other lewd treatises in the englyshe tonge, concernynge doctryne in matters now in question and controuersye, touchynge the hyghe poyntes and misteries of christen religion, whiche bokes, ballettes, rymes and treatises are chiefly by the Prynters and

28. I Edw. VI, c. 12.
29. CROSSE, op. cit., 62.
30. STEELE, Procl. No. 395.
31. A. W. POLLARD, op. cit., 8.
32. STEELE, Procl. No. 427.

Stacioners sette out to sale to her graces subiectes, of any euyll zeale, for lucre and couetous of vyle gayne," she charged and commanded her subjects not "to prynte any bookes, matter, ballet, ryme, interlude, process or treatyse nor to playe any interlude, except they haue her graces speciall licence in writynge for the same, vpon payne to incurre her highnesse indignation and displeasure."[33]

Mary's reign was not a happy one; she forced upon the people, much to their resentment, her husband, the Spanish King Philip; she failed completely in her attempt to force her religion on the nation; and she found it necessary to redefine restrictions on the press in increasingly harsh terms.

On June 13, 1555,[34] she issued a proclamation prohibiting books by certain authors and any other book "conteynynge false doctryne, contrarye, and agaynste the Catholique fayth, and the doctryne of the catholyque Churche." It further forbade books "concernyng the common seruyce and mynystration, set forth in englyshe, to be vsed in the churches, of this realme, in the tyme of Kyng Edward the sixt," a reference to the two Protestant prayer books of 1549 an 1552, prepared principally by Cranmer.

Mary's last proclamation, June 6, 1558,[35] was short and to the point, consisting of three sentences. It made the mere possession of unlawful books a capital offense.

But the most important official act of Mary's reign—indeed, possibly the most important single act in the history of Anglo-American copyright—occurred the year before this last angry proclamation: on May 4, 1557, Philip and Mary granted a charter to the Stationers' Company. The partnership between the company and the government, one interested in protecting property, the other in controlling the press, was to last for over a hundred years.

33. A. W. POLLARD, op. cit., 9.
34. STEELE, Procl. No. 461; I ARBER 52.
35. STEELE, Procl. No. 488; I ARBER 92.

3

The Stationers' Company

Operation of the Company

THE FOCAL point of the history of copyright is the Stationers' Company, whose records date principally from May 4, 1557, when the company received its charter from Philip and Mary.[1]

1. The principal records of the Stationers' Company for the period here involved are the REGISTERS, containing book entries and designated as REGISTER A, B, C, D, E, F, and G, respectively, transcribed by EDWARD ARBER, A TRANSCRIPT OF THE REGISTERS OF THE COMPANY OF STATIONERS, 1554–1640 A.D. (1876), and EYRE & RIVINGTON, A TRANSCRIPT OF THE REGISTERS OF THE WORSHIPFUL COMPANY OF STATIONERS, 1640–1708 A.D. (1914), and COURT BOOKS B and C, records of the transactions of the Court of Assistants, the governing body of the Company; COURT BOOK B was transcribed by W. W. GREG & E. BOSWELL, RECORDS OF THE COURT OF THE STATIONERS' COMPANY, 1576–1602 (1930); hereafter referred to as COURT BOOK B; and COURT BOOK C was transcribed by WILLIAM JACKSON, RECORDS OF THE COURT OF THE STATIONERS' COMPANY, 1602–1640 (1957), hereafter referred to as COURT BOOK C. The records of the book entries fall into two periods, those from 1554 to 1571, and those from 1576 to 1708. There is a hiatus of five craft years between REGISTERS A and B, and book entries for this period, 1571–76, are lost. In addition, there are no court records prior to 1576, and COURT BOOK B is, in fact, a portion of REGISTER B, which Arber was not allowed to print. REGISTER A, strictly speaking, is not a register of book entries, but a book of the warden's annual cash accounts; besides book entries, it includes lists of fees for such things as miscellaneous receipts, the presenting of apprentices, the making of freemen, and fines for breaking of ordinances, as well as payments made by the company. The book entries in REGISTER A were transcribed from other books of original entry. Greg has suggested the following explanation for the absence of court records prior to 1576 and the loss of the book entries: In 1557, the company began its records in two volumes, a WARDEN'S BOOK now known as REGISTER A, and a CLERK'S BOOK, essentially a minute book, which was in fact COURT BOOK A, now lost. In July 1571, on the appointment of a new clerk, the details of revenue, including the entrance of copies, being largely

The unbroken history of the stationers goes back to 1403, when the Mayor and Aldermen of London granted a petition by writers of text-letter, illuminators, bookbinders, and booksellers to form a guild.[2] As early as 1542,[3] the stationers had requested a charter, which indicates that the trade at that time was already well-organized. That request for incorporation had been refused.

According to the preamble of the charter granted in 1557, Philip and Mary incorporated the stationers to provide a suitable remedy against seditious and heretical material printed by schismatical persons. Such material, they felt, moved the sovereign's subjects not only against the crown, but also against the "faith and sound catholic doctrine of Holy Mother Church."[4] There is little reason to doubt that the preamble expressed the true reasons for the granting of the charter, although there has been some question whether the initiative for incorporation came from the stationers or the government.[5]

The charter itself, however, is dominated by the idea of suppressing prohibited books, and Mary's motive in granting it, whatever the source of the initiative involved, was to obtain an effective agency for censorship. Her last angry proclamation in 1558 indicates that probably even in 1557 she was becoming desperate for an effective means to control the press. On November 5, 1558, a bill for the restraint of the press was introduced in the House of Lords. It carried an impressive

---

administrative in nature, were turned over to the clerk for keeping in the CLERK'S BOOK, *i.e.*, COURT BOOK A. The WARDEN'S BOOK was at this time reserved for summary accounts only. The clerk continued to use his minute book for its original purposes, and rather than acquire a new book, he used it also for those entries theretofore made in the WARDEN'S BOOK, *i.e.*, REGISTER A, including the registration of copies. By July 1576, the CLERK'S BOOK was full, and a new one, now known as REGISTER B, was acquired in which records were carried on in the same manner as in the previous five years. When REGISTER B was filled, at different times for the various sections, the records were split up and resulted in REGISTER C, begun in July 1595, the first volume of which is, strictly speaking, a register, and COURT BOOK C, begun in 1602, the earliest COURT BOOK extant. See GREG, INTRODUCTION, RECORDS OF THE COURT OF THE STATIONERS' COMPANY, 1576–1602, viii–x (1930).

2. See I ARBER 593.
3. BLAGDEN, THE STATIONERS' COMPANY 28 (1960).
4. I ARBER xxviii.
5. See A. W. POLLARD, *op. cit.*, 9–10, wherein he disputes Arber's contention that the initiative came from the stationers. See Arber's arguments at I ARBER xxvi–xxvii.

title: " 'That no Man shall print any Book or Ballad, &c unless he be
authorized thereunto by the King and Queen's Majesties Licence, under the Great Seal of *England*.' As this is the first Restraint to the
Liberty of the Press, which we have yet met with, it is the more
remarkable. Because it shows us, that the Art of Printing, which had
not then been much more than half a Century in Use, was become so
obnoxious to the Government that they were obliged to have Recourse
to an Act of Parliament to restrain it."[6] The Queen died on November
17, however, and Parliament was dissolved.

In any event, it is not likely that incorporation altered anything in
the internal organization of the Brotherhood of Stationers. Graham
Pollard points out, "Though the incorporation was of fundamental importance from a legal point of view, to the Stationers themselves it
was a means to an end, not an end in itself: it was but one incident
of many in the Company's expansion."[7]

Although the companies of London played an important and complicated role in the social, commercial, and political life of the city,[8] the
Stationers' Company in this respect was relatively unimportant. It
looms large in the history of copyright, but it was ranked far down
in the hierarchy of London companies. "Far from ranking with the
Grocers', the Mercers', the Goldsmiths', and the rest of the twelve
great livery companies of London," writes Marjorie Plant, "the Stationers' occupied a humble position among some forty minor companies. The explanation is to be found not only in their small
membership but also in their lack of wealth."[9]

The amount of attention the Stationers' Company received from the
government, however, was such that no other company "ever attained
the same degree of monopoly as that which the State thought it expedient to confer on the Stationers."[10] The reason for this, of course,
was the government's need to control the press.

The constitution and make-up of the Stationers' Company was
similar to that of the other companies, and while its monopoly was

6. 3 PARLIAMENTARY HISTORY 354 (1751).
7. Graham Pollard, *The Early Constitution of the Stationers' Company*, XVIII
THE LIBRARY, 4th ser., 235, 236 (1937).
8. See HAZLITT, THE LIVERY COMPANIES OF THE CITY OF LONDON (1892).
9. PLANT, THE ENGLISH BOOK TRADE 127 (1939).
10. UNWIN, THE GILDS AND COMPANIES OF LONDON 261 (1908).

more complete, the difference was one of degree. Its powers were, in fact, similar to the powers usually granted to companies for the regulation of their respective trades.

The officers of a London company were generally a master and a warden, elected for a year, who, together with the Court of Assistants, ruled the organization. The Court of Assistants was the central feature of the company, and it was more than a court in name. It had jurisdiction over the stationers, rendering judgments by which "unruly apprentices were whipped, journeymen on strike were imprisoned, and masters offending against regulations were fined."[11] And, more important, members of the company were forbidden to carry trade disputes to any other court before having appealed to the Court of Assistants.

Before 1557, the Court of Assistants had become an essential part of the administrative machinery of the larger companies, but the stationers' charter is said to be the first in which the court appeared as part of the original constitution of the company.[12]

A company was governed by ordinances which were generally drafted by the men of the trade themselves, subject to approval, and which generally conformed to a common type.[13]

The Stationers' Company conformed to the general pattern, and its high degree of autonomy in controlling the book trade was characteristic of the industrial and commercial life of London of the times. This fact enables one to bring into perspective the significance of censorship and press control in the development of copyright. It seems safe to say, in view of the autonomy given the London companies in matters of trade, that even without censorship and press control, the stationer's copyright would have developed substantially as it did. The govern-

11. UNWIN, op. cit., 28.
12. Id. at 219.
13. An example is the Hatters' ordinances of 1348, summarized by UNWIN, op. cit., p. 89: "(1) Six lawful men to be sworn to rule the trade. (2) None but freemen to make or sell hats. (3) None to be apprenticed for less than seven years. (4) None to take apprentices but freemen. (5) Wardens to search as often as need be with power to take defective hats before Mayor and Alderman. (5) [Sic] No night work. (6) None of trade to be made free of city or to be allowed to work if not attested by wardens. (7) None to receive another's apprentices or servant if not properly dismissed, or (8) who is in debt to previous master. (9) No stranger to sell hats by retail, but only wholesale and to freemen."

ment's interest in press control, however, resulting in enlarged powers for the Stationers' Company, did make the task of the stationers in controlling their trade easier.

Company powers were generally limited geographically, but the charter of the Stationers' Company gave it an almost complete monopoly of printing, together with powers of national regulation. It provided that "No person within this our realm of England or the dominions of the same shall practise or exercise by himself, or by his ministers, his servants or by any other person the art or mistery of printing any book or any thing for sale or traffic within this our realm of England or the dominions of the same, unless the same person at the time of his foresaid printing is or shall be one of the community of the foresaid mistery or art of Stationery of the foresaid City, or has therefore license of us or the heirs or successors of us the foresaid Queen by the letters patent of us or the heirs or successors of us the foresaid Queen."

At the head of the Stationers' Company was its principal officer, the master, assisted by the upper warden and under warden, all of whom held offices for a year, and who, along with the clerk, were members of the Court of Assistants.[14]

The Court of Assistants was the ruling body of the Stationers' Company. It promulgated rules and regulations concerning the ownership of copy and publishing, and entries in the court books indicate that the court's jurisdiction to settle disputes involving members of the company and problems of the book trade was generally recognized and asserted.

The master and wardens were given plenary powers of search at any time "in any place, shop, house, chamber, or building of any printer, binder or bookseller whatever . . . for any books or things printed, or to be printed, and to seize, take, hold, burn, or turn to the proper use of the foresaid community, all and several those books and things which are or shall be printed contrary to the form of any statute, act or proclamation. . . . "[15]

Below the wardens were the senior and junior renter wardens, who

14. GREG & BOSWELL, *Introduction*, RECORDS OF THE COURT OF THE STATIONERS' COMPANY, 1576–1602 xiv (1930).
15. I ARBER xxxi.

were not members of the court, and whose main job was collecting quarterly subscriptions from all members of the company. The renters were senior members of the livery, and the clerk, whose primary task was keeping the records of the company, was also apparently chosen from the livery. Below the livery came the main body of freemen, the commonalty or yeomanry, which was added to in one of four ways: the admission of apprentices upon their becoming free; patrimony, whereby the son of a freeman was admitted; translation from another company; and, rarely, by purchase.

The beadle, "the pivot upon which the Company worked," issued notices for meetings, kept or transcribed some of the records and books of the company, and was a useful assistant to the executive officers. He was chosen from the yeomanry. Parallel with the yeomanry, but having no access to the normal ladder of promotion, were the brothers, composed generally of aliens and foreigners. At the bottom were the apprentices.[16]

Traditionally, admission to the Court of Assistants was by service as under warden, and all wardens, past and present, were members of the court, but in 1557, the year of the company's incorporation, the court co-opted nine of the most senior freemen to make up a court of eighteen assistants. In July 1561, however, there was a return to the traditional method of admission; by this time, the assistants had established, contrary to the charter provision, the principle that the power of election of officers and of members of the court was in the court's hands, rather than in the general body, thus insuring the oligarchical nature of the company's government; court membership carried with it life tenure.[17]

The proceeding in the Court of Assistants seems to have been more in the nature of an arbitration than a law suit, as the aim of the court always appears to have been to maintain order rather than to exact punishment. In 1601, there was an action at law between two stationers concerning covenants for the workmanship of books in which the Court of Assistants intervened, and "by consent of both parties" the suit was ended and the matter submitted to the master and a warden of the

16. See the account of the company's organization at I ARBER xliii–xliv.
17. See BLAGDEN, op. cit., Appendix III, Membership of the Court of Assistants, 1556–1576.

company, who settled the dispute in an order which proved that any future controversies were to be submitted to this master and wardens of the company, "Any thinge to the contrary notwthstanding."[18] When William Ponsonby instituted proceedings in the Star Chamber against John Legatt, a freeman of the company who was printer for Cambridge, and a number of London booksellers, the Star Chamber referred the matter for decision to the Master of Requests and the Recorder of London, who, after hearing the cause debated by counsel, referred so much of the bill as concerned the three defendants who were stationers to the master and warden of the Stationers' Company.

These officers, after conferring with "theire Assistants," called the plaintiff and defendants before them.[19] In 1616 and 1617, when a suit involving copyright was filed in chancery, after plaintiff had rejected arbitration by the Court of Assistants, "Something like a meeting of the Court of Assistants was held in the Court of Chancery to serve as guidance to that Court for its judgement upon the issues raised. Indeed, it could not be otherwise, and both parties concerned invoked the evidence of representative Stationers upon the customs of the Company."[20]

It has been suggested that while members of the company were bound to submit disputes to the court, they were not bound by the award,[21] a suggestion which seems to be well founded. In a dispute where the court ordered one party to pay a debt due the other, the order provided that if the debt was not paid, "Then Askell hathe libertie to seeke his remedie by lawe."[22] Although this dispute apparently did not involve copyright, the entries concerning copyright controversies generally state the consent of the parties to be bound by the decision,[23] the decisions themselves often appear to be in the nature

18. COURT BOOK B, 84.
19. COURT BOOK B, 80.
20. Sisson, The Laws of Elizabethan Copyright: the Stationers' View, XV THE LIBRARY, 5th ser., 8, 11–12 (1960). This article is based on records at the Public Record Office of a Chancery Suit in 1616–1617, Barnes v. Man.
21. GREG, Introduction, RECORDS, xlvii, n. 1.
22. COURT BOOK B, 2.
23. E.g., an order of August 16, 1578, reads: "At a court holden this daye the said pties haue submitted them selfes to stand to thorder of the mr wardens and assistants or the moore pte of them concerninge the matter in question abouespified. & for all other demaunds betwene them And the said pties haue pmised to stand to the same order." COURT BOOK B, 7.

of a compromise,[24] and the disputes were often delegated to persons who almost surely acted as arbitrators.[25]

Graham Pollard points out that there were some printers and dealers in books who were not members of the company, as a freeman could follow a trade other than that of the company to which he belonged.[26] One of the early policies of the company was to bring all such persons into the company,[27] because in any dispute involving a nonmember, the Court of Assistants was without jurisdiction.

On January 27, 1598, the company undertook to share the costs of a suit in the Star Chamber which the partners in the grammar and accidence privilege were bringing against William Barley and Simon Stafford.[28] These printers were members of the Drapers' Company, and Stafford's press had been seized. The outcome of the suit was that the company admitted Stafford as a master printer—that is, one entitled to own a press—thus bringing him within the company's jurisdiction, and Stafford's press was redelivered to him upon his entering a bond not to print anything contrary to the decrees of the Star Chamber.[29]

The three principal groups within the Stationers' Company were the bookbinders, the booksellers, and the printers. The bookbinders were the oldest group, the printers the newest. The bookbinders' position in the trade and in the company was that of superior journeymen; the booksellers had not in 1557 fully exploited the new conditions for the trade created by the press; and in the middle of the sixteenth century,

24. E.g., an order of January 17, 1598/99, involved a controversy about the ownership of a book, two entrances of which had been made. Ordinarily, the first entrance would prevail, but the order provided, "nowe vppon the examination & consideration thereof yt is ordered and agreed that the said mr Binge mr Ponsonby and mr man shall pte and ptelyke betwene [them] in Three equal ptes, haue and enioye the said copye, nowe and at all tymes hereafter bearinge ratablie chargs for the same accordingly." COURT BOOK B, 67.

25. E.g., an order of June 21, 1596, reads: "The controu'sie for the booke of martirs is referred to the determinacon of [mr harrison] mr. Watkins, mr Newberry, Mr. wight and mr. Norton, They to cast vp thaccoumpt and determyne of it." COURT BOOK B, 55.

26. Graham Pollard. op. cit., 235, 249.

27. In 1600, thirteen drapers were translated to the Stationers' Company. See Blagden, The English Stock of the Stationers' Company, X THE LIBRARY, 5th ser., 163, 172 (1955).

28. COURT BOOK B, 60.

29. COURT BOOK B, 64, 68.

the printers came to be the dominant power among the stationers.[30] In 1557, the main investors in copies were printers; during the first year after the company was incorporated, only two persons other than printers entered copies in the register.[31]

The power in the Stationers' Company was soon to shift to the booksellers. Christopher Barker in his report on printing patents in December 1582 complained that the booksellers "being growen the greater and wealthier nomber haue nowe many of the best Copies" to the discredit of the printers.[32]

The Company's Role in Controlling the Press

The Stationers' Company was able to develop the concept of copyright because the government remained indifferent to the private ownership of copy.

Censorship was another matter entirely. Although the company's charter had been granted by the Catholic Mary, the Protestant Elizabeth confirmed it in November 1559,[33] without any change, and for substantially the same reasons it had been granted: so that the stationers might aid the government in controlling the press. The company's function in press control, however, was to be that of policeman rather than judge. The charter originally gave the company officials no duties in connection with the issuance of licenses; when Elizabeth confirmed the charter, she did not add any. And as in the case of earlier censorship provisions, so with Elizabeth's regulations: religion was the primary motivating factor. Her policy in religion "was to unite all sections of opinion in one national church,"[34] and it is significant that her first censorship regulations were a part of the Injunctions of 1559,[35] intended as a code of ecclesiastical discipline.

The Fifty-first Injunction was directly concerned with the printers of books. It made clear that the Stationers' Company was to fulfill a

30. BLAGDEN, THE STATIONERS' COMPANY 40 (1960).
31. Ibid.
32. I ARBER 114.
33. I ARBER xxxii.
34. CROSSE, op. cit., 80.
35. I ARBER xxxviii. An injunction is: "defined as 'orders given by administrative authority for the observance of church law and customs. . . . The practice runs back to a distant past, and is a valuable piece of administrative machinery.'" CROSSE, op. cit., 51, n. 2.

role as an instrument, not an arbiter, of press control, and it marks the beginning of a diffusion of responsibility for censorship. Under prior regulations, the power of censorship had been limited to the sovereign and Privy Council, but this injunction divided works into three classes: new books; pamphlets, ballads, and plays; and books on religion, politics, and government already printed, with licensers specified for each class of works.

New books were to be licensed by the Queen herself in writing, or by six of the Privy Council, or by two of the following: the Archbishops of Canterbury and York, the Bishop of London, the Chancellors of Oxford and Cambridge, and the Bishop and Archdeacon of the place of printing. Of these last two, the Ordinary was to be one.[36] Pamphlets, ballads, and plays were to be licensed by three members of the Court of High Commission within the City of London.[37]

Books on religion, politics, and government previously printed in England or abroad were referred to members of the High Commission in London.

The names of the licensors were to be added to the end of every book, and to all of these orders, "her majestye straightly commaundeth all manner her subiectes, and specially the wardens and company of Stationers to be obedyent." Excepted from the operation of the injunction were classical authors and textbooks, the first and last such exceptions to be made in the acts of censorship.

Just as the government had no interest in the ownership of copies, so we can assume that the Stationers' Company had no interest in censorship, except as a means of protecting their own self-interest. Edward Arber comments: "We must realize the strength, one might almost say the virulence of their trade competition. . . . So we must think of these printers and publishers as caring chiefly for their crowns, half-shillings, and silver pennies. They bore the yoke of licensing as best they could, but only as a means to hold themselves harmless from the political and ecclesiastical powers. Their business was to live and make money; and keen enough they were about it."[38]

36. "[T]he Bishop may be assumed to be Ordinary within his diocese." GREG, LONDON PUBLISHING 6 (1956).

37. "The reason for this distinction is not apparent and there is no evidence that it was ever recognized." Ibid.

38. II ARBER 11, Introduction.

The stationers were anxious to make the most of their position to enhance their monopoly, and in 1559 they acted to obtain even greater control of the book trade than their charter granted them by seeking approval of certain articles drawn up "in forme of lawe."

The articles, of which only the headings have survived, asked: (1) for confirmation of the charter; (2) "None to prynte oneless he be ffre of the stationers"; (3) that no one was "to be a comon bokeseller in London or Westmynster" until he gave bond to keep the orders of the stationers; (4) "Euery boke or thinge to be allowed by the stationers before yt be prynted"; (5) the stationers were free to make and change "orders for pryntinge and bokesellinge"; (6) the officers of the company to prohibit any from printing until "he fynde surties to observe the[i]r orders"; (7) the stationers to have authority to arrest every offender in London or Westminster and to commit him to prison until payment of a fine of a hundred shillings for every offense, "or more yf the greatnes of th[e]offence requyre"; (8) jailers were to have warrants to receive persons arrested by the stationers, and (9) the Chancellor of England was to award process if need be.[39]

These were extraordinary powers, even for an Elizabethan company; and they were refused, even though eventually the stationers were to exercise practically all of them, in some instances without legal sanction. The document containing the ill-fated proposals is undated, but the first request makes it obvious that it was prepared before Elizabeth confirmed the charter on November 10, 1559.

The first sentence of the Fifty-first Injunction, issued subsequently, may indicate why the proposals were rejected. It read: "*Item* because there is a great abuse in the printers of bokes, which for couetousnes cheifly regard not what they print, so thei may haue gaine, whereby arriseth great dysorder by publicatyon of vnfrutefull, vayne and infamous bokes and papers."[40]

The rejected proposals marked the first round in the continuing struggle of the stationers to enhance their monopoly. Although the full text of the proposals is lost, the headings indicate that the draftsmen possibly made a strategic error in seeking power in the name of the company. In later years, this error was to be avoided, and the

39. I ARBER 350.
40. *Id.* at xxxviii.

stationers were to become ardent lobbyists for decrees of censorship as a means to sustain their control of the book trade. It is significant that the stationers' proposals are much more severe than the censorship regulations of Elizabeth. And in the light of subsequent events, it becomes apparent that censorship in England—at least, the long continuation of censorship—might be viewed more as a product of the stationer's copyright than vice versa.

It was in 1566 that the government in effect first acknowledged that it would have to cooperate with the Stationers' Company to achieve any satisfactory degree of censorship. This was the date of the first Star Chamber Decree regulating printing, and it represented a *modus vivendi*. The government and company would work together—"the former providing the authority and the latter the local knowledge and the executive ability, the former being vulnerable to printed criticism and the latter to invasion of literary property."[41]

The document which marked the beginning of this cooperation was entitled "Ordinances decreed for reformation of diuers disorders in printing and vttering of Bookes," and was a set of recommendations by the Court of High Commission approved by the Privy Council at the Star Chamber in 1566.[42]

The decree consisted of only six paragraphs, but two of them contained regulations the stationers undoubtedly sought. The first paragraph prohibited the printing or importation of books contrary to statutes, laws, injunctions, letters patent, or ordinances; and the fifth paragraph specified broad powers of search for the wardens, or any two of the company appointed by the wardens.

Of the remaining paragraphs, the second provided the penalty: the forfeiting of unlawful books, loss of the right to engage in printing, three months' imprisonment, and a fine of ten pounds. The third imposed a fine of twenty shillings for every book unlawfully sold or bound. Paragraph Four provided that all forfeited books were to be brought to Stationers' Hall to be destroyed or made into waste paper, at the discretion of the Wardens. The money forfeited was to be divided equally, one half for the Queen's use and one half to the person

---

41. Blagden, *Book Trade Control in 1566*, XIII THE LIBRARY, 5th ser. 287, 289 (1958).

42. I ARBER 322.

who seized the books or first made complaint. Paragraph Six required all persons in the book trade to enter into recognizances to observe the orders.[43]

For the first time, the Stationers' Company then had the sanction of the Star Chamber to support its jurisdiction over the trade; and even more important, from the company's point of view, was the protection given to privileged books under letters patent, and the powers of search, for the battle against the secret printing of privileged copies was just beginning.[44]

The terms of the patents themselves specifically forbade the printing by any other person of the work reserved by the grant to the patentee,[45] and in one instance the letters patent provided that offenders were to be fined forty shillings.[46]

But desperate printers who were pirating works covered by the patents and contending invalidity of the grants were not likely to be deterred by the terms of the grants themselves, and it was on the 1566 Decree that the plaintiff based his action in the Star Chamber case of *Day v. Ward and Holmes*.[47]

This case, in which defendants were alleged to have infringed John Day's patent for the printing of the *A B C with the Little Catechism* was a part of the bitter controversy between privileged and unprivileged printers which was just beginning at the time of the 1566 Decree.

But the stationers had already begun to take a more active part in censorship than was warranted by the official decrees in a way in which they could assure control over the property of copies. Although neither the company nor its officers possessed the right to issue licenses, the wardens apparently considered themselves, and in effect were, the chief licensing agents for many years.[48]

43. *Ibid.*

44. Blagden, *Book Trade Control in 1566*, XIII THE LIBRARY, 5th ser. at 290 (1958).

45. See *e.g., Letters Patent to William Seres*, II ARBER 60. See Appendix I.

46. *License to John Day*, II ARBER 61. See Appendix I.

47. II ARBER 753.

48. See GREG, LONDON PUBLISHING, 46 (1956); and see KIRSCHBAUM, SHAKESPEARE AND THE STATIONERS at 33 *et. seq.* (1955) for an account of the wardens acting as official licensors.

About 1634, Archbishop Laud appointed Sir John Lambe, Dean of the Arches, Sir Nathaniel Brent, and Doctor Duck "Commissioners concerning the Printers of London."[49] This was done evidently with a view to preparing the Star Chamber Decree of 1637, for Lambe made some notes as to the former practice of licensing books, and according to these notes, prior to the Star Chamber Decree of 1586, books were licensed by the master and wardens, some few by the master alone, some by the Archbishop, and more by the Bishop of London.[50] Felix Kingston, the master of the company at the time, "Sayth yat before ye Decree the master and wardens licensed all, And that when they had any Divinity books of muche importance they would take ye advise of some 2 or 3 ministers of this towne."[51] This is confirmed by the entries in the registers themselves, and the practice of the wardens' licensing for the press seems to have continued until the Star Chamber Decree of 1637.

W. W. Greg distinguishes between two types of licenses in the Registers: domestic licenses, which were granted by officers of the company; and official licenses.[52] "The small class of purely official licenses is negligible," he states, "except for a few years about 1590, and may be largely due to carelessness on the part of the Clerk. A sharp rise in the final year reflects a curious arrangement by which the Wardens apparently washed their hands of all responsibility for ballads. After the peak in official licensing consequent upon the appointment of correctors, there was a decline to 1594–95, when authority passed almost wholly into the hands of the Wardens, followed by a dozen years of slow recovery. After that outside licensing maintains a generally high level till 1624–25, when the periods of slackness already mentioned sets in and in two yearly periods no more than half the copies entered bear official sanction. Lastly, in 1638–39, every copy bore official and almost all domestic approval."[53]

49. III ARBER 15.
50. Id. at 690.
51. Ibid.
52. GREG, op. cit., Ch. III.
53. Id. at 50–51.

4

The Stationer's Copyright

THE EXACT date of the origin of copyright in England we do not know, but it may have been sometime between 1518 and 1542. The first of these dates is that of the first book printed with a privilege from the sovereign,[1] and the second is that of the first attempt of the Brotherhood of Stationers to acquire a charter. The privilege granted by the sovereign was a clear manifestation of the possibility of protecting the rights involved in publishing a book. An important reason for the Stationers' acquiring a charter would be to strengthen arrangements that may have already been made within the brotherhood for protecting copies.

The date of origin, however, may have been still earlier, with little or no regard for the privilege granted by or the charter sought from the sovereign. There is evidence that by the time the company received its charter in 1557, the stationer's copyright was already in existence. An entry in the records of the company under the dates of December 9, 1554, to July 18, 1557, records a fine "for an offence Donne by master wallye / for conselyng of the pryntynge of *a breafe Cronacle* contrary to our ordenances before he Ded presente the Copye to the wardyns . . . "[2] And a document entitled "The Appeal of William Seres the Younger to Lord Burghley," dated December 1582, reported that " . . . yt appeareth by the auntyent orders of stacyoners hall [*by which Craft that preceded the Company is evidently intended*] that no copie of any boke grete or small should be prynted before yt was brought thether and beinge there allowed yt is our order that no man should

---

1. A. W. POLLARD, SHAKESPEARE'S FIGHT, 3.
2. I ARBER 45.

prynt any other mans copie."[3] The "auntyent orders" are an indication of the very early existence of the stationer's copyright. Whatever the precise date of its beginning, however, copyright in England almost certainly originated as the stationer's copyright.

The remarkable fact about the early copyright is not that the stationers originated it, but that they should continue to control it for a hundred and fifty years. Whether today we regard that copyright as a legal concept in the traditional sense, or merely as a quasi-legal concept based on custom is immaterial. The fact remains that when copyright was established as a formal legal concept by statute, the draftsmen of the statute used the stationer's copyright as their model. Clearly, the stationer's copyright was more than a mere forerunner of the statutory copyright. Despite the fact that the courts in interpreting the Statute of Anne lost the point and broke the continuity of development, the two copyrights functioned in the same way for the same general purpose of protecting published works. The judicial construction of the Statute of Anne, however, altered the premise on which copyright had developed and based statutory copyright on a different, and as matters developed, unsatisfactory, premise. That premise was that copyright is basically an author's right, whereas the stationer's copyright, of course, was based on the premise that copyright is basically a publisher's right.

The point is relevant today, for the same fundamental ideas of copyright that were transmitted to this country in the eighteenth century still prevail. And it is only by a study of the stationer's copyright that one can appreciate how the change of the underlying premise destroyed the integrated nature of a legal concept and made it into a series of fragmented rules.

The stationer's copyright was an integrated concept because it was created by businessmen in the book trade, supported in their monopoly by regulations of censorship, for their own limited purposes. The fact that the aims of the government in supporting the monopoly in no way conflicted with the aims of the stationers left them unhampered in their development and control of copyright.

Briefly, then, the stationer's copyright was a right recognized among members of the company entitling one who published a work to pre-

3. II ARBER 771, 772. (Interpolation by Arber.)

vent any unauthorized printing of the same work. The word "published" is here important, because the stationer's copyright was
essentially a right to be protected in the receiving of profits from
publication, without the fear of piracy. The following explanation by
a noted bibliographical scholar of the decline of the position of bookbinders within the book trade as a result of the creation of copyright
gives emphasis to this fundamental point:

> There are three stages in the price of a book within the trade: its cost of
> production, its wholesale price, and its retail price. Before there was copy-
> right, the retailer bought books from the printer at wholesale rates, which
> were kept in check by the possibility of piracy. The advent of copyright
> enabled the owner of a copy to print it, or have it printed, and then sell at
> wholesale rates without fear of being undercut. The owners of copyright
> were retailers inasmuch as they were members of the Stationers' Company,
> even though some were printers as well. Such retailers could obtain their
> own publications at the cost of production; and, by exchanging these with
> other publisher-retailers, they could stock their shops at a rate below the
> wholesale price. The ownership of copyright was thus a practical advantage
> to the retailer, against which the bookbinder, who owned no copies and had
> to buy at wholesale rates, could not compete. The decline of the bookbinders
> is thus a consequence of the creation of copyright. . . ."[4]

As the advent of copyright resulted in the decline of the bookbinder,
so it gave rise to the publisher. Copyright enabled the publisher—or
bookseller, as he was called—to become the most powerful element
within the book trade, and in turn to reduce the position of the printer
to that of a mere journeyman.

The decline of the bookbinder apparently dated from some time in
the reign of Henry VIII, 1509–47, for Christopher Barker, in his "Report on Printing Patents," in December 1582, tells us, "In the tyme
of king Henry the eighte, there were . . . Stacioners; which haue, and
partly to this daye do vse to buy their books in grosse of the saide
printers, to bynde them vp and sell them in their shops, whereby they
well mayntayned their families."[5]

At any rate, by the date of the company's charter, the bookbinders
were already reduced to their condition of superior journeymen.

4. Graham Pollard, *The Early Constitution of the Stationers' Company*, XVIII
THE LIBRARY, 4th ser., 235, 253–254 (1937).
5. I ARBER 114.

Since the stationer's copyright was a publisher's right, it is appropriate to consider briefly printing and publishing practices of the stationers, to consider in some detail the company's control of copies, and to consider also the printer's right, a right of the printer analogous to the copyright of the publisher. A complete understanding of the stationer's copyright necessarily entails an examination of the practice of entrance in the company registers, the procedure and form of entrance, and the significant question whether entrance was actually required. Finally, it is necessary to deal with the problem of the rights of the author under the stationer's copyright.

Printing and Publishing

The distinction between printing and publishing is the difference between mechanically reproducing a book and the right to have the book reproduced. In addition, there is another function necessary to publishing: the sale of the completed product.

Since these functions are all complementary, they are subject to various arrangements, and during the time of press control, there were four basic arrangements for the publishing of books.

In the early days of the company, when the printers were the most powerful group within the organization, the printer was also the publisher, and often bookseller as well.[6]

Gradually, however, as the book trade expanded, a group of trade printers grew up who depended upon printing works for publishers, primarily booksellers,[7] creating the second basic arrangement for publishing. This was the arrangement which led to the increase of the booksellers' power, and in 1582, Christopher Barker, in his famous report, was complaining of the booksellers' growing position in the book trade. "The Booksellers being growen the greater and wealthier nomber haue nowe many of the best Copies and keepe no printing howse," he wrote, "neither beare any charge of letter, or other furniture but onlie paye for the workmanship. . . . "[8]

---

6. Shaaber, *The Meaning of the Imprint of Early Printed Books*, XXIV THE LIBRARY, 4th ser., 120, 123 (1944).
7. BLAGDEN, THE STATIONERS' COMPANY 74 (1960).
8. *Report on Printing Patents, December 1582*, I ARBER 114.

The two other basic arrangements for publication were the printer-publisher who arranged for his productions to be sold by a bookseller; and, finally, the strict publishing arrangement with a division of labor between the three principal groups of the book trade, the publisher, the printer, and the bookseller. This last arrangement, however, was a development of the seventeenth century, and not very common.[9]

These four arrangements for publishing were, of course, subject to variation, and partnerships in publishing ventures were common.[10] Some partnerships are known to have existed; others were undoubtedly in the nature of a joint venture. It has been suggested, for example, that a printer might purchase a copy and register it as his own to secure the workmanship, while relying on another for capital to finance his venture,[11] and that an impecunious bookseller might act likewise with a view to distribution.[12]

Whatever the business arrangements involved, the basic essential to publishing was the stationer's copyright, which protected the publisher in getting a return on his capital investment. Without this, any arrangement for publishing would have been too risky a venture.

That the publisher could legally protect his published books from being pirated by another did not, however, automatically mean that he had a legal right to print or publish the book in the first place. There were too many diverse interests to be reconciled to allow the ownership of copy to entail an absolute right of publication. Primary among these was the government's interest in censorship.

The Company's Control of Copies

From the Injunctions of 1559 to the final expiration of the Licensing Act of 1662[13] in 1694, with the exception of a few years during the Civil War, the Interregnum, and the last half of the seventeenth

9. There are about eighty examples of this arrangement for publishing books according to the imprint which are also entered in the Stationers' Registers. It exists as early as 1544, but 92 percent of the examples are after 1599. Shaaber, *op. cit.*, 134.

10. Shaaber, *op. cit.*, *passim*.

11. *Cf.* entrance at III ARBER 92: "Thomas Creede Entred for his copie . . . This copie to be alwaies printed for Nicholas Linge / by the seid Thomas Creede as often as it shalbe printed."

12. Greg, *Entrance, License, and Publication,* XXV THE LIBRARY, 4th ser., 1, 16 (1944).

13. 13 & 14 Car. II, c. 33.

century, all books printed in England were required to be licensed.[14]

But while the government regulated printing, the Stationers' Company regulated publication. On December 4, 1586/7, a company regulation designed to provide sufficient work for compositors limited the edition of an unprivileged book to 1250 copies. The ordinance also provided that no standing type should be used "to the hindrance of the Iornemen Printers: But that there shalbe asmanie Iournemen emploied from time to time in printinge" as there would be if no type was kept standing.[15] And on January 19, 1598, the company established by ordinance the sale price of books, with the penalty for violating the set rates being the loss of copyright in the book so sold: "And thereupon the same booke & books shalbe newly printed & disposed according to the discretion of the mr wardens & Assistents or the moore pate of them."[16] On February 23, 1612, the court ordered that when any printer or owner of a copy sold the whole impression of a book or copy to any freeman or brother of the company, the book should not be printed again unless by consent of the one buying the impression, or permission of the "Mr wardens & assistants or the more pte of them."[17]

An important aspect of the company's regulation of publication was the control which it exercised over the disposition of copies. The stationer's copyright was limited to members of the company,[18] and on the death of the owner, the copyright was at the disposal of the company. An order of December 17, 1565, provided that upon the

14. After the Injunctions of 1559 came the Star Chamber Decrees of 1566, 1586, and 1637. During the Civil War Period, acts regulating the press were the Ordinance of 1643. 1 FIRTH & RAIT, ACTS AND ORDINANCES OF THE INTERREGNUM, 184–187 (1911); the Ordinance of 1647, *Id.* at 1021–1023; the Ordinance of 1649, II FIRTH & RAIT, *op. cit.*, 245–254; and the Act of 1653, *Id.* at 696–699. Orders of the Lord Protector regulating printing were issued on August 28, 1655, reprinted in CLYDE, THE STRUGGLE FOR FREEDOM OF THE PRESS FROM CAXTON TO CROMWELL, Appendix E, pp. 323–337 (1934). The Licensing Act of 1662 was renewed, 16 Car. II, c. 7; 17 Car. II, c. 4, until the dissolution of the Cavalier Parliament in 1678, and was revived again for seven years in 1685, 1 Jac. II, c. 17, and renewed for the last time in 1692, 4 & 5 William & Mary, c. 24.

15. COURT BOOK B, 25.

16. COURT BOOK B, 59. For an example of the ordinance applied, see COURT BOOK C, 2.

17. COURT BOOK C, 57.

18. See order of January 19, 1598, limiting entrance of copies to members of the company. COURT BOOK B, 59.

death of the licensee—that is, the owner of the copyright gained by entrance, or the expiration of a privilege—no person was "to emprente or cause to be emprented the same Copye wthoute especiall lycence obtayned of the Mr Wardens and assesstaunts of the sayd Company:" The granting of a new license was to be according to the following rules: No new impression was to be granted until all books printed under the prior license were sold. Copies which consisted of a life interest were to be granted to the widow of the freeman for as long as she remained a widow and remained hers if she remarried within the company. Persons who took copies according to this ordinance were to verify the titles of the copies and the number of printed books remaining unsold. "All suche grants nots and determinations of any prvilege or intereste/and certificates of bokes vnsolde to be entred in the bokes of this Companye in suche sorte and wth lyke fees to the clerk as in and for the entries of previlege ys vsed to be."[19]

That these regulations were adhered to is indicated by orders in the books of the company. By order of the Court of Assistants, Joan Cooke, on October 5, 1607, succeeded to her deceased husband's half-interest in certain copies with Samuel Macham. Court Book C, page 27, records: "It is ordered that shee shall haue [half] of the booke wch Sam: Macham hathe prynted . . . And like [wise] for all the reste of the Copies that were entred to him and her husband that shee shall haue the halfe of euerye ympression [hereafter] bearinge halfe the Charge thereof / And yf she Marrye in the Companye then her intereste to contynue still accordinge to like proporcon in all the said books, But yf shee Marrye out of the Companye then her said intereste to Cease. . . . "

But Mrs. Barret, a widow who married out of the company, assigned her copies to Mr. Parker, and they, by order of the court, were entered to him.[20]

A stationer who married a stationer's widow was apparently entitled to her copies: an entrance of April 11, 1636, Court Book C, page 280, states that "Nicholas Vavasor Came to this Cort. and desired that the Copies lately appertayning vnto Leonard Beckett deceased (whose

19. Reprinted in Blagden, *The English Stock in the Stationers' Company*, X THE LIBRARY, 5th ser., 163, 177–178 (1955), Appendix I, from Liber A, *Orders of Parliament & Ld. Mayor*, f. 8ᵛ.

20. COURT BOOK C, 183.

widd he hath married) might be Entred vnto him in the Hall Booke of the Entrance of Copies, wch. the Table granted and haue ordered the same Copies to be Entred vnto him reserving euery mans Right."

If a widow's copies were undisposed of at her death, they became the property of the company,[21] by reason of the general rule that the death of a stationer put all his copies at the disposition of the company.[22]

The extent of the company's control over the disposition of copies is indicated by an entry in Court Book B on March 1, 1596, pertaining to the copies of a deceased stationer, Henry Byneman, who had died in 1583. At the motion of the husband of Byneman's widow, the copies of Byneman not otherwise disposed of were ordered to be entered to Valentine Syms, "who was servant to" Byneman. As to those copies which had been disposed of, Syms was given the printing of them "for the behoof of suche psons as they belonge vnto." As these copies became available "by death or otherwise," Syms was to have them entered to him, "prouided yt for so many of yem as are alredy graunted to any meere printer exercisinge printinge, the said val shall not clayme the printinge thereof from any suche printer."[23]

The Printer's Right

In this order we have an example of the "printer's right" to print copy, a right separate and distinct from copyright and which was "negotiable like an ordinary Copy."[24]

The printer's right originated in the economic difficulties of the company, a condition caused by an increasing number of workmen and the concentration of the best copies by printing patents into a few hands. The situation was magnified by the difference in the economic position of the small master printer, who wanted work for his press, and the bookseller. "Since the bookseller did not have to invest in printing-equipment he was more likely than the printer to have money to invest in publications; and since capital tends to breed capital the

---

21. See COURT BOOK C, 307.
22. See COURT BOOK C, 188; cf. COURT BOOK C, 87.
23. COURT BOOK B, 53.
24. Blagden, *The English Stock of the Stationers' Company*, X THE LIBRARY, 5th ser., 163, 172 (1955).

gulf between the bookseller investing in copyrights and the printer investing in type was likely to widen."[25]

One of the results of these difficulties was the Star Chamber Decree of 1586, which dealt with the problem from the government's
point of view; but the Stationers' Company found it necessary to take
other steps. Four of these steps were the encouragement to print unclaimed copies for the company;[26] the encouragement of printing
syndicates composed for several stationers to publish copies gained by
entrance;[27] copies controlled by letters patent;[28] and, finally, an attempt
to bring all printers and dealers of books into the company as members.

Because of the light it sheds on the stationer's copyright as being a
publisher's right, the most interesting aspect of the policy was the
emergence of the printer's right. As early as 1558/9, there is an entrance to John Tysdale to print a book for Richard Jugge, John Judson,
and Anthony Symthe,[29] and thus the practice was not without precedent. It was not, however, until after 1584, when John Harrison,
Junior, obtained the copy of a work, "Prouided that Robert waldegraue
shall have the printinge of euery ympression hereafter to be printed,"[30]
that the printer's right appears with enough frequency to be established as a separate right.[31]

25. Id. at 166.
26. See, e.g., III ARBER 157, "Symon Stafford Entred vnto hym for one Impression onely and no moo: to prynt for the Company. . . . "; similar entries to Felix
Kingston, III ARBER 101; Thomas Purfoot Senior "vpon condycon yat no other
partie haue Right vnto yt." III ARBER 137; and to Thomas Creede, III ARBER 103,
and Cutbert Burbye, II ARBER 671.
27. See II ARBER 422, where Henry Bynneman's entrance was conditioned on
the proviso that he "shall from tyme to tyme according to his good discretion
chose and accept any fyve of this cumpanie to be parteners with him in the
Imprintinge of these bookes."
28. See II ARBER 505, an entrance to the Master and Wardens "to th[e]use of
this Corporation" for the printing of The psalms of David in meter in the Scottish,
French, Dutch, and Italian language.
29. I ARBER 95.
30. II ARBER 435.
31. See, e.g., II ARBER 596, as to books entered to Thomas Adams, where "yt
is agreed (they) shalbe printed by John Charlwood for the said Thomas Adams: as
often as they shalbe printed." On July 6, 1589, the Court granted to Robert Robinson the right of printing Corderius' Dialogues "during the contynuance of the
lres patents graunted for the pryntinge thereof." One of the conditions expressed
was that Robinson should always "prynte the same booke as the Copye of the
said mr Harryson and mr Byshop," the patentees. COURT BOOK B, 32.

The printer's right was to the printer what the copyright was to the publisher, in that they both provided economic protection—the former for the craftsman, the latter for the entrepreneur. The value of the right is seen in those transactions where the vendor of the copyright reserved the right to print the works which were the subject matter of copyright.[32]

The order pertaining to Byneman's copies discussed above, where Valentine Syms was granted the printer's right of copies already vested in others, shows that copyright did not necessarily entail the printer's right.

The division of the two rights in this manner is almost conclusive evidence that the essential element of copyright was not the right to print, but the right to protection, once the book was published, in order to secure the profit from the sale.

When Edward White sold his copies to Thomas Pavier and John Wright on September 1, 1619, the contract was for the sale of the copies for seven years, which were to be entered to the vendees, but the provisions of the contract show that the sale of the copies was in the nature of an assignment of the privilege to publish the works.[33]

Entrance in the Registers

Entrance, as the term implies, signified the entering of the title of a work, together with the name of the person who was entitled to publish it, in the register book of the Stationers' Company. It was the form the stationer's copyright took, but there is some question whether entrance was necessary for copyright. Before dealing with this problem, however, it is necessary to deal with the procedure and form of entrance.

32. See, e.g., II ARBER 608, Thomas Scarlet to print books he and William Wright sold to Thomas Man; II ARBER 650, John Danter to print works he sold to Cuthbert Burbye; III ARBER 289, Simon Stafford to print works he sold to John Wright.

33. The contract provided "ffor the Consideracons herein expressed I haue sold vnto Thomas Pavier and John Wright for seauen yeares theis Copies vnder written which I desire maie be entred for their Copies, for that time soe the Condicons on their partes be performed." The conditions were, first, that White receive eighteen pence per ream for every impression printed within fourteen days after the books "shalbe finished." Secondly, White reserved the right to determine the number of printed books remaining in the hands of Pavier and Wright unsold "and if they shall not haue aboue the number of 150 bookes of anie sorte that then they

From the entries, we can gather that the procedure for obtaining copyright was for the stationer to present a copy—that is, a manuscript—licensed by the official authorities to the company wardens for the endorsement of their permission, after which the owner would submit the approved copy for entering on the register.[34] This remained the basic procedure throughout the existence of the stationer's copyright,[35] but we cannot assume that it was invariably adhered to. The form which entrance took on the register, however, did not remain the same.

The earliest forms of entrance, although they varied somewhat, were "Owyn Rogers ys lycensed to prynte a ballett Called *have pytie on the poore*,"[36] or "Recevyd of lucas haryson for his lycense for pryntinge of *a generall pardon forever*," with the notation of the fee.[37] The use of the term "license" has tended to create confusion, because of the

shall within one moneth after notice giuen or left in writeinge with them or either of them, reimprinte the said copies, which if they shall not doe or Cause to be done that then it shalbe Lawfull for me to dispose of them as I thinke fitt." Thirdly, White reserved the right to designate the printer "prouided the same Printer shall doe them as well, and for as reasonable a price as another will (bona fide) print them for." If the said printer "shalbe found to print anie more then the said Thomas and John shall agree for, and shall not doe them well and as reasonable for price as another will, that then it shalbe Lawfull for them to put them to print for the terme limitted, and vnder the Condicons expressed to whome they thinke fitt, so that I maie both knowe the printer & haue libtie to come into the printing house to see what nomber shalbe done from time to time vpon anie ympression of the said seuerall books." Finally, Pavier and Wright were to have the right to "ymprinte anie other copies that belonge vnto me vpon the same Condicons that are formerlie expressed." COURT BOOK C, 112–113.

34. In 1854, there is an entry reading, "Abraham Cotton Receaued of him for printinge A ballat intituled *A warnynge to wytches* entred by commaundement from master warden newbery vnder his own handwrytinge on ye backside of ye wrytten copie." II ARBER 440. A similar but less detailed description is given in an entry at II ARBER 432, dated June 5, 1584. *Cf.* entries at II ARBER 325, "Lycenced Vnder the handes of the Wardens," and at II ARBER 342, "lycencid by master Tottell and master Cooke vnder their handes in the tyme of their beinge wardens," several years earlier. If several works were allowed at the same time, apparently only one of them needed to be endorsed. II ARBER 432. In 1597, there was an order of the Court of Assistants stating the requisites for orderly printing as "aucthoritie" from an official licenser, "lycence" from the wardens, and "entraunce" in the REGISTER, COURT BOOK B, 57.

35. See entries for 1675–1708 in III EYRE & RIVINGTON which usually note "whereunto the hand of Master Warden . . . is subscribed."

36. I ARBER 96.

37. I ARBER 150.

connotations of censorship. It seems to be here used, however, in the sense of permission by the company, as indicated by a few entries, principally those under the dates of July 19, 1557, to July 9, 1558, which contain the clause, "and for his lycense he geveth to the house" a fee.[38] Where books were licensed by an official licenser, in the early entries, the term "auctorysshed by" was generally used,[39] although in later entries, the term "license" did come to be used to signify approval of the licensing authorities.

Changes in the form of entrance begin to occur about 1580, with the word "copy" replacing the words "to print." On September 5, 1580, an entry read, "Lycenced for his copie,"[40] and on July 27, 1580, there is the first of the rather curious entries reading, "Tollerated vnto him."[41] This form occurs fairly frequently for not quite two years, until March 10, 1582,[42] after which it disappears. Two minor variations of this entry infrequently used about the same time were "admytted vnto him"[43] and "allowed vnto him."[44] The reason for these anomalous forms is not clear. They may be simply a manifestation of the process of change, or they may be an early form of a conditional entrance, as later, entries were frequently made on condition that the copy belong to no one else, or with a proviso reserving every man's right.

The use of the word "copy" in the entries appears infrequently until about 1584, when such entries as "Graunted vnto him A copie,"[45] and "Receaued of master barker for A Copie,"[46] appear. Entries in these forms appear with greater frequency in 1585[47] and continue to appear with irregular frequency until some time in 1588, when they begin

---

38. See, e.g., I ARBER 78. Cf. the following use of the term license: "Recevyd of John hollender for his fyne for that he went from his master without lycense." I ARBER 183.

39. See, e.g., I ARBER 299. Official licenses are rare in REGISTER A. There are only about fifty among 1600 entries. Greg, *Entrance, License, and Publication*, XXV THE LIBRARY, 4th ser., 1, 8 (1944).

40. II ARBER 373.

41. II ARBER 375.

42. See II ARBER, 377, 382–87, 391–94, 396, 397 and 407.

43. II ARBER 378–379.

44. II ARBER 424.

45. II ARBER 430.

46. II ARBER 434.

47. II ARBER 444.

to predominate, and when it becomes obvious that the form "Entered for his copie" will prevail. By 1589, this form was so common that any other appears anomalous,[48] and in 1590, it is clear that the form of the entry in the Registers has evolved into: "John wolf. Entred for his copie. a book intituled *an admonicion to MARTIN MARPRELAT and his mates*: Aucthorised vnder the bysshop of Londons hand."[49]

The entries tended to vary somewhat, particularly as to the amount of information they contained, but it is necessary only to change the word "authorized" to "licensed" and add the name of the author to have the basic form used until March 7, 1709 (o.s.), the date of the last entrance before the enactment of the Statute of Anne.[50]

There was, however, one other subtle change.

Entries of assignments occur very frequently in the later registers, and sometime in the 1640s, the use of the terms "book" or "copy" in the disjunctive begin to appear in the entries of assignments, *i.e.*, "Assigned over unto him . . . this booke or copie . . . "[51] instead of "Assigned over unto him . . . this copie . . . . "[52] This new form continues to occur[53] with increasing frequency[54] until, by 1663, it is the accepted form; and on October 31, 1663, it is adopted for original entries, which from that time read "Entred for his copie under the hands of Master Roger Le Strange and Master Luke Fawne warden a booke or coppie intituled *Birinthea, a Romance* written by J.B."[55]

The form of the stationer's copyright, then, evolved from that of a license to print, to the ownership of copy, to the ownership of a book.

The change, however, was one of form only, not substance; and it is in the earliest form of entrance that we see the true nature of the

48. II Arber 513–536.

49. II Arber 538.

50. A new by-law of the company created a change in the method of entrance in 1682, requiring the entrance to be witnessed, and signed by the person to whom the copy was entered. III Eyre & Rivington 129. This form was followed until March 31, 1687, after which it ceased to be used generally, III Eyre & Rivington 319, although it occurs spasmodically thereafter. The change does not seem to have affected the concept of copyright in any way. The by-law is printed at I Arber 26.

51. I Eyre & Rivington 272, June 2, 1647.

52. I Eyre & Rivington 10, January 23, 1640.

53. I Eyre & Rivington 370, 373, 402, 404, 411, 417, 426.

54. II Eyre & Rivington 99, 169, 187, 190, 191, 192, 195, 197, 204, 205, 206, 209, 215, 219, 220, 222, 226, 227, 228, 232, 236, 238, 265, 284, 294, 295, 300, 306, 311, 324, 327, 330, 331.

55. II Eyre & Rivington 331.

stationer's copyright as permission of the wardens which entailed protection—not for the work itself, but protection for the right of one to publish the work. That this remained the nature of copyright is illustrated by a particularly full entrance to Charles Harper for the copyright for the laws of the Island of Jamaica in 1684, which reads in part: "These are therefore to authorise and impower Mr Charles Harper bookeseller to print the said *Booke of Laws* made for the use of that Island of Jamaica (from whome wee have received sattisfaccon for the same) and alsoe to forbid all other psons whatsoever to print the same without his leave first obteined, witnesse o[u]r hands the day and yeare within."[56]

The copyright of statutes presumably was no different from any other copyright. But more significantly, while books, ballads and pamphlets constitute the great majority of copyrighted works, there are also entries for maps,[57] pictures,[58] bills of lading,[59] and various legal forms,[60] as well as statutes.[61]

Entrance as a Requirement for Copyright

Although entrance on the company registers was the form of the stationer's copyright, there is some question as to whether entrance was necessary for copyright—a problem which has a direct bearing on

56. III EYRE & RIVINGTON 244.

57. See, e.g., entry to Gyles Godhed at I ARBER 211, 212, which includes "*The mappe of Englond and Skotlande*"; II EYRE & RIVINGTON 50, entry to Thomas Warren, "*The mapp of the citty of London* in 7 sheets."

58. See, e.g., I ARBER 212, II EYRE & RIVINGTON 33, 41, 195.

59. "Master Nich. Bourne. Entred for his copie (under the hand of Master Norton warden), all *Bills of Lading* in English, Ffrench, Dutch, Spanish, and Italian, to bee imprinted, being cutt in copper." II EYRE & RIVINGTON 40.

60. "Master Thos. Newcomb and Master Jno. Bellinger. Entred for their copies . . . certain formes of blank bonds or Obligacons & Conditions wth other Blankes suited to sevall occasions, engraven on copper plates, to be printed or drawn off with a rolling presse. . . . " II EYRE & RIVINGTON 317. See entry to Master Ambrose Isted, II EYRE & RIVINGTON 459 ("*a blanck certificate for takeing of the Sacramt*"); III EYRE & RIVINGTON 335 ("*All sorts of blanck pollices of Insurance on Ships Goods and Merchandize or any other thing relating thereunto.*"); see also II EYRE & RIVINGTON 460; III EYRE & RIVINGTON 60, 69.

61. "Master Henry Hills and Master John Field Entred for their copies Severall Acts made this present Parliament, begun at Westminster 17 day of September 1656. . . . " II EYRE & RIVINGTON 141. See similar entry at II EYRE & RIVINGTON 258 ("the severall Acts, Orders Proclamations, Votes & Resolves made by the late Parliamt and hereafter mentioned. . . . ").

the nature of the stationer's copyright. Bibliographical scholars disagree on this point. Until recently there were three principal views: that entrance was essential to copyright;[62] that copyright could be established by virtue of publication alone;[63] and that publication was necessary to establish copyright firmly.[64]

More recently, the view has been expressed that entrance was not necessary to legalize printing and publication, "but only to safeguard copyright."[65] These differences as to entrance boil down to the question of whether entrance was the copyright or only evidence of the copyright, and the views expressed may not be as divergent as might first appear, for the bibliographical scholars seem to be talking about two different things.

There is apparently no question but that entrance established copyright, for an entrance of April 12, 1595, to Henrie Olney is crossed with the notation, "This belongeth to master ponsonby by a former entrance And an agrement is made between them whereby Master Ponsonby is to enioy the copie according to the former entrance."[66]

But it seems likely that entrance was not the operative element and was not a formal requirement for copyright from the beginning of the company. An entrance of four ballads to Edward White on August 16, 1586, was made on the condition "yf any of these belonge to any other man. then this entrance to be voide."[67] Similarly, two sermons were entered to Robert Waldegrave a few days later, on August 22, 1586, "vpon condicon that they be Laufull and belong to no other."[68]

62. "So far from copyright being obtained by the mere act of publication, as has sometimes been supposed, unregistered publication might involve both the confiscation of copy and punishment of the offender." GREG, LONDON PUBLISHING 69 (1956).

63. KIRSCHBAUM, SHAKESPEARE AND THE STATIONERS 69 (1955). See also Kirschbaum, *The Copyright of Elizabethan Plays*, XIV THE LIBRARY, 5th ser., 231 (1959).

64. Graham Pollard, *The Early Constitution of the Stationers' Company*, XVIII THE LIBRARY, 4th ser., 235 (1937).

65. Sisson, *The Laws of Elizabethan Copyright: the Stationers' View*, XV THE LIBRARY, 5th ser., 8, 18 (1960).

66. II ARBER 295. See the earlier entrance at II ARBER 666. See also the entrance to Thomas Purfoote of September 5, 1586. "Receaued of him for his lycence to prynte, *a merye and pleasant Prognosticacon*, whiche was an old Copie of James Robotham." The entrance is crossed out with the notation, "yt is Edward aldees copie before entred." II ARBER 456.

67. II ARBER 455.

68. *Ibid.*

And it was not until August 2, 1596, that failure to enter a copy was named as an offense incurring a fine, when John Hardye was fined for printing a book "without authority and entrance."[69] On March 7, 1597, Thomas Millington was fined for printing a book before "yt was Aucthorised and entred,"[70] but it was not until April 2, 1599, that printing "without entrance" was specified as the sole offense.[71] There is only one more like instance in Register B, in 1620, "for printinge a booke without entrance Contrary to th[e] orders,"[72] and there are two other instances where failure to enter is joined "without Alowance"[73] and "without Aucthoritie,"[74] as being the offense. By way of contrast, fines were imposed freely for various misconduct,[75] and for irregular printing.

The fines in the registers pertaining to printing generally fall into one of three categories: for printing without license,[76] for printing another man's copy,[77] and for printing a named work contrary to the orders of the house or with no reason given for the fine.[78]

In Register B, the offenses for unlawful printing for which fines were imposed are phrased as being "for printinge a booke contrary to order,"[79] "without order,"[80] "without lycense,"[81] "for printing a ballat

---

69. II ARBER 826.
70. *Ibid.*
71. II ARBER 829.
72. II ARBER 835.
73. II ARBER 833.
74. II ARBER 837.
75. Fines were imposed "for feythtyenge with a prentes." I ARBER 44; "for vncurtes wordes vnto" a brother of the house. I ARBER 45; "for byndynge of bokes in shepes lether / contrary to our ordenaunces," I ARBER 70; "for not commynge to the hall on the quarter Daye," I ARBER 72; for "late apperynge," I ARBER 157; for opening "his shoppe vpon the sondayes," I ARBER 158; "for stytchyinge of bokes whyche ys contrary to the orders of this howse," I ARBER 158; for binding an apprentice and "not presentyinge hym Accordynge to the orders of this howse," I ARBER 158; "for sellinge of Nostradamus," I ARBER 216–218; for binding "*premers* vnlawfully contrary to the orders of howse," I ARBER 239; and "for yat he served *premers* and *Catchschesmes* to the haberdasshers contrary to ye orders of this howse," I ARBER 390.
76. I ARBER 70, 71, 93, 274, 275, 367.
77. I ARBER 93, 184, 239, 275, 277, 315.
78. I ARBER 316.
79. II ARBER 826, 828, 830, 835, 836, 843, 860.
80. II ARBER 847, 851, 854.
81. II ARBER 822, 847, 848, 849, 850, 851.

belonging to Ric Jones,"[82] "for printinge a boke for Thomas butter before the wardens handes were to yt,"[83] "without license and against the commandement of the wardens,"[84] "without authoritie,"[85] "printinge a booke disorderly,"[86] "for that he hathe transgressed th[e] ordynaunces in printinge bookes Contrary to the same,"[87] "without aucthority and entrance,"[88] "without license and contrary to order,"[89] "without allowance,"[90] and "without lycence contrary to the Constitution."[91]

Unfortunately, these specifications of the offenses are not very precise, but the emphasis is on permission from the wardens and this seems to have been the essential element of copyright, making copyright a license from the company, with entrance being only the evidence of permission.

From this, we can infer that entrance was a custom rather than a formal requirement under the ordinances. Since the earlier ordinances have not survived, we cannot be sure on this point; but one of the proposed ordinances of 1559 was that "Euery boke or thing to be allowed by the Stationers before yt be prynted."[92]

There is no mention of entrance as such, and the first mention of entrance as a legal requirement in any connection seems to have been in an Order of the Court of Assistants on December 17, 1565,[93] dealing with the disposition of copies upon the death of the licensee, or expiration of a privilege. The order provided that "All suche grants nots and determination of any previlege or intereste / and certificats of boks vnsolde to be entred in the bokes of this Companye in suche sorte

82. II Arber 850.
83. II Arber 853.
84. *Ibid.*
85. II Arber 824, 854.
86. II Arber 822, 824, 826, 827, 828, 836, 857, 862.
87. II Arber 860.
88. II Arber 826.
89. II Arber 831.
90. II Arber 833.
91. II Arber 835.
92. I Arber 350.
93. See Blagden, *The English Stock of the Stationers' Company*, X The Library, 5th ser., 163, 177 (1955), where the order is reprinted as Appendix A from Liber A, "Orders of Parliamt & Ld. Mayor," f. 8ᵛ.

and with lyke fees to the clerk as in and for the entries of previlege ys vsed to be."

The words pertaining to the entrance of privileges "ys vsed to be" possibly give a clue as to the origin of entrance as being a record of privileges granted by the sovereign. A vestige of this former practice, if it were such, is seen in an entrance in 1558 or 1559 whereby "Rycharde Tottle broughte in a patente for pryntinge of bokes of Lawe / to be confyrmed and allowed by this howse. . . ."[94]

The entering of privileges was not required, but it is easy to see how, in earlier times before the company was chartered and its power enhanced, it would be a convenience to the patentees to have their privileges recorded, particularly since they were of limited duration, and how this practice would be carried over to the owners of copies which were not protected by letters patent. The evidence on this point is too slight to make this any more than conjecture, but it is consistent with the idea that entrance was at first only customary rather than legally required. If entrance was at first only a matter of custom, how-ever, there is sufficient evidence that the custom became a legal re-quirement, probably at first by reason of orders of the Court of Assistants rather than by formal ordinance approved by the govern-ment.

On April 10, 1597, an order of the court resulted in the destroying of Edward Aldee's press for printing "disorderlie wthout aucthoritie lycence [or] [and] entraunce;"[95] on April 13, 1603, an entry in Court Book C pertaining to a controversy over the printing of King James' *Basilicon Doron* entered to six stationers on March 26, 1603,[96] recites the printing of the work without "Aucthoritie licence or entrance" con-trary to the "order for lycensinge & entranc' of Copies;"[97] and on De-cember 7, 1607, an order aimed at preventing the entrance of copies for any other than members of the Company does two things: (1) limits the right of entrance to members of the Company; (2) forbids

94. I ARBER 95. *Cf.* the following entrance to Master Newbery and Master Den-ham: "Receaved of them for their licence and allowance to printe all these bo[o]kes followinge, whiche doe belonge vnto them by vertue of ye queenes pryviledge and grante . . . " II ARBER 438.
95. COURT BOOK B, 57.
96. III ARBER 230.
97. COURT BOOK B, 2.

any stationer to aid anyone to have, get, or print any copy or book which is not entered in the registers. The order is somewhat ambiguous and bears quoting for that reason. It reads: "Yt is thought meete and so ordered by a full Cour of the Maister, Wardens and assistants holden this day. That the wardens of this Company shall not hereafter assigne appoint or suffer to be entered or Registered in this Companye, Any Copye or booke whatsoeu', for any pson or psons but suche onely (& none other) as shalbe Resiant and dwellinge here amongst the Companye in and about the citie of London and be contributors to all charges of the companie. And that no prynter nor any other pson or psons of this Company Shall by any vnderhand or overt dealinge, assiste, further, Ayde, or Helpe any pson or psons to Haue gett or prynte any Copie or booke in pte or in all contrary to the true meaning of this order, or that shalbe to be prynted or Authorised here or els where beinge not first entred and registred in this Companie. Vppon payne to be punished for doinge to the contrary of this Last clause or Article, Accordinge to the qualitie of thoffence by Fine, Forfaiture, ymprisonment or otherwise accordinge to the discretion of the Maister, Wardens, and Assistents, for the tyme beinge or the moore pte of them."[98]

Finally, on September 27, 1622, the Court issued the following: "It is this daie ordered that noe Printer shall print anie booke except the Clarke of the Companies name be to it to signifie that it is entered in the hall Booke accordinge to order."[99]

That entrance was firmly established as a requirement by 1637, with a penalty of forfeiture for failure to enter possible, is shown by another order of the court which recited the grant of the copies of Mr. Allott, deceased,[100] to Mr. Legatt and Andrew Crooke "and soe to be entred vnto them according to the Custome of this Company in the Register booke of the Entry of Copies. Now forasmuch as notice hath byn giuen them to Enter their Copies but they hitherto haue neglected the same, But since the said grant to them doe print diuers of the said Copies. It is this day ordered. That if the said Legatt and Crooke doe not Enter their Copies betweene this and the next Cort.

98. COURT BOOK C, 31.
99. COURT BOOK C, 149.
100. See COURT BOOK C, 287.

leaue shall be giuen for the printing of them for the Companies vse."[101]

It would be comforting to know whether the word "custom" is here used to refer to custom, or whether it was used also to refer to orders of the court and ordinances of the company. It seems likely that the word referred to custom re-enforced by order. The reason for this conclusion is found in the company ordinance of 1682.

The same year in which Legatt and Crooke were ordered to enter their copies, the Star Chamber Decree of 1637 was issued, providing that no work should be printed unless it "shall be first lawfully licensed . . . and shall be also first entred in the Registers Booke of the Company of Stationers."[102] This requirement was carried forward in the subsequent licensing acts. The Ordinance of 1643 provided no book should be printed until officially licensed "and entred in the Register Book of the Company of Stationers, according to ancient custom."[103] The Act of 1649, however, simply provided for protection for books "duly entred in the Register Book of said Company," without making it a requirement.[104] The Licensing Act of 1662 provided "That no private person or persons whatsoever shall at any time hereafter print . . . any book or pamphlet whatsoever, unless the same . . . be first entered in the book of the register of the Company of Stationers in London. . . . "[105]

In 1679, however, the Licensing Act of 1662 lapsed and was not renewed again until 1685,[106] and the company got approval for new ordinances in 1678, 1681, and 1682, apparently as a result of the impending and subsequent collapse of the governmental machinery for press control. The Ordinances of 1678 do not mention entrance at all, but the Ordinances of 1681 have a lengthy provision providing protection for copies which are entered. This ordinance reads: "V. And whereas several Members of this Company have great part of their Estates in Copies; and by ancient Usage of this Company, when any Book or Copy is duly Entred in the Register Book of this Company,

101. Court Book C, 294. The copies were entered on July 1, 1637. IV Arber 387–388. Cf. Court Book C, 311.

102. IV Arber 530.

103. I Firth & Rait, Acts and Ordinances of the Interregnum 184, 185 (1911).

104. II Firth & Rait, op. cit., 245, 251.

105. 13 & 14 Car. II, c. 33, par. III.

106. I Jac. II, c. 17.

to any Member or Members of this Company, such Person to whom such Entry is made, is, and always hath been reputed and taken to be Proprietor of such Book or Copy, and ought to have the sole Printing thereof; which Priviledg[e] and Interest is now of late often violated and abused: It is therefore Ordained, That where any Entry or Entries, is, or are, or hereafter shall be duly made of any Book or Copy in the said Register-Book of this Company. . . . "[107]

The ordinance does not read as if entrance had ever been the subject of a formal ordinance. This is supported by the fact that on December 6, 1682, three years after the lapse of the Licensing Act, the company found it necessary to get approval for an ordinance making entrance a formal requirement, not only for a first printing, but any reprinting: "Whereas, It hath been the Ancient Usage of the Members of this Company, for the Printer or Printers, Publisher or Publishers of all Books, Pamphlets, Ballads, and Papers, (except what are granted by Letters Pattents under the Great Seal of *England*) to Enter into the Publick Register-Book of this Company, remaining with the Clerk of this Company for the time being, in his or their own Name or Names, All Books, Pamphlets, Ballads, and Papers whatsoever, by him or them to be Printed or Published, before the same Book, Pamphlet, Ballad or Paper is begun to be Printed, To the end that the Printer or Publisher thereof may be known, to justifie whatsoever shall be therein contained, and have no Excuse for the Printing or Publishing thereof; which Usage this Company now taking into their Consideration, do think that the due Observation thereof may be a means to prevent the Printing and Publishing of Treasonable, Seditious, and Scandalous Books, Pamphlets, Libels, and Papers, or Discover the Printers or Publishers thereof.

"It is therefore Ordained, That all and every Member or Members of this Company shall before the Printing or reprinting of any Book, Pamphlet, Ballad, or Paper (except what are granted under the Great Seal of *England* as aforesaid) in his own Person cause to be Entred into the Register-Book of this Company . . . in his and their own Name and Names in words at length, the Title of all and every Book, Pamphlet, and Paper, that he or they shall hereafter Print or Publish, or cause to be Printed or Published. And to which Entry he or they shall set and

---

107. I ARBER 22–23.

subscribe his and their respective Name and Names; upon pain of forfeiting to the Master, and Keepers or Wardens, and Commonelty of the
Mystery or Art of *Stationers* of the City of *London*, Twenty Pounds;
to be by them Recovered by Action of Debt, to their own use. . . . "[108]

A Suggested Solution

Even though there is substantial evidence that entrance came to
be a strict requirement, there is equally substantial evidence that only
between sixty and seventy percent of London-printed books were regularly entered in the registers,[109] and that the proportion of printed
books entered fluctuated violently from year to year. This disparity can
be accounted for in part by the failure of the system, so to speak, but
the degree of the differences, resulting in divergent opinions by emi-
nent scholars, requires further explanation.

It is, in fact, this variation between theory and practice which may
give the clue to the real nature of the stationer's copyright. The two
conclusions that entrance was essential to copyright and that copyright could be acquired by publication only could both be wrong, because they proceed from the assumption that the ownership of copy
and copyright were synonymous.

The ownership of copy itself does not seem to have provided protection upon publication; and entrance in the register book does not
seem to have been conclusive of the right to protection, but only evidence of this right. In 1620, John Bill, in writing of Bishop's publication
of Fulke's *Answer to the Rhemish Testament*, entered December 9,
1588, at II Arber 510, said: " . . . he (Bishop) had ye printing of yat
copie to him and his Assignes. and this appeares by witnesses as also
by ye Registry of ye Stationers hall where this was entred before ye
master and wardens of ye Stationers at a court the[n] holden as all
copies which are bought by Stationers are And this entry in ye hall
booke is the commun and strongest assurance yat Stationers haue, for
all their copies. which is the greatest parte of their Estates."[110] Under
this view, copyright was the permission of the wardens, for it was only
license from the wardens that guaranteed protection for published

108. I ARBER 26.
109. Greg, *Entrance, License and Publication*, XXV THE LIBRARY, 4th ser., 1, 7
(1944); GREG, LONDON PUBLISHING 68 (1956).
110. III ARBER 39.

works. The early practice of the Brotherhood of Stationers in granting copyright, described in "The Appeal of William Seres the Younger to Lord Burghley," December 1582, does not mention entrance. " . . . no copie of any boke grete or small should be prynted before yt was brought thether and beinge there allowed yt is our order that no man should prynt any other mans copie."[111]

If this is correct, the dispute over whether books which were published and not entered in the registers were or were not copyrighted takes on less significance. The registration of his copyright was apparently at the choice and will of the stationer,[112] because it was primarily for his protection. There were undoubtedly many instances where a published work once on the market was no longer of any value, and not worth the fee and effort of having it registered. Nor does the fact that entrance became a strict requirement affect the conclusion as to the essential nature of copyright, because entrance remained evidence of the copyright, not the copyright itself. The instances where failure to enter a work resulted in a forfeiture of the copyright are evidence of this, for these decisions were the enforcement of a penalty, and not to the effect that the copyright never existed.

On the other hand, it is not surprising that some books were apparently published without entrance and when later the copyright was transferred were entered on the register. These books may have been copyrighted—that is, published with the permission of the wardens— or they may have been published simply by virtue of the ownership of the manuscript, without a copyright. That, in the latter instance, the wardens should, in effect, grant retroactive copyright is not surprising, since the condition precedent was present and no damage to another's interest would result.

The Rights of the Author

The author was not a member of the Stationers' Company, and he had no role in developing and shaping the stationer's copyright. Yet, the importance of the author to copyright is such that a consideration

111. II ARBER 771, 772.
112. Sisson, *op. cit.*, 18.

of the rights of the author during the period of the stationer's copyright is necessary to an understanding of that copyright. The present assumption seems generally to be that the stationer's copyright precluded a recognition of any rights of the author.[113] Such a conclusion is not surprising, for during the Elizabethan period, when they were held in low esteem, "authors as a whole, including professionals like Nashe, never quite made up their minds whether they were professionals or amateurs."[114] And authors continued to rely on patrons for support until the eighteenth century.

Still, to say that no rights of the author were recognized during the time of the stationer's copyright is to view the problem in a too simplistic manner. The relationship between authors and the stationers existed on a much more complex and sophisticated level over too long a period of time. Despite the company's rule, renewed on December 7, 1607, limiting the right of the entrance to members of the company,[115] from which, of course, authors were excluded, there are recorded occasions of the grant of copyright to the author for his own works. On

---

113. See MILLER, THE PROFESSIONAL WRITER IN ELIZABETHAN ENGLAND 137 (1959). *Cf.* "So far as the author was concerned, no rights existed; in a few cases, it is true, a royal patent was granted to a particular individual giving him a monopoly of his work for a specified period, but those exceptions only serve to accentuate the general case." Aldis, *The Book Trade, 1557–1625* in 4 CAMBRIDGE HISTORY OF ENGLISH LITERATURE 446–447 (1909).

114. MILLER, *op. cit.,* 140. *Cf.* the following, Nashe's dedication of THE TERRORS OF THE NIGHT to Mistress Carey: "As touching this short glose or annotation on the foolish Terrors of the Night . . . A long time since hath it line suppressed by mee: vntill the vrgent importunitie of a kinde frend of mine (to whom I was sundrie waies beholding) wrested a Coppie from me. That Coppie progressed from one scriueners shop to another, & at length grew so common, that it was readie to bee hung out for one of their signes, like a paire of indentures. Wherevppon I thought it as good for mee to reape the frute of my owne labours, as to let some vnskillful pen-man or Nouerintmaker startch his ruffle & new spade his beard with the benefite he made of them." Quoted in A. W. POLLARD, SHAKESPEARE'S FIGHT WITH THE PIRATES, 32 (1920). Pollard comments: "Although the booklet was being so repeatedly copied by different scriveners not only did none of them make a second copy and sell it to a printer, but Nashe does not seem even to have considered the possibility of this being done. It is solely the benefit or pay which the 'vnskillfull pen-man' might make by producing manuscript copies that he grudges him. Yet in 1594 a pamphlet by Nashe had probably as high a selling value as any other book of the same length that was being put on the market." *Ibid.*

115. COURT BOOK C, 31.

March 1, 1618, license was given to Reynold Smith "to ymprint his table & Computacon that he hath made and to sell them wthout interruption of the Company;"[116] and on September 5, 1631, John Standish "became a Sutor to the Mr. Wardens & assistants for leave to print" his book, "the Psalms of David accorded to the french & Germaine verses and tunes." The Court of Assistants granted, "That an impression of a 1000 of them shall be printed at the Charge of the author." For this privilege, Standish was to give only "a quarterne of the said bookes vnto the Company," for after the impression was sold, the copyright was to go to the partners of the English Stock.[117]

That the relations between the stationers and authors were cooperative rather than competitive is illustrated again by an entrance of November 19, 1661, to Henry Herringman which carries the following notation: "This entrance was importunately desired to be cross't out by Mr Herringman, who, as he had no hand in printing it, so he protests not to have knowne the nature of it sooner, & that he did it only to secure it to ye authour on his request."[118] Unfortunately, as with most entries, the details are unavailable to us, but the custom of stationers' entering copies for others was apparently not an unusual one. After 1640 there are several entries which contain the statement that the work is published by a person, occasionally the author, other than the stationer to whom the copy was entered.[119]

This practice was probably the result of cooperation with the author of a work to which the copyright was not financially attractive to enable him to have it published by underwriting the cost of printing. Evidence of such an arrangement appears in reference to a theological work by Henry More, which appeared in 1675 under the title of *Henrici Mori Cantabrigiensis Opera Theologica*.[120] More's account of the terms of the agreement clearly implies that he is seeking a publisher, and that the arrangement was to be such as to prevent the publisher from suffering a loss. The impression was to be five hundred copies, of which

116. *Id.* at 107.
117. *Id.* at 231–232.
118. II EYRE & RIVINGTON 304.
119. I EYRE & RIVINGTON 392; II *Id.* 166, 222, 265, 307; III *Id.* 27.
120. McKerrow, *A Publishing Agreement of the Late Seventeenth Century*, XIII THE LIBRARY, 4th ser., 184 (1932).

More was to have twenty-five without cost. As to the remainder, he apparently had the alternative of buying one hundred copies outright at fifteen shillings each, with the hope of selling at the regular publisher's price of twenty shillings; or he could purchase only so many books as he could dispose of, but pay the price the bookseller paid, sixteen shillings per copy. The account reads: "I hav 25 copies that cost me nothing, and buy 100 copies of ye 500, and not at such a rate as they usually sell such small Impressions at the booksellars, yt is twice the value of what they cost at the printing house, but onely half as much againe in yt proportion that 3 is to 2, so yt if a book for example stand them at the printing house papyr and printing 10 s. I shall pay fifting shillinges, and thought this was a better way than to pay one fifth part lesse then ye booksellers would sell it for. But if I hav any book myself it will not prove very much I hoope."[121]

This type of arrangement, or a similar one, was probably fairly common, for there are examples of books with imprints showing that the book was printed for the author, who presumably bore the expense of publication.[122] Most of the examples are books of limited interest, "mathematical text-books, picture books, and the like,"[123] in which copyright would be unattractive financially. Even so, such examples further indicate that the relationship between authors and stationers was not a simple one.

The complexity of this relationship, the unique conditions under which it occurred, and the long period of time over which it existed preclude any simple answers to the problem of the rights of the author.

Of the two basic types of rights, property rights and personal rights, it is the former which the stationers most clearly and obviously recognized in the author.

The basic aspect of the property right was the right of the author to be paid for his work, and the evidence indicates that the stationers recognized this right from the beginning. This does not mean, of course, that piracy from authors did not exist under the stationer's copyright as it did under statutory copyright, for the career of the

121. *Id.* at 184–185.
122. Shaaber, *The Meaning of Imprint in Early Printed Books*, XXIV THE LI-BRARY, 4th ser. 120 (1944).
123. *Id.* at 137.

most infamous literary pirate in the history of the book trade, Edmund Curll, extended some thirty years after the passage of the Statute of Anne in 1709.[124] But during the Elizabethan period, "the appropriation of literary rights without permission or payment, which we call piracy, in so far as it can be proved, was largely concerned with the works of dead authors, or of men whose rank would have forbidden them to receive payment for their books."[125]

As early as November 11, 1559, there is evidence of an explicit recognition of the author's right to payment. The grantee in a "License to John Day" was given the privilege of printing "*the Cosmographicall glasse* compiled by William Cunningham doctor in Physicke as also duringe the tyme of seven yeares all suche bookes and Workes as he hath Imprinted or hereafter shall imprinte beinge deuysed compiled or set oute by any learned man at the paymente costes and Charges onely of the saide John Daye . . ."[126]

In 1620, "John Bill's Representation of the *History of Doctor Fulke's Answer to the Rhemish Testament*,"[127] written about 1588, recounts how George Bishop subsidized the author for nine months and paid him forty pounds for the copyright of his work.[128]

In 1602, there is a record of a dispute between Mr. Burbie and Mr. Dexter concerning the printing of the *English Schoolmaster*, wherein it was ordered, "And all charges aswell to the Aucthor as otherwise to be equally borne betweene them pte and pte like,"[129] and in 1619, when Thomas Jones and Lawrence Chapman printed a work without the consent of the author's wife, the Court of Assistants ordered them to pay her twenty shillings "for a recompence."[130]

But the clearest example of recognition of the company for legal liability to an author for printing his works without compensation is found in an agreement entered into on March 4, 1615, between the company and James Pagett of the Middle Temple, who sold the company "A certaine number of books Called A promptuarye or Reper-

124. A. W. POLLARD, *op. cit.*, 33.
125. *Id.* at 32.
126. II ARBER 61.
127. Entered on December 9, 1588, to G. Bishop. II ARBER 510.
128. III ARBER 39.
129. COURT BOOK B, 88.
130. COURT BOOK C, 119.

toyre generall of the yeare books of the Comon Lawe of Englande."[131]
Pagett was apparently one of three authors of the work, with Thomas
Ashe and Sergeant Jones.[132] The company paid three hundred pounds
for the books, and Pagett entered into a covenant to save the company
harmless from the other authors, i.e., "Tho. Ashe and his assigns."

The right of an author to receive payment for his works is such an
elementary right that the major point can be easily overlooked. It was
necessary for a stationer to obtain the author's permission to publish
his work, and thus for copyright, even though the copyright was
granted by the Stationers' Company. Several orders of the Court of
Assistants substantiate the point. On December 6, 1625, there is an
order pertaining to certain works by Mr. Farnaby. Raffe Rounthaite
had entered the works, which he printed for Philemon Stephens and
Christopher Meredith.[133] It was ordered that the entry be crossed out
and the copy be left to Mr. Farnaby "to dispose of to some other of
the Company to whom he will." Stephens and Meredith were ordered
to give Mr. Farnaby "for 750 wch was last printed to recompence him
for the printing of it against his will 45 s. to be paid the last day of
Candlemas terme."[134]

On August 10, 1632, there is an entrance in the Register to John
Waterson "crost out by his owne consent and resigned to the Author";[135] and on January 19, 1632, there is an entry in Court Book C
where the author complained of Mr. Harrison's printing his work,
whereupon Harrison resigned his interest.[136]

On June 4, 1638, we find the following instructive entry: "Mr.
Clarke brought mr Chillingworths booke called the Religion of Protes-
tants a Safe way to Saluation (wch booke was printed at Oxford) &
desired the same might be entred to him haueing the Authors and
the printers. Consent. wch being Shewed in Cort. It was ordered that
the said booke should be entred vnto him accordingly."[137]

The stationers, in acknowledging a duty to pay the author and to

131. COURT BOOK C, 82.
132. *Id.*, n. 1.
133. See IV ARBER 123.
134. COURT BOOK C, 191.
135. IV ARBER 282.
136. COURT BOOK C, 245.
137. COURT BOOK C, 310.

obtain his permission before acquiring a copyright, recognized the author's initial property right in his works. To that extent, their conduct presaged what was later to become known as the common-law copyright of the author, the right of first publication.

The difficult problem, however, is whether the stationers recognized the author's personal rights. Part of the difficulty is semantic, for the term "rights" may be used with any number of meanings—for example, to mean an inchoate right, a legal right, or a natural right. When we speak of a well defined body of rights such as property rights, there is little difficulty.

The common law has traditionally been oriented to property rights and has always given them definitive protection.

Personal rights are more comprehensive than property rights, and such rights have been less favored by the common law. Thus, the term "personal rights" is often used to indicate either an inchoate right or a natural right rather than a legal right. Used as meaning an inchoate right, the term designates a relationship which is a matter of special concern and which should be, or may be, but is not definitively protected by law. Used to mean natural right, the term designates a relationship which should be, and in fact may be, protected by law by reason of the nature of the relationship. For the most part, the term "author's rights" is here used to indicate an inchoate right or a natural right or both.

The personal rights of the author as author, however, are unique, because of the unique nature of his work. The author, here used as the exemplar of the artist, is a creator, and as such his work differs from that of others. First, his work is an extension of his personality; second, his work constitutes contributions to the culture of society. Since his contributions to society are unique and particularly valuable, it is to the interest of society to give special protection to the author's personal interest in those contributions. The author's relationship to his works is such that he should be given a degree of continuing control sufficient to enable him to protect the integrity of his work. The point is, perhaps, more graphically illustrated by reference to the artist. A distorted painting is more readily manifest than a distorted manuscript and few would dispute the propriety of enabling the artist to prevent the distortion of his paintings, or the sale of reproductions of his paintings which had been distorted. So with the author, whose creations are no less an extension of his personality. These rights of the author and artist are personal to them to protect their personality, but they are based on the fact of their creation. Thus, these personal rights can best be identified as creative rights, which can be defined as continuing rights of the author necessary to insure and maintain the integrity of the work he has created by preventing its distortion by others.

The answer to the problem of the stationer's recognition of the author's creative rights is not so readily apparent as the answer to the problem of his property rights. Clearly, there was no well defined body of creative rights enforceable in courts of law or even in the Court of Assistants. But just as clearly, the stationers respected the unique interest an author as author has in his works, even though they perhaps did so as a matter of self-interest.

In considering this problem it will be helpful to remember that the stationers, as businessmen, were primarily interested in themselves and their profits; any creative rights of the author they recognized were a by-product of the copyright they shaped to their own ends and purposes. The initial question, then, is whether such rights were consistent with the aims and purposes of the stationers and their copyright.

The answer is yes, for the stationer's copyright was literally a right to copy—that is, a right to reproduce a given work for sale. The basic purpose of this right was to provide order for the book trade by establishing a method to enable publishers to have the exclusive right to publish a work without competition as to that work. And the sanctions for copyright came from the company, for it was the company, not the author, which granted the copyright. From the stationers' viewpoint, copyright was protection against rival publishers, not against authors, and the existence of continuing rights of the author in his work was consistent with the existence of copyright in the stationer.

The extent of these rights in the author is not clear, but it is almost certain that the stationers recognized the right of the author, and by implication, only the author, to alter and revise his work despite the existence of copyright. An entrance of October 24, 1586, of Dr. Bright's *A Treatise of Melancholie* to Master Byshop and John Wyndett contains the following note: "Memorandum that master Doctour Bright hathe promised not to medle with augmenting or alteringe the saide book vntill th[e] impression which is printed by the said John Windet be sold."[138] Had the stationers not recognized the right of an author to alter his work, the securing of Doctour Bright's promise would have served no purpose.

And that the point was the right of the author, rather than his power to do so, is supported by those entries of works "newly Altered and enlarged" by the author,[139] which presumably entitled one to an additional copyright. On June 5, 1610, for example, there is an entry to Master Mann, senior, and Jonas Mann of "*Three sermons, or certayne sermons preached in Oxfordshire*, the first by master Robert Clever, and the Twoo last by master John Dodd heretofore published and nowe newly corrected by the Authors wherevnto is added another *sermon* of master Clever *on Psalme* 51."[140] And on December 9, 1611, there is an entrance to Samuell Macham of a work in Latin by "Joseph Hall Theologiae Doctore" followed by the following entrance: "*Item Entred for his Copy the same booke to be printed in Englishe yf ye Author please to haue it translated.*"[141]

This entrance, incidentally, is an example of a common practice during this period indicating the limited nature of the stationer's copyright and by implication, a recognition of the author's creative right. The practice was that of entering a work before it was written, or more often, translated. Such entries carry the condition that the work is to be approved by the licensing authorities before it is printed.

The above examples, of course, are not conclusive as to the existence of the author's creative rights. On the other hand, neither are they exhaustive, for other entries of similar import are to be found in the registers, and there is no way of knowing the many unrecorded instances that may have occurred. While we cannot assume that the stationers always and invariably respected the author's creative interest, neither did they always enter their copies in the register, nor did they always respect each other's rights. Many variable factors undoubtedly influenced the stationer in his attitude toward a particular

138. II ARBER 457.
139. III ARBER 406.
140. *Id.* at 435.
141. *Id.* at 473.

author and his actions in regard to any particular work, of which the rules, regulations, and customs of the company were only a part.

Not the least of these additional factors would be the nature of the work involved, its lasting value, its potential market, and its acceptability to the licensing authorities. A sermon was undoubtedly treated differently from a ballad, and a play differently from a dictionary. Moreover, the entries do not inform us of the underlying transactions. Thus, on June 7, 1608, John Fflaskett assigned to John Bill "*A Dictionarie* in Ffrenche and Englishe Collected first by C. Holyband and sythenc[e] Augmented or Altered by Randall Cotgrave."[142] A reasonable inference here is that Cotgrave "augmented or altered" the work with the consent of Holyband, but perhaps not. We do not know. Still, the fact of the notation indicated that there was no unwarranted meddling with the author's work.

In addition to the entries and orders in the company records, there is one further factor of broader scope which tends to confirm the recognition of author's rights by the stationers. This was the nature of the conveyance from the author to the publisher.

Of two points about the author's conveyance, we can be certain: it was not a conveyance of copyright, but it was more than the sale of a manuscript.

On the first point, the author could not, of course, convey a copyright, for only the company granted copyright.

On the second point, the conveyance had to be more than the mere sale of a manuscript; the stationer was not interested in the manuscript for its intrinsic value, but only for the purpose of publishing.

Again, however, the author could not convey the right to publish, for the printing of a work was subject to the laws of censorship. The ostensible dilemma to which these factors lead is easily resolved by a return to the basic premise—that the stationers recognized a duty on their part to pay the author and to obtain his permission to publish his work. That permission, from a legal standpoint, was a negative rather than an affirmative one. The author's conveyance was in effect a negative covenant—that is, a contract not to object to the publication of the work, rather than a contract granting a right to publish it.

142. *Id.* at 381.

The point is illustrated by Milton's contract for the publishing of *Paradise Lost*.[143] The contract recites that John Milton "hath given, granted, and assigned, and by these (presents) doth give, grant, and assigne, unto the said Sam[ll]. Symons, his executors and assignes, All that Booke, Copy or Manuscript of a Poem intituled Paradise lost, . . . now lately Licensed to be printed . . . "

This language, similar to the language of a deed, implies complete ownership of the work, but its effect was to convey title to the manuscript actually turned over to the purchaser. The essence of the contract is the covenant on the part of Milton. "And the said John Milton . . . doth covenant with the said Sam[ll]. Symons, . . . that hee . . . shall at all tymes hereafter have, hold, and enjoy the same, and all Impressions thereof accordingly, without lett or hinderance of him, the said John Milton, . . . And that the said Jo. Milton, . . . shall not print or cause to be printed, or sell, dispose, or publish, the said Booke or Manuscript, or any other Booke or Manuscript of the same tenor or subject, without the consent of the said Sam[ll]. Symons . . . "

The significant point is that Symons required Milton to promise that he, as author, would not interfere with the publishing of the work. Such promises would hardly have been necessary if copyright had been deemed to give the copyright owner all rights in connection with the copyrighted work.

A more sophisticated example of the conveyance of the author is found in the sale by James Thomson, the poet, of his works, which were the subject of litigation in *Millar v. Taylor* and *Donaldson v. Beckett*, the two landmark cases in English copyright law. The contracts are discussed in a report of the *Donaldson* case,[144] and are revealing because there are two conveyances, one from the author to a bookseller, and one from a bookseller to another bookseller. The first contract, from Thomson, the author, to Millar, the bookseller, was in 1729, whereby Thomson "did assign to Millar, his executors, administrators and assigns, the true copies of the said tragedy and poem, and the sole and exclusive right and property of printing the said copies for his and their sole use and benefit, and *also all benefit of all addi-*

---

143. The contract is transcribed in 6 MASSON, LIFE OF JOHN MILTON 509–511 (1946).
144. 2 Bro. P.C. 129, 1 Eng. Rep. 837, 838.

tions, corrections, and amendments which should be afterwards made in the said copies."[145]

The second contract, from Millan, a bookseller, to Millar in 1738, conveying other works of Thomson originally sold to Millan, included "all the right, title, interest, property, claim, and demand of the said John Millan to or in the said copies."

By virtue of these agreements, "Andrew Millar became lawfully entitled to all the profits arising by the printing and publishing of the several poems . . . and to all the sole and exclusive property and right of printing copies of them, and of vending and disposing of the same."[146]

The emphasis on the right of printing and the benefit of additions and alterations of the author in the conveyance from Thomson contrasted with the emphasis on profits in the conveyance from Millan highlights the limited nature of the stationer's copyright. More important, however, the implication here that the author retained sufficient control over his work to make additions, corrections, and amendments—note the language, "which should be afterwards made" —notwithstanding the ownership of copyright in another is a clear example of the recognition of author's creative rights.

Further, it points up the value of analyzing the author's conveyance in terms of a negative covenant rather than the sale of his work. The distinction is more than one of semantics, and it is helpful because we have here a unique example of a chattel being conveyed not for its intrinsic value, but to enable the purchaser to exercise the right which is actually being conveyed. The manuscript is more than a symbol, of which a stock certificate is an example, but less than the object of purchase, of which a book itself is an example.

Thus, to say that the conveyance of the author was the sale of his work is to imply that the author divested himself of all his interest and rights in his works. To say that the conveyance is essentially a negative covenant is to imply, first, that the author retained rights in his work; and, second, that the agreement not to object to the publishing of the work is an agreement not to object to the publishing of the work as the author wrote it. In other words, the most reasonable

145. *Ibid.* (emphasis added).
146. 2 Bro. P.C. 130, 1 Eng. Rep. 838.

inference is that the author retained certain rights in connection with his work despite the existence of the copyright in the stationer.

The reasonableness of this inference is supported by other factors, individually insignificant, but collectively persuasive. The stationers, as businessmen, had no reason to alter an author's work; from their standpoint, there was only one thing to do with a manuscript, and that was to publish it. Altering the work was not only unnecessary for the protection against the piracy of published works for which copyright was designed—it was inimical to copyright.

The stationer's copyright was deemed to exist in perpetuity, copyright was often owned jointly, and it was frequently sold and assigned. The idea that the copyright owner was the owner of the work to do with as he pleased would have almost surely precluded the negotiability of copyright, for the value of the copyright was determined by the marketability of the book.

To maintain its value, a book had to be a good copy—that is, one which was faithful to the author's creation as he had written it. Moreover, since altered works were eligible for copyright, the practice whereby copyright owners could change the work presented a real danger that other stationers could, by altering or hiring a hack to alter a particular work, acquire a competing copyright. Mutual respect for each other's rights required that the stationers not interfere with the works to which they held the copyright.

The integrity of copyright, which was of paramount importance to the stationers, depended in large measure upon the integrity of the underlying work. The most effective way to maintain that integrity was to deny the copyright owner the right to meddle with the work itself in any way. Any altering of the work was to be done by the author, and as to this right of the author, the stationers probably had little choice. They had no jurisdiction over the author and could not control his activities in regard to his work, except by means of contract, which explains the promises exacted from the author in their conveyances to the booksellers. There were, then, very practical reasons for the stationers to recognize the author's creative rights, to protect the integrity of their copyright by maintaining the integrity of the copyrighted work and also to protect their copyrights from a subtle form of piracy.

The evidence available to us clearly indicates that the stationers recognized the author's property rights. They recognized also other rights of the author, rights which can be called creative rights, although the term undoubtedly did not occur to them. That such rights may not have been fully developed need hardly concern us, for their existence at all shows that the stationers were aware of the continuing interest of the author in his works by reason of the fact that he created them. And it is this point which confirms the other evidence as to the limited scope of the stationer's copyright.

Unfortunately, the stationers' recognition of the author's creative rights did not survive the statutory copyright. While the stationer's copyright was a publisher's right, the statutory copyright became an author's right. As such, it came to embrace all the rights of an author in connection with his published work. The change was more significant than has been generally recognized, for it was this change which denied to copyright a body of consistent fundamental principles.

There were such principles for the stationer's copyright, because that copyright was consistent in purpose and function. The purpose was to protect the publisher and the function was to provide order for the book trade.

The purpose of the statutory copyright came to be to protect the author and the publisher, and its function came to be to provide order for the book trade and to prevent monopoly.

The uniting of these purposes and functions, consistent to some degree, inconsistent to a larger degree, within one legal concept destroyed the unity of that concept. Thus, the failure of the Anglo-American courts to develop and recognize separate and apart from copyright, as did the stationers, the author's creative rights, had very practical consequences.

Why the courts failed to do this and what the consequences were becomes apparent only in the light of subsequent events in the eighteenth century. But before dealing with these events, we turn first to other aspects of the early history of copyright, the printing patent and the problem of censorship and press control.

5

The Printing Patent

THE PROMINENCE of the stationer's copyright in the history of copyright tends to obscure the fact that it was only one of two copyrights in England prior to the Statute of Anne. The other was the printing patent, a right to publish a work granted by the sovereign in the exercise of his royal prerogative.

By the end of the seventeenth century, the granting of printing patents had for all practical purposes ceased, and it was the stationer's copyright which served as a model for the statutory copyright. But in the early days of the Stationers' Company, the printing patents were the more desirable of the two copyrights, and understandably so— they covered the most profitable works to be printed; and, as grants of the sovereign, they offered more secure protection than the stationer's copyright. In case of conflict, the printing patent prevailed over the stationer's copyright. In "John Bill's History of Doctor Fulke's *Answer to the Rhemish Testament*"[1] is a narrative which shows how the grant of a patent to the deceased author's daughter prevailed over the stationer's copyright. It is plaintive in tone: "And because ye words of the patent are doubtfull whether they looke backwards and forwards or only for the tyme to com[e] she by colour of ye sayd letters patents and by great meanes, intends to tak[e] away not only the copie but also those bookes which we haue printed, before ye said grant from his Maiestie at ye price of paper and printing." The author expresses his conviction that the king did not know of the stationer's copyright, and expresses hope for the opportunity to prove that he is rightfully entitled to the copyright.

1. III ARBER 39.

The priority given to the printing patent resulted from the fact that it was a governmental copyright, while the stationer's copyright was a private copyright. This distinction led to other differences. Generally, the stationer's copyright was granted only to stationers in connection with a particular work upon the proper showing to the wardens and it was deemed to exist in perpetuity. The printing patent, as a grant of the sovereign, was not limited to stationers, although stationers were the most frequent recipients; it was limited in time, and there were two types of printing patents, general and particular.

The general patent was a privilege to print a certain class of works, usually for life, such as law books,[2] primers and books of private prayer,[3] and almanacs and prognostications.[4]

The particular patent was limited to the printing of a specified work for a limited period, usually seven or ten years.[5] But the life term for the general patent and the terms of seven and ten years for the particular patents were not invariable.[6] Indeed, since the patent was granted at the will of the sovereign, probably none of the provisions was invariable.

The patent to John Day on November 11, 1559, for example, gave Day the right to print "or cause to be imprinted" the *Cosmographical Glass*, for his life, as well as "during the tyme of seven yeares all suche bookes and Workes as he hath Imprinted or hereafter shall

2. Granted to Richard Tottell on January 12, 1559, II ARBER 15.

3. Granted to William Seres on July 3, 1559. See Appendix I. A subsequent patent for the same was granted to Seres, with a revision to his son, William, for their joint lives on August 23, 1571. II ARBER 15.

4. Granted to R. Watkins and James Robertes on December 3, 1588. II ARBER 16.

5. See, *e.g.*, the license to John Bodleigh for printing the English Bible "for terme of Seven yeares next ensuyng the date of thes our letters patentes . . . " II ARBER 63, and Letters Patent to Thomas Vautrollier on June 19, 1574, to print certain named Latin works for a term of ten years. II ARBER 746.

6. The patent to Watkins and Robertes for *Almanacs and Prognostications*, a general one, was limited to twenty-one years, and Nicasius Yetsweirt, Secretary of the Privy Council for French, was granted the reversion of Tottell's law patent for thirty years from November 18, 1577. II ARBER 15–16. On April 18, 1573, Thomas Vautrollier received a particular patent for printing Lloyd's translations of Plutarch's *Lives* for eight years, II ARBER 15, and letters patent to Richard Wright of Oxford on May 25, 1591, gave him the right to publish the History of Cornelius Tacitus in English for life. II ARBER 16.

imprinte beinge deuysed compiled or set oute by any learned man at the paymente costes and Charges onely of the saide John Daye."[7]

The differences between the two copyrights, however, did not prevent them from having essentially the same function of protecting a published work from piracy and being for the benefit of the publisher instead of the author. The similarity between the two in this respect is indicated by the report of a Royal Commission appointed to inquire into the controversy within the Stationers' Company in the 1580s. The report said that when works are not covered by a privilege—that is, a patent—"the companie do order emongest them selves that he which bringeth a booke to be printed should vse yt as a priviledge."[8]

To the stationers, the major difference between the two copyrights was probably simply that the printing patent was more profitable and carried more prestige.

Despite the importance of the printing patent to the stationers during the sixteenth and early seventeenth centuries, the similarity of its function to that of the stationer's copyright and its decline in the latter part of the seventeenth century would make it of only academic interest, except for one major factor: because the printing patents were so profitable and because they were limited to a favored few, they led to the rise of monopolists within the company itself.

The problem of monopoly which has always plagued copyright had an early beginning, for the privileges, as they were called, caused much difficulty in the Stationers' Company. Later, in the eighteenth century, the monopoly of the booksellers was based on the stationer's copyright, but the difficulties in the two periods were very similar. An understanding of the earlier monopoly aids in an understanding of the latter. And an understanding of the earlier is aided by a brief review of its ultimate source, the royal prerogative.

The Printing Patent and the Royal Prerogative

The right of the king to grant printing patents seems to have been assumed without any question in the sixteenth century. It was a part of the royal prerogative, which has been defined as "the power of the

7. II ARBER 61. See Appendix I.
8. II ARBER 784.

king to do things which no one else could do, and his power to do them in a way in which no one else could do them."[9] This definition is not very precise, but the value of the concept to the sovereign lay in its indefiniteness. "It is commonly asserted that one of the major differences between the Tudors and the Stuarts lay in their treatment of the royal prerogative: where the Stuarts spoilt acceptance by defining, the Tudors by not analysing reserved to themselves a large undefined power."[10]

The prerogative was of the law, not above it;[11] it comprised "those rights enjoyed by the king which acknowledged his superior position and enabled him to discharge the task of governing,"[12] and was derived from the common law, not Parliament.[13]

In regard to the press, there was not likely to be much question concerning the royal prerogative in the sixteenth century. Printing was a new industry, and the control of the press, in view of the religious controversy, would probably have been deemed essential to enable the sovereign "to discharge his task of governing" by any disinterested judicial tribunal, even though at first this need was not realized.

The new book trade received recognition by the crown in 1485 when Henry VII appointed Peter Actors as the first royal printer in a grant which was remarkably free of any restrictions,[14] and it was not until

9. ADAMS, CONSTITUTIONAL HISTORY OF ENGLAND 78 (1921).

10. ELTON, THE TUDOR CONSTITUTION 17 (1960). "But in truth the difference lay more profoundly in the content given to the term, not in any mere attitudinizing over it. . . . " Ibid.

11. "Tudor royal prerogative was a department of the law which conferred upon the ruler certain necessary rights not available to the subject. The Stuarts saw their prerogative very differently: to them it comprised those rights bestowed by God for which they were answerable to God only. Their prerogative was not part of the law: it was over and above it, or were over and against it." Id. at 18.

12. Id. at 17.

13. " . . . Parliament maketh no part of the king's prerogative, but long time before it had his being by the order of the common law. . . . " William Stanford on the King's Prerogative (1548) reprinted in ELTON, op. cit., 18–19.

14. "Grant for life to Peter Actoris, born in Savoy, of the office of Stationer to the King; also licence to import, so often as he likes, from parts beyond the sea, books printed and not printed into the port of the city of London, and other ports and places within the kingdom of England, and to dispose of the same by sale or otherwise without paying customs etc., thereon and without rendering any accompt thereof." Reprinted in JUDGE, ELIZABETHAN BOOK-PIRATES 6 (1934).

the imminent crisis in religious matters precipitated by Henry VIII's desire for a new wife (and by Martin Luther) that the matter of press control became urgent.

The printing patent, however, was only one type of letters patent granted by the sovereign, and the nebulous nature of the prerogative makes it difficult to distinguish the basis of the printing patent from the basis of the industrial patent.

In fact, the granting of the printing patent seems to have been originally merely an aspect of the patent system in general, which originated as a means of encouraging industrial development in England. The earliest grants were letters of protection given to foreigners for the purpose of introducing new industry. The first authenticated instance of such a grant is the letters of protection to John Kempe and his company in 1331.[15] This was not the grant of a monopoly, but a declaration of a policy in favor of the textile industry, with a general promise of like privileges to foreign weavers, dyers and fullers who should settle in England and teach their arts to those willing to be instructed therein.[16]

There were similar grants to others throughout the fourteenth and fifteenth centuries. "In 1336 similar letters were issued (10 Ed. III, Dec. 12) to two Brabant weavers to settle at York in consideration of the value of the industry to the Realm. In 1368 (42 Ed. III, p. I) three clockmakers of Delft were invited to come over for a short period . . . The first instance of a grant made to the introducer of a newly-invented process will be found in letters patent dated 1440 (18 H. 6 Franc. 18. m. 27) to John of Shiedame, who with his Company was invited to introduce a method of manufacturing salt on a scale hitherto unattempted within the kingdom. Twelve years later, in 1452, a grant was made in favour of three miners and their Company, who were brought over from Bohemia by the king on the ground of their possession 'meliorem scientiam in Mineriis' (Rymer, xi. 317)."[17] Legal justification for such grants is found in the citation from the Year Book, 40 Ed. III, fol. 17, 18, recognizing the Crown's power to grant privileges for the

15. Hulme, *The History of the Patent System under the Prerogative and at Common Law,* XII L.Q.R. 141, 142 (1896), hereafter cited as *The Patent System.*
16. *Ibid.*
17. Hulme, *The Patent System* 143.

sake of the public good, although prima facie they are clearly against common right.[18]

The earlier grants were "no more than passports,"[19] but the letters granted John Kempe were the beginning of a deliberate and vigorous policy which was pursued with substantial results.[20]

Under the Tudors, however, the patent system underwent a change by reason of the inclusion of monopoly clauses in the grants which perverted the medieval policy of encouraging industry.[21] It is the monopoly clauses which distinguish the Elizabethan grants from the earlier ones, and they "appear to have been borrowed from continental precedents, where the industrial privileges followed close upon the heels of the printer's copyrights."[22] The patent system was consistently abused by Elizabeth, who made many grants for purely mercenary reasons to enrich the royal purse.[23]

The extent of this abuse is reflected in Hulme's analysis of the lists of grants submitted to the Committee of Grievances in 1601. This list included fifteen dispensations, seven copyright patents, and seven industrial monopolies. The dispensations, which were grants with a *non obstante* clause, included licenses "(a) to traffic in forbidden articles, (b) to perform acts prohibited by the penal statutes, (c) offices delegat-

---

18. *Ibid.*

19. CARR, SELECT CHARTERS OF TRADING COMPANYS, 28 Selden Society lvi (1913).

20. Fox, MONOPOLIES AND PATENTS 45 (1947).

21. Hulme, *The Patent System* 144.

22. Hulme, *The History of the Patent System under the Prerogative and at Common Law. A Sequel*, XVI L.Q.R. 44 (1900), hereafter cited as *The Patent System, A Sequel*.

23. See Fox, *op. cit.*, 70. Cf. the following from the speech of Sir Robert Wroth during the debate on monopolies in 1601. " 'There have been divers Patents granted since the last Parliament; these are now in Being, *viz.* The Patents for Currants, Iron, Powder, Cards, Ox-shin Bones, Train-Oyl, Transportation of Leather, Lists of Cloth, Ashes, Anniseeds, Vinegar, Sea-Coals, Steel, Aquavitae, Brushes, Pots, Salt-Petre, Lead, Accidences, Oyl, Calimin-Stone, Oyl of Blubber, Fumachoes, or dryed Piltchers in the Smoak, and divers others.'

"Upon Reciting of the Patents aforesaid, Mr. *Hackwell* stood up and asked thus: 'Is not Bread there? *Bread quoth one, Bread quoth another; this Voice seems strange quoth another; this Voice seems strange quoth a third*; No, quoth Mr. *Hackwell*, But if Order be not taken for these, Bread will be there before the next Parliament.' " 4 PARL. HIST. 462.

ing to an individual the dispensing power of the Crown in respect of a given statute."[24]

The "monstrous development," as Hulme said, was the delegation of the dispensing power to an individual, and the grant was subsequently voided by the courts on the ground "that when a statute is made by Parliament for the good of the commonwealth, the King cannot give the penalty, benefit, and dispensation of such Act to any subject; or give power to any subject to dispense with it, and to make a warrant to the Great Seal for licenses in such case to be made . . . "[25]

This was in 1605; but in 1597, after a bill against monopolies had failed to pass, Elizabeth requested Parliament not to "take away her Prerogative, which is the chiefest Flower in her Garden, and the principal and head Pearl in her Crown and Diadem," promising that the monopolies "shall all be examined to abide the Trial and true Touchstone of the Law."[26] And in 1601, it was apparently only the direct intervention of Elizabeth that prevented the enactment of a monopoly statute. She delivered a speech in Parliament during the debate on monopolies, after which the debate ceased and Parliament returned to the consideration of the Subsidy Bill, which had "laid dormant"[27] during the debate.

Thus, under Elizabeth, letters patent became merely monopolistic grants, and there was little distinction made between industrial and printing patents. The fusion of the two types is seen in the grant of a monopoly for importing, selling, and making playing cards, which was voided in *The Case of Monopolies*.[28] The renewal of the patent had been given to Ralph Bowes on June 13, 1588, for twelve years,[29] and was granted to Edward D'Arcy on August 11, 1598.[30] The patent was

24. Hulme, *The Patent System, A Sequel* 54.
25. The Case of Penal Statutes, 7 Co. Rep. 36, 77 Eng. Rep. 465 (1605).
26. 4 PARL. HIST. 420 (1751).
27. *Id.* at 479–83.
28. 11 Co. Rep. 84b, 77 Eng. Rep. 1260; Moore (K.B.) 671, 72 Eng. Rep. 830; Noy, 173, 74 Eng. Rep. 1131. The patent for cards was apparently one of the most objectionable. In the debate on monopolies in Parliament in 1601, Secretary Cecil said, "The Patent for Cards shall be suspended and tryable by the common law." 4 PARL. HIST. 472.
29. II ARBER 16.
30. *Ibid.*

primarily an industrial one, but because it involved printing, the Stationers' Company considered it a printing patent. On June 25, 1588, just twelve days after the grant, Bowes was received into the company as a freeman at his request,[31] and the moulds for printing cards were entered to him in the register.[32] On November 3, 1600, the court entered an order that D'Arcy, upon showing his letters patent, "shall haue entred as mr bowes had the ij sutes of moulds for playing cards wch were entred to mr Bowes xj Octobr' 1588."[33]

However, when D'Arcy, "a groom of the Privy Chamber to Queen Elizabeth," sued "T. Allein," a haberdasher, for the infringement of the patent, the patent was treated solely as an industrial one. The plaintiff argued that the Queen had a right to make the grant because (1) playing cards were not a necessary merchandise, but objects of idleness; (2) the Queen had a prerogative to control the use of matters of recreation and pleasure; and (3) the Queen, in regard of the great abuse of cards, might suppress them entirely, and thus might moderate their use.

The defendant contended that the grant was a monopoly, and against the common law for four reasons: (1) all trades are profitable for the commonwealth; (2) a monopoly gives the patentee the sole trade for his private benefit, not for that of the commonwealth, thus interfering with the lawful occupations of various persons; (3) the Queen was deceived in her grant, because it will be employed for the private gain of the patentee to the prejudice of the public good; and (4) the grant was one of first impression and was a dangerous innovation, because it was granted to one "inexpert in the art and trade."[34]

The argument in the case given in one report shows the theoretical basis for the granting of letters patent:

Now therefore I will shew you how the Judges have heretofore allowed of monopoly patents, which is, that where any man by his own charge and industry, or by his own wit or invention doth bring any new trade into the realm, or any engine tending to the furtherance of a trade that never was used before: and that for the good of the realm: that in such cases the King

31. COURT BOOK B, 29.
32. See II ARBER 503, 512.
33. COURT BOOK B, 79. The date, 11 October, is error for 18 October.
34. The Case of Monopolies, 11 Co. Rep. 84b, 77 Eng. Rep. 1260 (1604).

may grant to him a monopoly patent for some reasonable time, until the subjects may learn the same, in consideration of the good that he doth bring by his invention to the commonwealth: otherwise not.[35]

The abuse of the royal prerogative, however, continued to be such that it finally resulted in the enactment of the Statute of Monopolies.[36] This statute struck directly at the prerogative by providing that letters patent "ought to be and shall be for ever hereafter examined, heard, tried and determined by and according to the Common Laws of this Realm, and not otherwise." Section VI, however, provided "That any Declaration before-mentioned shall not extend to any Letters Patents and Grants of Privilege for the Term of fourteen Yeares or under, hereafter to be made, of the sole Working or Making of any manner of new Manufactures within this Realm . . . "

The most significant aspect of the statute from the standpoint of copyright is that it did not apply to letters patent "concerning Printing." The reason for this exception is not clear, but the same exception was also made for the "Digging, Making or Compounding of Salt-Petre or Gunpowder, or the Casting or Making of Ordnance."

Whatever the reason for excluding the printing patents from the operation of the Statute of Monopolies, the saving of the prerogative in this regard indicates that the reasons for the printing patent differed from those for the industrial patent. However, caution is the first word to be used in attempting to ascertain the basis of the printing patent prerogative. It would be easy to assume that the basis was a need to control the press. The religious controversy, past, present, and future, supports this idea. Moreover, the exception for the making of materials for war in the same section of the statute that saved the printing patents indicates that the security of the state was involved. And it is true that the power of the sovereign to control the printing of bibles and books of religion would serve the ends of censorship. Even so, it does not seem that the need for censorship fully explains the prerogative.

The first printing patent was apparently granted in 1518, for a book "on the Latin sermon preached by Richard Pace at St Paul's Cathedral

35. Noy at 182, 74 Eng. Rep. 1139.
36. 21 Jac. I, c. 3.

on the peace between England and France."[37] This was some years before the need for stringent press control was realized, and Henry VIII in his proclamation of November 16, 1538, made clear the distinction between a royal grant and a license to print. The proclamation provided that no person was to print any book in the English tongue unless upon examination made by some of the Privy Council, or other as his highness should appoint, "they shall haue lycence so to do, and yet so hauynge, not to put these wordes *Cum priuilegio regali*, without addyng *ad imprimendum solum*, and that the hole copie or els at the least theffect of his licence and priuilege be therwith printed, and playnely declared and expressed in the Englyshe tonge vnderneth them."[38]

This language meant that every book required a license, but this license was not to be used as indicating a royal privilege for printing. The words "Cum priuilegio regali" were restricted by the addition of "ad imprimendum solum," which must be construed " 'only for printing,' *i.e.*, they did not, unless this was expressly stated, confer the royal approbation and they did not in themselves prohibit piracy, though the 'whole copy' or 'effect' of the privilege, when it is printed as the Proclamation directs, probably always contains this prohibition."[39] This distinction between a printing patent and a license to print from censorship authorities seems to have continued. A royal grant never relieved the grantee of the duty to have his works approved by the licensing authorities.

In fact, the real basis of the prerogative over printing seems to have been simply an aspect of royal power, assumed when that power was despotic. Its survival for so long is explained by the context of the times, and when the issue of the prerogative came before the courts, it was gradually delimited. How this was done is seen in a group of cases,

37. A. W. POLLARD, SHAKESPEARE'S FIGHT 3.
38. *Id.* at 6.
39. *Id.* at 7. "Incidentally we may note that while a license to print and a privilege carrying with it protection against piratical competition ought to have been kept clearly distinct, the one word 'priuilegium' seems to have been used as a Latin equivalent for both, the reason being, I believe, that King Henry VIII, who re-wrote this clause with his own hand, was not in the least concerned at the moment with the commercial effect of the proclamation, but only with maintaining his own right of censorship." *Id.* at 6.
40. III ARBER 42.

beginning in 1666 and ending in 1775, which made the royal prerogative over printing into a proprietary interest of the sovereign in a few
types of works, *e.g.,* bibles, as head of the Church, and law reports
as head of the State. The subjects in controversy were generally,
though not always, works which had been granted to the Stationers'
Company in letters patent from James I in 1603[40] and in 1616.[41]

In the first of these cases dealing with rights under a printing patent,
The stationers v. The Patentees, Atkins's Case,[42] the House of Lords
recognized the royal prerogative over printing in its fullest form by
sustaining the patent. The case concerned a dispute over the printing
of law books between the Stationers' Company and the law patentees,
and the basis of the argument of counsel for the patentees was the
king's prerogative to control printing. "The King hath a general prerogative at common law . . . time out of memory; the publishing of
books, and the art of writing and communicating is as ancient as time
it self, and at first subjected to the supream authority . . . The Kings
prerogative over printing is necessary as to religion, conservation of
the publique peace, and necessary to preserve good understanding between King and people."[43]

In 1667, in *The Stationers' Company v. Seymour*[44] the company sued
defendant in an action of debt for printing Gadbury's Almanac without their leave. The defendant did not contend that he had any property
in the copy, but only that the company's patent was void. The court
held for the company on the ground that the almanac had no author,
and the King had the property in the copy which he could grant. Shortly
thereafter, both patents for law books,[45] and "*English bibles* and
psalms,"[46] were held to be legal.

In 1681, in *Stationers' Company v. Lee,*[47] the company obtained an
injunction to stay the selling of primers, psalters, almanacs and sing-
ing psalms imported from Holland, for which it had the patent. The
argument proceeded upon narrower grounds than theretofore. "The

41. III ARBER 679.
42. Carter 89, 124 Eng. Rep. 842 (1666).
43. Carter, 89, 90, 124 Eng. Rep. 842, 843.
44. 1 Mod. 256, 86 Eng. Rep. 865; 3 Keble 792, 84 Eng. Rep. 1015.
45. Roper v. Streater, cited, Skinner 233, 90 Eng. Rep. 107 (1672).
46. Mayo v. Hill, cited, 2 Show. K.B. 260, 89 Eng. Rep. 928 (1673).
47. 2 Show. K.B. 248, 89 Eng. Rep. 927.

King hath always had and exercised his prerogative in printing of *these and some other books* . . . The King is head of the Church and has a particular prerogative in ecclesiastical affairs, and therefore in printing of *primers, &c.* he has a particular prerogative in restraining and licensing prognostications of all sorts; and were it otherwise it would be of dangerous consequence to the Government."[48]

The Stationers' Company v. Parker,[49] in 1685, was an action by the company against Parker, who pleaded a grant to Oxford for printing "omnes & omnimodes libros," and a subsequent grant "to print tam libros content. in charta to the stationers of London, quam alios non prohibit." The basic question was whether the king by his subsequent charter had given power to the university to print works notwithstanding. The defendant argued that "the king had power to grant the printing of books concerning religion or law," which was an interest, but not a sole interest. The prerogative is one of power and the prohibition being an act of government, determines with the death of the king. Further, what the king has prohibited, he may also enlarge. The court "enclined for the defendant, and said, that if it was not for *Seymour's case,* which they thought a hard case, they would have given judgment upon this argument" for defendant.

In 1775, in *The Stationers' Company v. Carnan,*[50] the delimitation of the king's prerogative over printing was completed. The case was stated out of Chancery for a ruling by Common Pleas on a point of law. The defendant had printed an almanac or prognostication, and the company sought an injunction. The defendant argued that "none of the true grounds on which a prerogative copyright can be founded appear in the present case. Codes of religion and of law ought to be under the inspection of the executive power, to stamp an authenticity upon them. Therefore Bibles, Common Prayer Books, and statutes are proper objects of exclusive patents. But almanacks are not of this kind."[51]

The court ruled: "1. That the grant made to the plaintiffs, the Stationers' Company, was restrained to such almanacks and prognosti-

---

48. 2 Show. K.B. 258, 259–60; 89 Eng. Rep. 927, 928 (Emphasis added).
49. Skinner, 233, 90 Eng. Rep. 107.
50. 2 Black. W. 1004, 96 Eng. Rep. 590.
51. 2 Black. W. 1007–1008, 96 Eng. Rep. 592.

cations as should be licensed or allowed by the Archbishop of Canterbury, the Bishop of London, or either of them for the time being. 2. We are of opinion, that the Crown had not a prerogative or power to make such grant to the plaintiffs, exclusive of any other or others."[52]

The Printing Patent and the Stationers' Company

The book trade in England prior to 1774 was continually plagued by the booksellers' monopoly. Even though copyright itself was a monopoly of only one book, the perpetual existence of copyright made it a means to a monopoly of the market. A profitable copyright enables one to purchase other copyrights and since power breeds power, it is not difficult to see how perpetual copyright could enable a small group to establish their control over the trade by controlling the most profitable copyrights.

This is substantially what happened to the book trade in England, a process which can be attributed in part to the printing patent, which was monopolistic in the sixteenth century in a way the stationer's copyright was not. It was this fact that made the printing patent so important to the Stationers' Company. The point seems to be contradictory, since conceptually the stationer's copyright was no less monopolistic than the printing patent, and appears to be even more so, as the printing patent was granted for only a limited period of time. There are, however, two points in regard to the printing patent which made the difference.

First, the printing patent might cover a class of works, rather than a single work, and it was these general patents which were the most objectionable.

Secondly, the printing patent usually covered works which for copyright purposes had no author. Except for the printing patent, the works would be available to any printer or publisher.

The extent to which the stationer's copyright would have been allowed, in the absence of the printing patent, to tie up such profitable works as the *ABC* (the first English school book), the Bible, the prayer books, and almanacs is conjectural. But in view of the difficulties resulting from the patents for such works, it does not seem likely that

52. 2 Black. W. 1004, 1009, 96 Eng. Rep. 590, 593.

the stationer's copyright would have been sufficient to prevent competitive publications of such works.

It was resentment against the printing patent that led to the controversy within the Stationers' Company during the 1580s. The fight was against the patentees, and it may be significant that during the entire controversy there seems to have been no resentment expressed against the stationer's copyright, apparently because the stationer's copyright was available to the insurgents. When John Wolfe, one of the insurgents, affirmed openly in Stationers' Hall that it was lawful for all men to print all books "what commandment soeuer her Maiestie gaue to ye contrary,"[53] he was speaking against the printing patents.

The controversy within the company during the 1580s is significant in copyright history for two reasons. One of its results was the Star Chamber Decree of 1586, which enhanced the power of the Stationers' Company. The other reason is that this controversy represents the first effort to deal with the problem of copyright monopoly, and the events of the struggle illustrate the real nature of the monopoly problem of copyright. The printing patent was objectionable primarily because it made exclusive the right of publication to works that would otherwise be available to all printers for publication. The patented works were, for the most part, works which today would be in the public domain. Thus, the monopoly problem of copyright arises when the concept is such as to foreclose competition. Insofar as the printing patent was concerned, competition was foreclosed by an arbitrary grant of the sovereign.

The problem of monopoly was again an issue in the eighteenth century when the booksellers were battling for perpetual copyright. By this time, copyright had been in existence long enough to create essentially the same problem that resulted from the printing patents. The continual existence of copyrights of classical authors foreclosed competition in the publication of classical works of literature. In both periods, the essential problem was how copyright should affect works to which no single publisher could reasonably claim the exclusive right to publish.

In the sixteenth century, the basis of the monopolists' power was the

---

53. II Arber 781.

printing patent; in the eighteenth century, the basis of the monopolists' power was the power to control in perpetuity the publication of such works as those of Shakespeare, Milton, and Dryden.

The importance of the controversy in the 1580s warrants a detailed treatment of it. The following material deals with the two phases of the dispute, the report of the royal commission inquiring into the dissention and efforts of the company to secure legislation.

The controversy resulted from economic difficulties caused by the monopolistic printing patents. The Stationers' Company failed to realize the increasing significance of the concept of copyright, which was bringing about a shift in the balance of power in the company away from the industrial section, i.e., the printers and bookbinders, towards the commercial section, the booksellers.[54]

The company was changing from a membership of small entrepreneurs to one of large capitalists, and one of the precipitating causes of the friction was the large number of apprentices who came to their freedom during 1571–76.[55] These former apprentices who had the means to set themselves up in business were prevented by printing patents from publishing books which they could otherwise have secured from an author, paying him well and making a profit for themselves.[56]

As usual in such instances, the workmen were the first to feel the pinch of economic difficulties, and the first phase of the controversy was concerned with their complaints.

The situation had become sufficiently serious by August 1577 (?) to warrant a petition to Lord Burghley entitled, "The griefes of the printers glasse sellers and Cutlers susteined by reson of privileges granted to privatt persons,"[57] showing common cause against monopolies. As related to printing, the document complained that privileges would be the ruin of the printers and stationers, "being in nomber. 175.," because the printing patents covered works which had been available for printing to all members of the company prior to the grants.[58]

54. See Blagden, *The English Stock of the Stationers' Company,* X THE LIBRARY, 5th ser., 163, 166 (1955).

55. II ARBER 16.

56. *Ibid.*

57. I ARBER 111.

58. *Ibid.*

The patents specifically complained about in the petition were those of John Jugge, as Queen's Printer, for Bibles and Testaments, of Tottel for law books, of John Day for the *ABC* and *Catechisms*, of Robertes and Watkyns for *Almanacs* and *Prognostications*, and Thomas Marshe for Latin school books.

There is no indication that anything came of this petition; but a couple of months later, in October, the company reacted to a petition of the bookbinders complaining of their difficulties by a harmless order providing that: (1) bookbinders who were Englishmen and freemen of the City should have work before strangers and foreigners; (2) bookbinders should perform their tasks promptly; and (3) infringers of the ordinances should be imprisoned or punished as the master and wardens thought proper.[59]

But the court seems to have considered the complaint an effrontery, for on January 7, 1578, there is an entry of recantation signed by six persons, which declared that the undersigned persons complained against the wardens and ancients, and "the same was not Done accordinge to their Duetie for wch they are sorie."[60]

Shortly thereafter, however, the court began to take the complaints more seriously, because it made an unasked-for, and again, harmless, concession in response to "The peticons of the poore men of this Companie for their Relief," on January 27, 1578.[61] The petition, apparently on the part of both bookbinders and printers, requested: (1) more work; (2) that no work be put to foreigners or strangers; (3) that the petitioners may be well and truly paid for their work; (4) that the printers and others of the company not be allowed to have an excessive number of apprentices "to the hindrance of poore freeman of this mystery," and (5) that "the ffrenchmen and strangers beinge Denizens maie not haue excessiue nomber of appntics."

The court responded in typical fashion, promising more work and saying that if any workmen had cause of complaint for poor pay, the master and wardens would provide a speedy remedy; but significantly, because this was a policy matter, the court said it could not reasonably grant that no work was to be put to foreigners or strangers; however, any brother being grieved could complain and he would have

59. COURT BOOK B, 3.
60. *Ibid.*
61. COURT BOOK B, 4.

remedy. The complaint about excessive apprentices was "reasonable but the complainte is too vncertaine and generall." The reply to the petition about Frenchmen and denizens having an excessive number of apprentices was more circumspect, and from the answer one may guess that the reason for the circumspection was that the foreigners were being used by members of the company as a convenient loop-hole to circumvent a company regulation limiting the number of ap-prentices. The court answered that the foreigners had no apprentices, but had apprentices of other men appointed to serve them to learn their art. This could not "sodenlie be remedied," but the best relief possible was to be given by the master and wardens to "the saide poore bretheren."

Then followed the concession. It was, further, "aboue the saide peticons charitablie offered and ordred by this companie" that poor brothers should be allowed "anie laufull copie wherevnto noe other man hathe righte or whereof there is noe number remayninge by the fourmer printer vnsold,"[62] that is, which nobody else wanted. The concession, if it can be called that, was characteristic of the company, whose policy seems to have been not to take any action until abso-lutely necessary, and then to take as little action as possible so as not to disturb the *status quo*.

"The Petition of the Poor" is a convenient point to mark the end of the first phase of the controversy; and it is apparent from the com-pany's response to the various petitions, increasingly attentive though it was, that the difficulties of the workmen were a nuisance, to be ignored if feasible. If that could not be done, the workmen were to be pacified with as little inconvenience to the company as possible. This was very different from the attitude manifested toward the troubles of the patentees by the Courts of Assistants in October 1578, near the beginning of the difficulties.

The designation of the works in the printing patents was not always sufficiently clear to prevent an overlap. This had happened in regard to a patent of the two William Seres, father and son, for various books

62. Court Book B, 4–5.

to which John and Richard Day claimed the right. The Day patent had been assigned to other stationers, and in settling the dispute, the court awarded a life interest in various copies to eighteen named persons, who were to pay Seres and his son one shilling for every impression. This nominal sum sustained the Seres' ownership, for upon the death of the grantees, the copies were to return to the original patentees, without the usual widow's rights.[63]

Had the company been as much concerned with the plight of the workmen as with the plight of the patentees, it is likely that there would have been no second phase of the controversy, but this would have meant affirmative action in regard to the printing patent. Possibly, the ruling fathers of the company were wise enough to realize that Elizabeth would brook no interferences with "the chiefest flower in her garden," and that they could not have done anything directly had they wanted to. At any rate, it is not likely that they wanted to, and in the face of the company's inaction, there was little that the unprivileged members could do except resort to self-help.

The second phase of the conflict involved more than mere petitions, for it was characterized by secret printing presses and the pirating of privileged works. The controversy thus spread beyond the confines of the company, because the government was not willing that secret printing presses should exist for whatever reason, and particularly at this time, because of the "rising tide" of Puritanism. The government's concern was undoubtedly welcomed and encouraged by the company, as this concern was a means to increase its power.

In May 1583, the Bishop of London, in his report of the search for secret printing presses, stated that the master and wardens informed him that the books for printing not covered by printing patents were

63. Liber A, f. 36ʳ, reprinted in Blagden, *The English Stock of the Stationers' Company*, X THE LIBRARY, 5th ser. 163, 181, Appendix III (1955). Another agreement between John and Richard Day and William Seres the Younger was entered into on October 29, 1578, although it was not signed until January 18, 1579. The gist of the agreement was that Seres would not interfere with the Days' printing of the "psalmes of David in meter with notes." The agreement contained the signature, in addition to those of the Days and Seres, of Henry Denham, assignee of the elder Seres, who was deceased. Liber A, f. 37ʳ, reprinted in Blagden, *op. cit.*, 184, Appendix IV. Still another order between these same parties can be found in COURT BOOK B, 9, dated January 28, 1580.

not sufficient "to maineteigne anye man,"[64] a confession with an ul-
terior motive.

The success of the insurgents in pirating privileged works was such
that it brought forth action from both the company and the government. The company attempted to deal with the pirates, prosecuted
them in the Star Chamber, persecuted them otherwise; and, as a last
resort, took steps to spread the benefits of the patents, particularly
among the pirates—once they reformed—and to make more copies
available to the use of the whole company. The government appointed
a Royal Commission to look into the difficulties, and the commission's
report served as a prelude to the Star Chamber Decree of 1586.

The insurgents were a well-organized group—a Secret Combination,
as Arber called them—whose membership was representative of the
various groups within the company. Their leader was John Wolfe. In
1583, Christopher Barker and Frauncis Coldocke, wardens at the time,
named Wolfe's principal cohorts as John Charlewood and Roger Ward,
printers; Henry Bamford, compositor; Franck Adams, "a maker of
writing Tables"; William Lobley, a bookbinder; and Abraham Kidson,
Thomas Butter, and William Wright, booksellers, all of whom "are
greatly animated by one Master Robert Neak, a lawyer."[65]

Wolfe, the outstanding figure in the controversy, was not even a
stationer, but a member of the Fishmonger's Company. His first copy
was entered on May 16, 1579, upon condition "that he shall haue it
printed by Jhon charlwood."[66] His role as leader against the system
of printing patents apparently resulted from a sense of personal injustice, not from a conviction that the system was inherently bad.
Soon after setting up in business, Wolfe sought a printing patent, and
it was only after this request was refused that "he printed what pleased
him best," which meant the lucrative copies of Francis Flower, Thomas
Marshe, John Day, William Seres, and Christopher Barker.[67]

Once he began his campaign, however, Wolfe managed to convey

---

64. I ARBER 246. The Bishop reported that "there were found sundrie presses
and furniture for printinge in secrete corners and Darke cellers, and those vsed
in printinge thinges forbidden to them to prynte." *Ibid.*

65. II ARBER 779.

66. II ARBER 353. However, Wolfe was apprenticed to John Day on March 1562,
for ten years. I ARBER 172.

67. II ARBER 781.

a sense of moral outrage and indignation directed to the system of privileges, and the success of the pirates was undoubtedly due in large measure to this feeling, and to the fact that the piracies were apparently limited to privileged works. There is no indication that books protected by the stationer's copyright were interfered with, although this may have been because such works were not as valuable as those protected by patents.

Christopher Barker's notes on the behavior of Wolfe[68] show the leader of the insurgents as a thorough demagogue, whose aim was the abolition of the printing patents, but the account also shows how deeply the grievances against the printing patent were felt. Wolfe's announced position was that he as a free man had a privilege as great as anyone, and that he would print all the books of the patentees if he lacked work. He affirmed openly in Stationers' Hall that it was lawful for all men to print all books " 'what commandement soeuer her Maiestie gaue to ye contrary,' " and even after a reconsideration of these remarks, continued his former conduct saying " 'he will liue.' " He often made disloyal speeches of the Queen's government, and without naming the Queen, announced, " 'She is deceaued,' 'she shall know she is deceaued,' Also 'she is blindly lead, she is deceaued.' " In response to an admonition that he as one man should not presume "to contrarie her Highnesse gouernmente," Wolfe made his oft-quoted remark: " 'Tush,' said he, 'Luther was but one man, and reformed all ye world for religion, and I am that one man, yat must and will reforme the gouernement in this trade,' meaning printing and bookselling."

In view of Wolfe's actions later in becoming a member of the company and sharing in the patents, his words cannot be taken at face value; but before he gave over his task of reform, he supported his words with actions other than pirating, self-serving though they were. When he was in prison, which was at least twice, he "resorted vnto him diuers poore men of sundry companies, as vnto one to be a meane to make them rich." He and his confederates vowed "to withstand her Maiesties grantes wholy," and one of the confederates, Franck Adams, said, " 'he bound in 100ˡˡ to follow that cause.' "

Wolfe gathered disorderly crowds and made speeches, and collected money from "poore suiectes, perswading them to overthrow all priui-

68. See II ARBER 781–82.

ledges," because, he said, " 'his purse was not able to maintaine so great a Cause as yat they had in hand.' " He and his confederates were accused of incensing the meaner sort of people throughout the city as they went so that it "became a common talke in Alehouses, tauernes and such like places, whereupon insued dangerous and vndutifull speaches of her Maiesties most gracious gouerment."

As a result of all this, the poor of the company were "animated against their Elders, were ready to offer vs violence, euen when we were together in our Common Hall studying to do them good. yea our seruants also aswell Apprentices as Journeman became disobedient, and our Apprentices married wiues, and for a time did what they list."[69]

Christopher Barker was not a disinterested witness, for as the Queen's Printer, with the sole right of printing the Bible, the Book of Common Prayer, and the Royal Statutes and Proclamations, he offered the biggest and best target for piracy. He had even complained against printing and patents before he became a patentee,[70] and when the above account was written, Barker had already engaged in fruitless negotiations with Wolfe.

Although Wolfe's first copy was not entered in the Company register until May 1579, less than two years later—by March of 1581—he had already published enough of Barker's works to make the latter anxious to come to some sort of terms. Barker gave Wolfe work on condition that he not print any more of other men's copies, and that he translate to the Stationers' Company from the Fishmongers; but Wolfe's work, to the value of eighty pounds, was "so vntruely and euilly done" that it brought discredit to Barker, and the attempted compromise failed. Wolfe continued to pirate copies and refused to translate. Barker again conferred with him on May 14, 1582, but Wolfe's price had increased in the meantime. He demanded five apprentices, which was more than the Stationers' rules allowed, but which Barker promised to help him in obtaining. Barker further promised Wolfe "good and gainefull copies," and to help him procure a loan of twenty pounds upon good security. As to the printing of his works, Barker said that "you and I will reasonably agree." Wolfe denied hav-

---

69. Ibid.
70. He was a signatory to "the griefes of the printers," August 1577. I ARBER, 111.

ing any more of Barker's copies in printing, but "his seruants were in work of ye same, as within .4. houres after was manifest. Whereupon Barker gaue him ouer, as a man unreasonable to deale withall."[71]

Prior to Barker's fruitless interview with Wolfe in May, John Day, on February 7, 1582, filed a bill in the Star Chamber against Roger Ward and William Holmes alleging their piracy of the *ABC*, for which Day held the patent, contrary to the Star Chamber Decree of 1566.[72] The action was obviously a test case, and the facts brought out in the interrogatories give more concrete evidence as to the success of the piracies. Not only did Ward admit to printing ten thousand copies of the *ABC*,[73] he accomplished the feat while imprisoned,[74] which shows the high degree of organization among the insurgents. Ward's defense was the familiar complaint that because "a verye small number in respecte of the rest of the Companye of Stacioners Prynters havinge gotten all the best bookes and Coppyes to be printed by themselfes by Priuyledge" the rest of the poor printers, by reason "of pretended Priuiledges . . . can scarce earne breade and Drinke by their trade . . . "[75]

Despite the action against him, Ward's contumaciousness continued. On October 25, 1582, his wife and servants refused to allow stationers to search his house for illegal presses,[76] and in August 1583, the master, wardens and ancients of the company appealed to Lord Burghley against him.[77]

By the fall of 1582, matters were coming to a head. The company had obviously been acting against the insurgents in ways other than court actions and negotiations, for in October 1582, twenty-one persons in a petition to Lord Burghley, endorsed "The Stationers of London against ye priviledged persons," complained that Thomas Norton was unfairly letting his position as counsel to the Stationers' Company prejudice his advice as City Remembrancer.

Said the petition, "Wherevpon we are now by all meanes possible

71. II ARBER 780.
72. Day v. Ward and Holmes, II ARBER 753.
73. II ARBER 760.
74. II ARBER 756.
75. *Ibid.*
76. II ARBER 776.
77. II ARBER 785. Ward's activities continued at least until 1586. See COURT BOOK B, 20, for an order to seize and destroy his presses.

sought to be hindered by master Norton the Councellor, and who is alltogether hired agaynst vs, for that he sayth, he hath authority to imprison vs, except we will enter into such vnreasonable bondes, being coulored with an outward shew of good meaninge, as neither law nor Justice would permitte."[78]

A similar appeal to Sir Francis Walsingham, Secretary to the Queen and a member of the Privy Council, complained that the privileged men "haue taken away sundrie your saide oratours goodes of great value, committed some of their poore servauntes to diuerse prisons where some are yet remayning at ymportable charges to their great hinderaunce and vtter vndoing if this rigorous dealing be permitted."[79]

Some time prior to this, the Queen had appointed a Commission to inquire into the troubles of the Stationers' Company, and the Court of Aldermen appointed four of their number to report on the printers' complaints of poor wages and shortage of work.[80]

In December 1582, Barker submitted his famous report to Burghley on the printing patents of 1558–1582, in which he pointed out the decline of the printers' economic position because the booksellers, not having to invest any capital in fixed assets, "haue nowe many of the best Copies."[81] It was this development, according to Barker, which compelled the printers to procure grants from the Queen "of some certayne Copies, for the better mayntenance of furniture, Correctours, and other workmen, who cannot suddaynely be provided, nor suddenlye put awaye: and if they shoulde [be put away] must of necessitie, either wantt necessarie lyving, or print bookes, pamphlettes, and other trifles, more daungerous than profitable."[82]

In the meantime, the patentees had taken it upon themselves to spread the interest in their monopolies. Sometime before October 1582, Henry Denham, the assignee of William Seres, had taken "vij yonge men of the company of staconers to joyne with hym,"[83] and John Day

---

78. II ARBER 777.
79. II ARBER 778. The appeal is undated. Arber guesses it to be also in October 1582.
80. Blagden, *The English Stock of the Stationers' Company*, X THE LIBRARY, 5th ser. at 168. See *The Journeymen of the Stationers' Company appeal to the Privy Council*. II ARBER 770.
81. I ARBER 114.
82. I ARBER 115.
83. II ARBER 771.

had "dispersed" the *ABC* to "vij or Eight householders of the Companie."[84] On March 26, 1583, the Court of Assistants allowed Henry
Bynneman the entrance of certain copies on condition that he should
"from tyme to tyme accordinge to his good discretion chose and accept
any fyve of this cumpanie to be partners with him in the Imprintinge
of these bookes."[85] These actions were early steps against the trouble
caused by the patents at a time when the controversy was still raging.
In the same month, March 1583, the wardens made a supplication to
the Privy Council on behalf of the assistants and patentees against John
Wolfe and his associates.[86]

In July 1583, the Royal Commission made its final report.[87] The original appointees, Doctor Hammond and Thomas Norton, had been augmented by the Bishop of London, the Dean of the Arches, and the
Recorder of London, who assumed that matters had been brought
under control, because "Those that haue presses and complaine against
the patenties are not aboue iiij,"[88] and John Wolfe had "acknowledged
his error and is releved with worke." Wolfe had translated to the Stationers' Company and was formally entered into the Register as a
freeman *per redemptione* on July 1, 1583.[89]

The commission's report is particularly interesting because it is more
nearly a disinterested commentary of contemporaries on the printing
patent, and by inference the stationer's copyright, than any of the
other documents relating to the controversy, although it did manifest
a bias toward the *status quo*, as the commissioners were of the opinion
that "the complainants had no great cause to complaine at the beginning." The unprivileged members viewed the printing patent as a
monopolistic device which deprived them of work; the privileged members strongly urged its necessity as a means of preventing publications dangerous to the government. The commissioners' view was that
particular printing patents were a necessary means of maintaining
order in the book trade, but that the general patents should be abol-

84. II ARBER 775.
85. II ARBER 422.
86. II ARBER 778.
87. II ARBER 783–785.
88. II ARBER 784. Arber guesses the four to have been "J. Charlewood, R.
Waldegrave, R. Ward and possibly T. East."
89. II ARBER 688.

ished. The basic premise of the commissioners was that it was not proper for "sondrye men" to print one book, and when her majesty did not grant a privilege, "the companie do order emongst them selves that he which bringeth a booke to be printed should vse yt as a priviledge."

The commissioners recommended that the privileges should be maintained by putting into execution the Star Chamber Decree of 1566. Otherwise, there would be a lack of good type, "want of house-holders to set men a woorke," and no "great bookes of valew" would be printed. The report justified printing patents by listing "what helpes the complaynantes haue,"[90] and finding that the patentees claimed no more than their patents granted. The patentees had taken order to relieve the poor, and should enjoy the rest of their privileges without interruption. Significantly, however, the commissioners recommended: "Their Lordships to be a means to her maiestie that hereafter no generall title of bookes of Art nor scholle bookes except bookes per-teyning to her maiesties service be not Drawen into privilege."

This recommendation for the abolition of general printing patents is a startling concession to the unprivileged, and is an acknowledge-ment that the basic complaint against the patents was well founded. It also indicates that neither Elizabeth nor the stationers viewed the granting of patents as necessary for censorship. There is no indication in the various recommendations that the need for suppression of dangerous materials is a justification for printing patents.

The recommendation may, of course, have been mere window dress-ing, because it is difficult to think that the commissioners seriously thought that Elizabeth would dispense with the granting of general printing patents, which she did not.[91] That it was not mere window dressing is indicated by the recommendation following that "Marshe and vautroller having the sole printing of schole bookes maye be treated withall to chose some sortes and leave the rest."

90. "(a) They enioy Divers copies to them selues as fullie as the priviledged men (b) They haue any booke from the print which they procure to be made or translated (c) They haue libertie of Damaske paper and smale pamphletes. (d) They maye haue from the companie suche copies the[y] will requier which vpon Deathe of any or occurence of yeres fall voyde (e) Divers Stacioners that be honest men though the[y] haue no presses, putting their worke to other and translating of bookes get as great commoditie as they that haue priviledge" II ARBER 784.
91. See III ARBER 87.

Further, the other recommendations for limiting the excessive number of printers as to apprentices, against false printing, and controlling the prices of books are all directed to maintaining order in the book trade. These recommendations were consistent with censorship, of which the commissioners were cognizant (they recommended that press owners should "be bound" not to print forbidden things); but their justification in the report was order in the trade, particularly the recommendations against false printing and prices of books, which were directed to workmanship and monopoly.[92] The commissioners were not, of course, concerned primarily with censorship, but the report does give a perspective of the printing patent as a protective device for trade purposes rather than as an aspect of censorship.

Some of the recommendations of the commission were incorporated in the Star Chamber Decree of 1586, and they may have been responsible for the actions of the patentees shortly thereafter, on January 8, 1584, in giving up certain of their copies "for the use of the poor of the Stationers' Company." Not all of these copies were protected by patents, and many of them were practically worthless,[93] but again the action was characteristic of the company, which seems always to have been willing to take any necessary action to protect its basic position. This attitude is exemplified in the treatment of the insurgents, once they reformed. Most of the reformed dissidents were to share in the patents they had protested against, and John Wolfe subsequently became Beadle of the Company.[94]

The controversy, however, was not yet over. The death of John Day on July 23, 1584,[95] gave rise to a general uproar over the works, the *ABC with Catechism* and the *Psalmes of David in Meter*, covered by the patent to him and his son, Richard. Richard assigned the patent to Edward Whyte, Willyam Wright, Thomas Butter, Frauncis Adams,

92. "(9) Against false printing (a) Suche as offend to geue vp their presses and live as other workmen vntill they be better skilled (b) Everye printer to be bound not to withstand the searche of the warden (c) Bookes of Divinitie false[ly] printed the Printer to be punished at the Discretion of the Ancientes (10) Towchinge The prises of bookes. (a) That no printer sell bookes to any in greater nomber or at lesse then after the rate they sell to any Stationer (b) That no booke seller take vp whole impressions/" II ARBER 785.

93. See a list of the copies at II ARBER 786–789.

94. See COURT BOOK B, 24.

95. II ARBER 791.

and John Wolfe, all of whom had been insurgents against the printing patent. These parties filed a bill in 1585 in the Star Chamber against persons pirating the patented copies,[96] alleging the unlawful printing of 6,000 copies of the *Psalmes* and 20,000 copies of the *ABC*, but the bill was defective because it did not comply with the requirement that "the hand of a Serieant at the lawe or Reader in court and the word Reader to be put to it," and apparently the demurrer was sustained. Francis Flower and his assigns brought an action in the Star Chamber in November 1585, for the unlawful printing of 2,500 copies of the *Accidence*[97] and another action against other defendants for printing 2,000 copies of the grammar.[98]

The company by this time had taken steps to secure protection by legislation. On October 29, 1584, an order was entered by the court "That the wardens of this yere shalbe alowed out of the stocke of the hall for all suche somes of money as they shall employe about the pcuringe of an Act of pliamt for confirmacon of ye charter of the house or any other good aucthorytie on matters tendinge to ye comodyty of the house/"[99]

Apparently, the company continued its actions until 1586. On March 7, 1586, the Court allowed a charge of twenty shillings for a dinner for members of the Company to urge them "To attend before the counsell at the starrechaber in A cause concerninge the whole bodie of the Cupanye," and other sums were allowed "for chargs disbursed in the said cause in the [star] chamber."[100] The legislation sought was, of course, the Star Chamber Decree of 1586, and the attitude of the stationers toward the nature and purpose of the printing patent is perhaps best revealed in "The Arguments of the Patentees in Favour of Privileges for Bookes,"[101] a petition submitted on May 4, 1586, in support of the Star Chamber Decree issued the following June 11.

The attitude was not basically different from that shown in the report of the commissioners in 1584, but the petition emphasized the basis of the royal power. The petition contended that "All princes in

96. Day v. T. Dunn, II ARBER 790.
97. Flower v. Dunn, II ARBER 794.
98. Flower v. Bourne, II ARBER 800.
99. COURT BOOK B, 16.
100. COURT BOOK B, 18.
101. II ARBER 804.

Christendom, where printing is vsed, doo graunt privileges, somme for yeres som for life and som in fee," and this is a prerogative exercised since printing was first introduced in England.

Further, it was necessary for the commonwealth that none but those authorized by the Queen should print, otherwise "it maie be a meanes, that heresies, treasons, and seditious Libelles shall often bee dispersed. . . . " The patents also allowed the patentees sufficient profits to be able to print books "which are more beneficial to the common wealth, than proffitable to the prynter." The patentee was compelled to keep prices within reason by the Statute of 25 Henry VIII, and if his workmanship be poor, then a condition could be annexed to the patent for forfeiture.

However, the most revealing reasons given in support of the patents deserve to be quoted in full: "And further if priuileges be revoked no bookes at all shoulde be prynted, within shorte tyme. for commonlie the first prynter is at charge for the Authors paynes, and somme other suche like extraordinarie cost, where an other that will print it after hym, commeth to the Copie gratis, and so maie he sell better cheaper than the first prynter, and then the first prynter shall never vtter [sell] his bookes. Besides the Seconde prynter maie better the first ympression either by notes, tables, difference in paper or volume (as it is easier to amende then first to invent) which will also hynder the sale of the firste prynters bookes to his vtter vndoing. These inconvenyences seen euery man will strayne curtesie who shall begynne, so farre that in the ende all prynting will decaie within the Realme, to the vndoing of the whole company of Staconers."[102]

The arguments in the petition and the view of the royal commission that particular patents were a means of establishing order in the book trade (and that general patents should be abolished) indicate that a primary value of the printing patent was that it did help preserve order in the trade. In theory, of course, the stationer's copyright could have served this function, but it was a private affair of the company, and its weakness was that control of the disposition of copyrights was in the hands of interested parties. Moreover, the works which were in dispute were works which had already been published many times under patents. The printing patent, as a governmental copyright, was

102. II ARBER 805.

the most effective means of establishing a right to exclusive publication.

Thus, notwithstanding the existence of the stationer's copyright, the printing patent seems to have been necessary to maintain order in the trade. This may explain why printing patents were excluded from the operation of the Statute of Monopolies.

For present purposes, however, the real significance of the controversy is that it illustrates the fundamental purpose of copyright as it developed as a means of providing order in the book trade by protecting published works from piracy. As indicated above, the problem arises again in the eighteenth century. Complete disorder in the book trade arose with the final lapse in 1694 of the Licensing Act of 1662, and led to the enactment of the Statute of Anne. The primary purpose of that statute was to restore order to the trade and to destroy the monopoly of the booksellers by limiting the term of copyright.

This problem is dealt with later, but the problem of monopoly was bound to rise again. It was, in a sense, a continuing issue and it became a particularly live issue in the 1640s, after the abolition of the Star Chamber in 1640 nullified the Star Chamber Decree of 1637. Again disorder in the trade resulted, requiring new legislation.

Monopoly seems to have been the reason for disorder in the trade, because the nonmonopolists resented being foreclosed from the right to print works which they felt they had as much right to publish as the monopolists. The long delay in dealing with the issue directly is explained by the long-continued censorship acts, and by the fact that the company, shortly after the controversy of the 1580s, found a means of doing formally what it had been attempting to do informally in resolving the complaints of the insurgents. This was a means of spreading the benefits of the monopolies among the members of the company. It was the grant of patents to the company itself, made by James I in 1603, that made this possible, because it led to the creation of the English stock.

The English Stock

The English Stock was a publishing organization in the nature of a joint stock company which was formally organized in 1603 when James I granted a patent to the Stationers' Company for the sum of nine thousand pounds, raised by the sale of shares to members of the

Company.[103] The original letters patent, surrendered in 1616 for a larger one,[104] was based on three earlier patents which had been issued separately to William Seres,[105] John Day,[106] and Richard Watkins and James Robertes.[107]

Since the patent to the company conflicted with unexpired privileges, there was a considerable expense in payments which had to be made to various claimants beyond the initial investment of nine thousand pounds.[108] In addition, the stock also expended large sums in purchas-

103. The patent, for "psalters, psalms, prymers, Almanacks & other books" is reprinted at III ARBER 42. For an excellent account of the origins of the Stock, see Blagden, *The English Stock of the Stationers' Company*, X THE LIBRARY, 5th ser., 163 (1955). Blagden described the English Stock as a "book-producing and book-wholesaling organization run from Stationers' Hall. . . . "

104. Reprinted at III ARBER 679.

105. Seres received a patent on March 5, 1553, for the printing of Primers containing the Psalter. Shortly thereafter, he received a similar patent for the Catechism in English "with the brief of an ABC thereunto annexed." He lost these patents within a few months, Blagden, *The English Stock of the Stationers' Company*, X THE LIBRARY, 5th ser. at 164; but on June 3, 1559, he received them again for himself and his assigns for life. Later on August 23, 1571, he obtained a further grant for the joint lives of himself and his son and before he died, he leased it to Henry Denham. See II ARBER 15.

106. The *Psalms of David in meter* and the *ABC* with the little Catechism was granted to John Day in 1560 for seven years, was renewed in 1567 for ten years, and finally was renewed by letters patent on August 26, 1577, to John and his son Richard for the term of the longer life. II ARBER 753–754.

107. On May 12, 1571, Watkins and Robertes received a patent for almanacks and prognostications, which was renewed for the second time on December 3, 1588, for twenty-one years. II ARBER 16. See Blagden, *The English Stock of the Stationers' Company*, X THE LIBRARY, 5th ser., at 164.

108. The records of payment to the various claimants, which are probably incomplete, show the expense which this entailed. Six hundred pounds were paid for Verney Alley's patent for Psalms, COURT BOOK C, 68; an annuity of three pounds was given to Alice Wolfe, widow of John, for the ABC's for horn-books, COURT BOOK C, 13; and the estate of Richard Watkins was paid one hundred and sixty pounds for his privilege for almanacs, COURT BOOK C, 9. There is no record of payment to the partners in the Day and Seres privileges. Professor Jackson suggests such payments involved a considerable sum. JACKSON, *Introduction*, RECORDS OF THE COURT OF THE STATIONERS' COMPANY, 1602–1640, viii (1957). The absence of records may be explained by the fact that no such payments were made. The patent to the Company as to Primers, Psalters, and Psalms, reads "Any other priviledge or anye other order heretofore graunted or taken to the contrarie notwithstanding." III ARBER 42. Whether this amounted to a cancellation of the previous grants is not clear, but there was no such provision in connection with the almanacs and prognostications. However, the payment for Verney Alley's was

ing other patents from individual grantees, making the venture an extremely expensive one, a measure of importance to the stationers.[109]

The English Stock was only one of several stocks organized within the company. There were also the Latin Stock and the Irish Stock, as well as "The Ballad Partners," who were not organized as a stock-company.[110]

The English Stock was the first, however, and the most important, and the only one, apparently, which was continuously profitable. The date of its formal creation is a convenient one to mark the final outcome of the controversy of the 1580s, because the new letters patent served to solidify the position of the patentees and to insure for the company power to act as arbiter of the book trade, power which it had long sought.

There were two factors which led to the grant, political and economic. Elizabeth near the end of her reign had issued a proclamation renouncing monopolies, and in 1601 she abolished the most unpopular patents and left the decision as to the rest of the courts.[111] When James I arrived in England on May 6, 1603, he repeated Elizabeth's proclamation against monopolies, and the few months in which he adhered to this policy afforded a favourable opportunity to the companies to buy the grants, while there were no individuals competing in the same field.[112] Since royal grants to companies were not considered monopolies, such grants could be made without fear of criticism.

The economic factor was the dissatisfaction of the unprivileged in the Stationers' Company with the concentration of the patents in a few

---

apparently for a patent given to him on February 20, 1592, for the reversion of the patent to John and Richard Day for the *Psalms of David*, the *ABC with the Little Catechism*, and the *Catechism* in English and Latin compiled by Alexander Nowell. See the second grant in the Company, III ARBER 679. The answer is probably found in the fact that there was a real question of conflict between the wording of the various patents and the Company considered it a wise policy to purchase rather than contest.

109. For example, the Stock bought the law patent of Charles Yetsweirt from Bonham Norton and Thomas Wight, who had purchased it in 1599 from Yetsweirt. See COURT BOOK C, 13; COURT BOOK B, 70. For a list of books included in the English Stock on March 5, 1620, see the entrance at III ARBER 668.

110. See JACKSON, *Introduction, op. cit.*, xi–xiv.

111. Blagden, *The English Stock of the Stationers' Company*, X THE LIBRARY, 5th ser., at 176.

112. UNWIN, THE GILDS AND COMPANIES OF LONDON 301 (1908).

hands. The company had two alternatives in dealing with the economic difficulties: to seek to abolish the printing patent for individuals, particularly the general patents; or to attempt to spread the benefits of the patents among a larger number of persons.

It took the latter course, which, if successful, would mean more power for the company in controlling the publishing of books, because the patentees were theoretically outside the company's jurisdiction.

The new policies were manifested by the encouragement to the poor members to print unclaimed copies in the order of 1578, re-enforced by the patentees' gifts of copies in 1584 to the company for the use of the poor, the emergence of the printer's right whereby a printer could own the right to print a work although he did not have the right to publish it, and the encouraging of printing syndicates.[113]

The encouragement of printing syndicates was an aspect of the most important policy, which was to spread the economic rewards of the patents more equitably among members of the company. The impetus for this action came from the patentees themselves during the height of the controversy of the 1580s, probably as a matter of self-defense. Henry Denham, the assignee of William Seres, took "vij yonge men . . . to joyne with him,"[114] John Day dispersed his work to "vij or Eight householders of the Companie,"[115] and Richard Day assigned his patent to five of the malcontents on November 16, 1584.[116]

Although these steps were taken by individual patentees, the significance of the actions is that when the patents were assigned to several persons, disputes that arose would be settled by the company. This is what happened on January 18, 1585, when the Court of Assistants arranged with the assignees of Day that Thomas Purfoot, another malcontent, should have, during the life of the privilege, the printing of the first leaf of *The Little Catechism*, "wch he before printed As Assignee to Iohn daie deceased."[117]

---

113. On June 15, 1587, the company ordered that the *Statutes at Large*, a gift of Christopher Barker, be "printed if there can be found a convenient nuber of ye cupanie that will disburse the charge thereof," and the two volumes "of ye homilyes shall goo in hand to be printed And asmany of the cumpanie to haue ptes therein as will disburse the charge of the same." COURT BOOK B, 24.
114. II ARBER 771.
115. II ARBER 775.
116. II ARBER 791.
117. COURT BOOK B, 16.

As early as June 9, 1575, the company had attempted to organize printing "in common" for books controlled by letters patent.[118] The entry was based on an order of the Court of High Commission of June 8, with the assent of Richard Jugge, the Queen's Printer, that Jugge should have the right to print only "the byble in Quarto and the testament in decimo Sexto. And all other bibles in folio and testaments (excepted as before) to be at the libertie of the printinge of ye rest of the Stationers."

The Court of Assistants took this to mean that the copyright was in the company, because the master, wardens and assistants "ffor good order and quietnes to be had and vsed touchinge the saide Bibles and Testaments so licensed to be printed in common" ordered that no person should print the works granted unless he or they presented every such Bible or Testament to them for permission "to thintent that the Mr Wardens and adsistants in the grantinge of eury suche license, maie Inioyne and take order with the ptie and pties to whome any suche license shalbe graunted, for the good and sufficient imprintinge of eurye suche Bible and testament so to be prsented, as well with good pap and good woorkemanshippe, as with good correction."

The order also provided that those licensed to print works should submit any controversy to the court, and laid down rules to insure good workmanship and to prevent both price-cutting and price raising. In this order we see the elements of control which the company was to exercise more formally in connection with the English Stock,[119] but the arrangement as to the printing of the Bible was brought to an end, presumably because of the death of Jugge and the succession of Christopher Barker to the position of the Queen's Printer.[120]

It was the establishment of the partners in the Day and Seres patents

118. Liber A, f. 25[v] reprinted in Blagden, *The English Stock of the Stationers' Company*, X THE LIBRARY, 5th ser., Appendix II, at 179.

119. *Cf.* the following order of 29 July 1605: "Yt is ordered that no booke appteyninge to the pruileges of the Company shall hereafter neither in pte nor in all be putt to printinge or taken in hand by any printer or other to be printed Except it shalbe done with the consent of the Mr. Wardens. & Assistants or the moore pte of them, and the printer & the nuber of the ympression and the pryce for woorkmanship by them [first] appointed rated & sett Down/" COURT BOOK C, 14.

120. See Blagden, *The English Stock of the Stationers' Company*, X THE LIBRARY, 5th ser., 172.

that enabled the Stationers' Company to establish the precedent of control, making the granting of the patent of 1603 the next logical step. The exercise of the company's control is shown in the minutes of a partners' meeting on October 12, 1591, where it was ordered that action be taken against John Legatt of Cambridge for printing *The Psalmes of David in Metre*. It was agreed "by the pten's in mr Ric' dayes priulege" that John Wolfe (by now Beadle) should assist Richard Day in the prosecution. The treasurer was to meet all the charges out of the partners' "common stock" and recover from individuals in proportion to their holdings, all of which was done "accordinge to ye Iudgement of a Court of Assistants/"[121]

By 1594, the two patents were being run together under the general direction of the Court of Assistants by the Treasurer and the stock-keepers, who were elected annually.[122]

Once it was formally established, the English Stock was operated so as to maintain a strict control over the publishing of the books within its jurisdiction. The Stock was governed by the master and wardens and a committee of shareholders called the stock-keepers, two elected annually from each of the three classes of shareholders on the first of March—or, if that was a Sunday, on the second. There was also a committee of auditors chosen annually at the same time, two from each class; and a treasurer elected with them who was bonded and well paid for his services. The master, wardens, and stock-keepers, at their fortnightly meetings, apparently determined what books should be printed, the size of the editions, who should print them, and at what price the books should be sold. The stock-keepers kept the accounts,

---

121. COURT BOOK B, 39. *Cf.* the following order of August 16, 1591. "In full Court this Day / Iohn Charlwood Robert Robinson and Iohn wolf by consent of the pten's in mr Seres p'uilege are Chozen and appointed to defend the printinge of thold prymer against the newe printed by Scarlet for mr Tipper The chargs of the sute to be borne out of the stock belonging to the pten's in this p'uilege/" COURT BOOK B, 38.

122. See the two entries for March 18, 1594, one pertaining to Mr. Day's privilege, the other to Seres' privilege. "Mr. Daies pruilege. At this court many of the parten's in mr Seres and Mr. Dayes preuilegs being present: by voyces of the said parten's A. Treaserer, and ffoure stockekeps were elected: as followeth. . . . Mr. Seres p'uileg / Yt is agreed by the said pten's pnt that the lyke Course for eleccon of their stockkeps treasorers shalbe obserued, whiche is according to thentent of their arles of pten'ship" COURT BOOK B, 48.

delivered the paper to the printers, gave receipts, and paid the bills. Great care was taken that extra copies were not printed and retained for private sale,[123] and the company maintained close control of the ownership of shares, which were limited to fifteen assistants; thirty members of the livery, and sixty members of the yeomanry.

The shares were used as security for loans, but such transactions had to be approved by the courts,[124] and no shares could be transferred or sold without the court's permission.[125] Widows of shareholders were permitted to keep one share,[126] so long as they did not marry out of the company, and if a shareholder resigned or surrendered his share, the court might declare him ineligible to be elected to such part again, or to attend regular meetings of the stock or to take part in its business.[127]

The English Stock was only one of the many affairs of the Stationers' Company, and its creation by no means meant that the publishing of all books was under the company's copyright.

Printing patents were still held by and were available to individuals. Two notable examples are the patents for John Speed's *Genealogies* and Rider's *Dictionary*. Speed entered into a contract with the Company whereby the Company agreed to print the *Genealogies* with Bibles and to pay Speed a royalty of eight pence a copy.[128] The contract, entered into on November 21, 1615, was renewed from time to time[129] until Speed sold the patent to the Company in 1637 for seven hundred pounds.[130]

Rider's *Dictionary* was printed by a group of partners for many years without any formal organization as a stock company.[131]

The stationer's copyright, of course, remained available and there were other stocks, *e.g.*, the Latin and Irish Stocks, which proved to be unprofitable and short-lived; but of all the affairs of the company, the

123. JACKSON, *op. cit.*, x.
124. See, *e.g.*, COURT BOOK C, 247.
125. See, *e.g.*, COURT BOOK C, 164.
126. COURT BOOK C, 38.
127. See COURT BOOK C, 144, 275, 291.
128. COURT BOOK C, 78.
129. COURT BOOK C, 241, 295.
130. COURT BOOK C, 317.
131. See COURT BOOK C, 18, 175, 271, 330.

English Stock was the single most important one. It was the core of the company's power; when in the 1640s the company was again faced with internal difficulties, primarily complaints against individual monopolies and oligarchic rule, it managed to ride out the storm partly because of the English Stock. By this time, the shareholders numbered well over a hundred, included widows, and the capital investment amounted to 14,400 pounds.[132]

Although the printing patent was the important form of copyright in the early years, its importance waned with the delimitation of the royal prerogative over printing and with the development of literature. By the end of the seventeenth century, the stationer's copyright had become the more important of the two, and it was the stationer's copyright which was the basis for the statutory copyright. The printing patent, however, as the basis of the early monopoly within the company, established a tradition which was not only continued, but which was added to as the development of English literature made the stationer's copyright more valuable.

And monopoly was the single most important factor in the later development of statutory copyright. The major idea present in the printing patent not present in the stationer's copyright was the idea that copyright was a grant of the government. What effect this aspect of the printing patent had on the later development of copyright is conjectural, but it did provide a long history of government control of copyright. It may be that this idea of government control has had more influence in American copyright law than in English law, because of the joining together of the patent and copyright clauses in the Constitution.

From the printing patent, we turn now to the third of the four major legal concepts in the development of copyright: censorship and press control.

---

132. Blagden, *The Stationers' Company in the Civil War Period*, XIII THE LIBRARY, 5th ser., 1, 14 (1958).

6

Copyright and Censorship

"For that part which preserves justly every mans Copy to himself, or provides for the poor, I touch not," wrote Milton in *Areopagitica*, opposing the revival of censorship by Parliament during the Interregnum. He only wished that "thay be not made pretenses to abuse and persecute honest and painfull men, who offend not in either of these particulars." Milton thus recognized the value and importance of copyright, but he saw too that copyright was used as an excuse to renew censorship laws in order to protect the booksellers' monopoly of the trade. In his words, "Some old *patentees* and *monopolizers* in the trade of bookselling . . . brought divers glosing colours to the House, which were indeed but colours, and serving to no end except it be to exercise a superiority over their neighbors . . . that they should be made other mens vassalls."

Milton failed for the time in his plea for freedom of the press, but his tract provides a keen insight into the relationship of censorship and copyright. Censorship in England began without any reference to copyright, and there is little doubt that copyright would have developed without it. Copyright, however, became an instrument of censorship, a policy of the sovereign, with which the courts did not interfere. Except for censorship, the courts might well have imposed limitations on the early copyright to preclude its use as an instrument of monopoly; but the presence of censorship protected copyright from judicial interference, and the favored few, in using copyright to develop an oppressive and long-continued monopoly, caused it to be so associated with monopoly that even today copyright is deemed to be a grant of government, a privilege, not a right.

The stationers early perceived the value of censorship regulations to support their monopoly, and they never lost sight of the point. Indeed, their continual lobbying was such that the long-continued existence of censorship in England can be attributed in large measure to them, although they were not always successful in their efforts. Elizabeth I at first refused the company's request for more power, and the Fifty-first Injunction of 1559, Elizabeth's first act of censorship, ignored the stationers, except to command them especially to be obedient to the orders. The Star Chamber Decree of 1566, the next act of censorship, was less than satisfactory from the stationers' viewpoint. The company, however, became more successful in its efforts at acquiring power as the need for press control increased. The basis of their argument seems always to have been the need for order in the book trade. After the final lapse in 1694 of the Licensing Act of 1662, the disorder in the trade was such that the stationers sought new censorship legislation from Parliament. After they failed in this, they sought legislation designed simply to restore order to the trade. The Statute of Anne was at least in part the result of these efforts.

There were three major acts of censorship under the Tudors and Stuarts: the Star Chamber Decrees of 1586[1] and 1637[2] and the Licensing Act of 1662.[3] In addition, there was a series of ordinances regulating the press during the Civil War Period and the Interregnum, the main ones being the Ordinances of 1643,[4] 1647,[5] and 1649.[6]

The Star Chamber Decree of 1586

The Stationers' Company took advantage of the controversy within the company during the 1580s as an excuse to secure more power through new legislation to control printing. As early as 1584, an entry in Court Book B allowed the Wardens "all suche somes of money as they shall employe about the prcuringe of an Act of pliamt,"[7] and for

---

1. II ARBER 807.
2. IV ARBER 528.
3. 13 and 14 Car. II, c. 33.
4. I FIRTH & RAIT, ACTS AND ORDINANCES OF THE INTERREGNUM 184–187 (1911).
5. I FIRTH & RAIT, 1021–1023.
6. II FIRTH & RAIT, 245–254.
7. COURT BOOK B, 16.

the year 1586–87, there are two entries in Register A for the receipt of "Contrybution of certen of the Companye toward the charges of the suynge out of the newe orders of the Starre Chamber, as was agreed vpon by order of Courts."[8] In 1584, the company was undoubtedly seeking to take advantage of the report of the Commission of the Privy Council appointed to inquire into the controversy. The Commission made its final report on July 18, 1583,[9] and it was clearly a forerunner of the Star Chamber Decree of 1586; but the company's initiative alone was not enough, as shown by the failure of its earlier efforts in 1559 and 1562, and the promulgation of the Decree in 1586 was apparently due primarily to John Whitgift, who became Archbishop of Canterbury in 1583.

Whitgift was "an uncompromising opponent" of puritanism, and just prior to his becoming Archbishop, the puritan doctrine had been making great strides among the clergy of the Church of England. One source of embarrassment to the government and danger to ecclesiastical doctrine was the success of the secret printer, thought to be principally Robert Waldegrave. Waldegrave was one of the insurgents in the Stationers' Company, and he published puritan tracts under the name of Martin Marprelate. Whitgift found it necessary to adopt stringent measures to stem the puritan tide, the most important of which, for present purposes, was his procuring the 1586 Decree from the Star Chamber.[10]

"The new Decrees of the Starre Chamber for orders in printinge" was issued on June 23, 1586.[11] The decree is a relatively short one, consisting of nine items, as compared with thirty-three for the decree of 1637. Its substance is correctly reflected in the title: it was a decree for regulating printers and publishers; there is no mention of either writing or authors in the document. The preamble makes clear that the concern was with "contentyous and disorderlye persons professinge the arte or mysterye of Pryntinge or sellinge of bookes," and indicates that the prime mover in the promulgation of the decree was the

8. I ARBER 518, 524.

9. II ARBER 783.

10. See Wilson, *The Marprelate Controversy*, III THE CAMBRIDGE HISTORY OF ENGLISH LITERATURE, 425–426 (1911).

11. There are three copies of the Decree, in STATE PAPERS DOMESTIC ELIZ. vols. 190 and 192, and another in LANSD. MS. 905. Arber printed the oldest text, from 190 S.P.D. ELIZ., Art. 48. Note, II ARBER 807.

Archbishop of Canterbury. All persons "vsinge or professinge the arte, trade or misterye of pryntinge or sellinge of bookes" were to be governed by the rules set forth, and Her Majesty charged the Archbishop of Canterbury "and the righte honorable the Lordes and others of her highness prvye Councell" with the responsibility of enforcing the regulations. "Wherevpon the said moste reverend father and the wholle presence sittinge in the honorable Courte" decreed the regulations to be "dulye and invyolablye kepte and observed."

Item one of the decree provided for the registration of all existing printing presses with the master and wardens of the Stationers' Company; future presses were to be registered within ten days after they were set up. Item two limited printing to London and its suburbs, except for one press each at Cambridge and Oxford, and provided that presses were not to be maintained in any secret or obscure corner, but were to be kept in open places, so as to be accessible to searches to be made by the master and wardens of the company. Resisting search or concealing the existence of any printing press was specifically forbidden.

The provisions of item three, limiting the number of printing presses and providing a procedure for the choosing of persons to own presses, were rather involved. They provided that no person who had set up a printing press within the past six months should continue to use it until the "excessiue multytude of Prynters hauinge presses already sett vp" should be diminished "to so small a number of maisters or owners of printinge houses" that the Archbishop of Canterbury and the Bishop of London should think it "requisyte and convenyent for the good service of the Realme" to have more presses established. When this occurred, the Archbishop and Bishop were to notify the master and wardens of the company, and the new printers were to be chosen from among free stationers. Within fourteen days after the election, the master, wardens, and at least four assistants of the company were to present the person so chosen to the members of the Court of High Commission—or six of them, of whom the Archbishop of Canterbury or the Bishop of London was to be one—who were to approve the choice; the candidate could then "be master and governour of a presse and printinge howse." The person chosen to be queen's printer was exempted from this procedure.

Item four contained the licensing provisions, and it is this provision which shows the extent to which the draftsmen of the decree were concerned with the mechanical process of printing rather than the creative process of writing. It provided that "no person shall ymprynt or cawse to be ymprinted, or suffer by any meanes to his knowledge his presse, letters, or other Instruments to be occupied in pryntinge of any booke, work, coppye, matter or thinge whatsoever" unless the works were properly licensed. No work was to be printed except as approved according to the Injunctions of 1559, and by the Archbishop of Canterbury or Bishop of London. The requirement of the approval by one of the two ecclesiastics was apparently a convenient means of brushing away the cumbersome procedure of the Injunctions. An exception was made for the queen's printer, and for persons "pryviledged to prynte the bookes of the *Common Lawe.*" The law books were to be approved by the two chief justices and chief baron, or two of them. The paragraph further prohibited the printing of books against any statutes or laws of the realm, or injunctions or letters patent, "or contrary to any allowed ordynaunce sett Downe for the good governaunce of the Cumpany of Staconers." The penalty for violations of the first three items of the decree, concerned with the ownership of presses, involved a year's imprisonment. The penalty for printing a book without license was six months' imprisonment.

The remaining portions of the decree were designed to implement the first four items. Item five provided a penalty of three months' imprisonment for the binding or selling of books printed contrary to the decree; item six gave the wardens of the company, or any two of the company deputed by them, the power to make search and seize all unlawful books (to be delivered to Stationers' Hall) and to bring offenders before the Court of High Commission; item seven gave the wardens the power to search for and to carry away all presses, type and other instruments used contrary to the decree. The wardens were required to take order from the assistants before "Defacinge, burninge, and destroyinge all the sayd letters, presses, and other pryntinge Instruments," and the material so defaced was to be redelivered to the owners again within three months after the seizing thereof. Item eight, "for the avoydinge of the excessyve nomber of Prynters," limited the number of apprentices to three, for persons who had been master or upper warden; two, for under wardens and members of livery; and one, for members of the yeomanry. The queen's printer was permitted to have six apprentices. Item nine limited the printers at Oxford and Cambridge to one apprentice each, but they were allowed to use any journeyman "being freeman of the cytte of London without contradiccon."

The theory of controlling the printing presses underlying the 1586 Decree was a sound one. So long as the printing presses were limited in number and under the watchful eye of the government, the matter of individual licenses was not of great significance, as dangerous writings not printed and distributed offered little threat to the government or established religion. Moreover, the concentration of control on the mechanical reproductions of books left a wide degree of latitude for members of the book trade, and to a large extent the government could depend upon the self-interest of the stationers in wanting to please the government so as to maintain their monopoly. The government in 1586 was not so much interested in what was printed as what was not printed, which meant that censorship under Elizabeth was basically a power to disapprove, rather than a power to approve. This theory of censorship was to undergo a change under the Stuarts, but the Star Chamber Decree of 1586 remained the mainstay of censorship in England for fifty years.

The Star Chamber Decree of 1637

Notwithstanding the actions of the government, it was Arber's opinion that the press under Elizabeth "was probably the freest in Europe; as free indeed as the political situation at that time would admit of."[12]

The Stuarts were different. Where Elizabeth was concerned with the public good, the Stuart kings were concerned with personal exaltation; they aimed that they should be the personal embodiment of the state, with everything depending upon their personal will. James I told Parliament, " . . . The state of monarchy is the supremest thing upon earth: for kings are not only God's lieutenants upon earth and sit upon God's throne, but even by God himself they are called gods.

12. III ARBER 11.

. . . I conclude then this point touching the power of kings with this axiom of divinity, That as to dispute what God may do is blasphemy, . . . so is it sedition in subjects to dispute what a king may do in the height of his power."[13]

It is not surprising, then, that the productions of the printing press after 1603 came under a more stringent supervision as a part of the policy of government. "[U]nder the early Stuarts . . . the Press was under *surveillance*; being watched with increasing jealousy as well by the government as by the hierarchy,"[14] as shown by the fact that the entries of copies in the registers of the company from the accession of James I to 1640 are much fuller, more precise, and usually include the names of the two sponsors, the licensing clergymen and a warden of the company, or the two wardens themselves.

It was not, however, until the second Stuart king that the most significant Stuart document relating to printing was promulgated, the Star Chamber Decree of 1637. Once again, the decree was promoted by the Stationers' Company for its own benefit, and was granted by the government out of necessity.[15] The clerk of the company was given a gratuity of fifteen pounds for extra work involved in procuring the decree[16] and a gratuity of twenty pounds was given "for his Loue & kindnes to the Company" to the Attorney General,[17] who had drafted the decree with the advice of the Lord Keeper, Archbishop Laud, and others.[18]

The company had failed in its ambitious bids for power in 1559 and 1562, but the Star Chamber Decree of 1586 had given it a large part of what it wanted. The patents granted to the company by James I and the consequent creation of the English Stock, however, made protection of copies of even greater importance. The powers the company

13. Speech of James I before Parliament, 21 March 1610, from PROTHERO, STATUTES AND CONSTITUTIONAL DOCUMENTS, 1558–1625, 293–294 (1913).

14. III ARBER 15.

15. An early draft of the decree contained only eighteen clauses which omitted much of what the stationers particularly wanted. The decree itself contains thirty-three clauses, with those provisions the stationers desired. See BLADGEN, THE STATIONERS' COMPANY 118, n. 1, 118–125 (1960). For example, Items XXV and XXVI, pertaining to searches, were omitted in the draft.

16. COURT BOOK C, 298.

17. COURT BOOK C, 300.

18. BLAGDEN, THE STATIONERS' COMPANY 118 (1960).

had were not sufficient "for dealing successfully either with infringers of the Company's rights (cheap and popular books being particularly vulnerable)" or with criticism of the church and state.[19] The government was willing to grant the company its wishes because the Decree of 1586 had been found, according to the preamble of the new decree, *"by experience to be defectiue in some particulars;"* but, with commendable caution, it was provided *"the said former Decrees and Ordinances shall stand in force with these Additions, Explanations, and Alterations following, viz."*[20]

Even though the 1637 Decree contained substantially all of the provisions of the 1586 Decree, the two documents are different in scope and theory. The aim of the 1586 Decree was not so much to control the output of the press as it was to prevent the publication of dangerous books. The 1637 Decree, on the other hand, was a stringent scheme for censorship, not merely control of the printing press. It is a far more comprehensive and detailed document than the earlier decree, and the difference between the two regulations is manifested in their provisions dealing with offenders. The earlier decree provided specific penalties, varying with the offense committed; the 1637 Decree provided only that the Court of High Commission should inflict such punishment as it thought fit for the offense committed. The later decree not only regulated the ownership of presses, it contained a more comprehensive scheme for licensing and provided detailed regulations for the sale and importation of books, and for type founders and makers of presses. The broadened scope of the later decree is undoubtedly due in part to the stationers.

The first paragraph of the 1637 Decree forbade the printing, selling, importing, or binding of "any seditious, scismaticall, or offensive Bookes or Pamphlets, to the scandall of Religion, or the Church, or the Government, or Governours of the Church or State, or Commonwealth, or of any Corporation, or particular person or persons whatsoeuer . . . " This comprehensive beginning was carried over into Item II, which provided that no one should imprint any book or pamphlet "vnlesse the same Booke or Pamphlet, and also all and euery the Titles, Epistles, Prefaces, Proems, Preambles, Introductions, Tables,

19. *Ibid.*
20. IV Arber 529.

Dedications, and other matters and things whatsoeuer thereunto annexed, or therewith imprinted . . . " should be lawfully licensed and
"also first entred into the Registers Booke of the Company of
Stationers. . . . "

This provision was followed, in Item III, by the designation of
persons authorized to license books. They were, for law books, one of
the chief justices or the chief Baron; for books of history, or any other
book of state affairs, one of the Secretaries of State; for books concerning heraldry, titles of honor and arms, or otherwise concerning
the office of the Earl Marshall, the Earl Marshall; and all other books
"whatsoeuer," the Archbishop of Canterbury or Bishop of London.
The chancellor and vice-chancellor of both of the universities were
authorized to license books printed at the universities, but were not
to license books of law or matters of state. In all instances, the official
licensers had the power to appoint one to act for them.

The procedure for obtaining a license was given in Item IV. Each
licensee was to have two written copies of each book, one of which
was to be retained to insure that the copy was not altered, the other
returned to the owner. The licenser was required to testify that there
was nothing in the book contrary "to Christian Faith, and the Doctrine
and Discipline of the Church of *England*, nor against the State or
Gouernment, nor contrary to good life, or good manners, or otherwise. . . . " The license was to be imprinted in the beginning of the
book with the name of each licenser.

Items V, VI, and VII dealt with the importation of books. Every
importer of books was required to submit a written catalogue of all
imported books to the Archbishop of Canterbury or Bishop of London; all packages of imported books were to be opened only in the
presence of the Archbishop or Bishop with the master or one of the
wardens of the company; and no book to which the copyright was
held, either by patent or registration in the company's register, was
to be imported.

Item VIII required that the names of the author, printer, and publisher of all books, ballads, charts, and portraits were to be printed
thereon. Item IX forbade the use of the "marke or vinnet" of the
Stationers' Company or any person without the consent of the owner;
and, in Item X, only persons who had been apprentices in the book

trade for seven years were allowed to deal in any way with "Bibles, Testaments, Psalm-books, Primers, Abcees, Almanackes, or other booke or books whatsoeuer."

The remaining twenty-three items of the decree were primarily devoted to provisions covering the industrial section of the book trade to implement the policy of complete control. The importation of books in the English language was forbidden, "for the better incouraging of Printers in their honest, and iust endeauours in their profession. . . ."[21]

Only freemen of the Stationers' Company could import books in any language.[22] No press was to be established without notice to the master and wardens of the company;[23] and no press was to be forged or type cast, or imported without notice to these officials.[24] Only twenty master printers, excepting the king's printer and the printers for the universities, were to be allowed a press. Future master printers were to be named by the Archbishop of London or six "other high Commissioners."[25] Printers were required to post bond in the sum of three hundred pounds as surety not to print or allow to be printed any but licensed books.[26] Printers who had been master or upper wardens of the company were allowed three presses; all other printers were limited to two.[27] No book was to be reprinted without a new license,[28] and the number of apprentices allowed was limited.[29] Because secret printing had been caused by lack of employment for

21. Item XI.
22. Item XII.
23. Item XIII.
24. Item XIV.
25. Item XV.
26. Item XVI.
27. Item XVII.
28. Item XVIII. Greg interpreted this provision to mean not that a book had to be licensed for each printing, but only that every work, old or new, had to be licensed after the passing of the decree. GREG, LONDON PUBLISHING, 13. The language of the provision is ambiguous and reads in full: "XVIII. *Item,* That no person or persons, do hereafter reprint, or cause to be reprinted, any booke or bookes whatsoeuer (though formerly printed with licence) without being reuiewed, and a new Licence obtained for the reprinting thereof. Always provided, that the stationer or Printer bee put to no other charge hereby, but the bringing and leauing of two printed copies of the book to be printed, as is before expressed of written Copies, with all such additions as the Author hath made." IV ARBER 533.
29. Item XIX.

journeymen printers, the master and wardens of the company were required to take special care that all journeymen printers free of the company be set to work within the company,[30] under penalty of imprisonment for failure to do so.[31]

The printers of the universities were not limited in the number of apprentices they could have, but they were not to allow their journeymen printers to go to London for employment, unless the printers of London so requested, without prejudice to their own journeymen.[32] Master printers could employ only free men or apprentices of the trade.[33] If a person other than an allowed printer set up or worked at any press, he was to be set in the pillory, whipped through London, and suffer any other punishment deemed proper.[34] The master and wardens of the company, or any two licensed master printers appointed by the Archbishop of Canterbury or Bishop of London, were given authority to search for illegal printing,[35] and to seize illegal books to bring them to the Archbishop of Canterbury or Bishop of London.[36] Only four founders of type for printing were allowed,[37] who were to be limited in the number of apprentices they could have.[38] Provisions similar to those requiring journeymen printers to be put to work were also included for journeymen founders;[39] employment in the casting of type was limited to journeymen apprentices, with an exception for a boy "pulling off the knots of mettle hanging at the ends of letters when they are first cast. . . ."[40]

Persons convicted of violating provisions of the decree, in addition to other punishments, "shall before such time as he or they shall be discharged, and ouer and aboue their fine and punishment, as aforesaid, be bound with good sureties, never after to transgresse, or offend in that or the like kinde, for which he, or they shalbe so conuicted

30. Item XX.
31. Item XXI.
32. Item XXII.
33. Item XXIII.
34. Item XXIV.
35. Item XXV.
36. Item XXVI.
37. Item XXVII.
38. Item XXVIII.
39. Item XXIX.
40. Item XXX.

and punished, as aforesaid." Forfeited books, except those ordered to be burnt, and the forfeitures already granted by letters patent, were to be divided and disposed of as the High Commission saw fit, always providing that one moitie be to the king.[41] Importation of books was limited to the port of the City of London.[42]

Finally, as there was an agreement between Sir Thomas Bodley, founder of the library at Oxford, and the Company of Stationers that a copy of each book printed be sent to the library, the decree made this practice a matter of law.[43]

The Star Chamber Decree of 1637 was short-lived, for the Long Parliament abolished the Star Chamber by an act of July 5, 1641,[44] but it was more important that its short existence would normally indicate. Charles II revived it in 1662 under the guise of the Licensing Act. Without the decree of 1637, Parliament in 1662 would have had to return to the decree of 1586, a seventy-six-year-old precedent for censorship; and it seems likely that except for the later decree, there might have been no Licensing Act at all.

Charles II had been restored to the throne for two years before the Licensing Act was passed, and even then the act was limited to two years. This is not to say that Charles would not have engaged in censorship—this he did, as early as 1660, when the government appointed Sir John Birkenhead Surveyor of the Press and issued an order in council dated June 7, 1660, instructing the Stationers' Company to seize copies of certain antimonarchial tracts.[45] But without the 1637 Decree as a precedent, censorship might have been left to orders in council. The 1586 Decree was basically a regulatory document designed to safeguard the state religion, and as such would not have been a satisfactory precedent in 1662; but the 1637 Decree made censorship a political instrument of despotic government, and in 1662, Charles, a newly restored monarch not wishing to return to his travels, was

41. Item XXXI.
42. Item XXXII.
43. Item XXXIII.
44. 16 Car. I, c. 10. The Court of High Commission was abolished at the same time. 16 Car. I, c. 11. The effective date of both acts was August 1, 1641.
45. See Walker, *The Censorship of the Press During the Reign of Charles II*, 35 HISTORY, n.s., 219 (1950).

extremely sensitive to political criticisms. He was thus easy prey to the lobby of the Stationers' Company seeking new press regulations to renew their power.

Acts and Ordinances of the Interregnum

The abolition of the Star Chamber did away with the complex system of press control built up over the years and marked the beginning of the end of censorship in England. The end was a long time in coming, for a practice so deeply ingrained in history was not to be easily eradicated; and the Stationers' Company was to do its part to delay the end as much as possible, because copyright depended for its protection on government support.

There has been some suggestion that the Long Parliament (1640–1653) intended that the press be free, even though it did not intend that freedom to be extended to the authors of "papistical books."[46]

In 1641, Parliament set up a Committee of Printing, not to control the press, but to deal with specific complaints of disorder in the book trade.[47]

It was not until 1643 that Parliament passed the first licensing act of the Interregnum, "An Ordinance for the Regulating of Printing."[48] The principal impetus for the act came from the Stationers' Company, for reasons similar to those which had motivated the company before and which again prompted it to petition Parliament for a new act in 1703, 1706, and 1709: protection of the stationers' property.

After the abolition of the Star Chamber and High Commission in 1641, the Stationers' Company encountered new difficulties, centered, as was the controversy leading up to the Star Chamber Decree of 1586, on monopolies. Monopolies in 1641, however, were considerably more important to a larger number of people than in 1683, when the principal concern was the privileges granted to individuals. In 1641, there were two kinds of monopolies—corporate and private—because

---

46. CLYDE, THE STRUGGLE FOR THE FREEDOM OF THE PRESS FROM CAXTON TO CROMWELL 55 (1934).

47. See BLAGDEN, THE STATIONERS' COMPANY 146 (1960).

48. I FIRTH & RAIT, 184–187.

of the joint stocks organized within the company from 1603 to 1640, first and most imporant of which was the English Stock.[49]

In 1641, the Stationers' Company unsuccessfully sought from the Committee for Printing certain patents to be "put into the whole Companyes hands for the Common good of the Realm,"[50] and shortly thereafter the unpopularity of the company's monopoly was reflected in a pamphlet entitled "Scintilla, or a Light broken into darke *Warehouses*," criticizing the monopolistic practices of the stationers.[51] The pamphlet was directed primarily against seven private patents, principally the Irish, Scotch, and law patents, and those of the king's printers. The complaints expressed are typical ones against monopolies, restricted supply, and excessive prices. The pamphlet, however, stopped short of attacking the English Stock, a corporate rather than a private monopoly. "Here I could open another window, but I see many poore stand within to keep it shut, and I will not adde misery to their affliction."[52] The pamphlet, aimed at reform within the Stationers' Company, made three suggestions for corrective measures to be made by Parliament: (1) to enforce the statute of 25 Henry VIII, c. 15, concerning prices of books; (2) to change the composition of the oligarchic court of assistants; (3) to allow the printing of copies entered to the company which the company itself did not publish.

This document serves as a prelude to the controversy of 1643–45, concerning which two documents are of special interest. These are two petitions to Parliament, one in January 1643,[53] and one in April 1643.[54]

The first of these documents reflects the nature and reason of the controversy within the company, indicated in the *Scintilla* pamphlet. The Committee for Printing had directed a new impression of the Bible, and eleven men had sought to acquire the monopoly for the printing. These men were accused of being patentees and monopolizers of the most valuable books to the "great detriment of the Kingdome,

49. See JACKSON, *Introduction*, RECORDS OF THE COURT OF THE STATIONERS' COMPANY, 1602–1640. (1957).

50. BLAGDEN, THE STATIONERS' COMPANY 131 (1960).

51. IV ARBER 35.

52. IV ARBER 38.

53. I ARBER 583.

54. I ARBER 584.

and to the ruine and destruction of this poore Company."[55] The prayer
of the petition was that the House of Commons order the printing of
the Bible for the benefit of the whole company.

The second petition is of particular interest because it reveals the
extent of the stationers' desire for censorship and press control, upon
which they insisted their prosperity depended. After stating the importance of printing for the advancement of learning, the petition
continued, "Neverthelesse it is not meere Printing, but well ordered
Printing that merits so much favour and respect, since in things
precious and excellent, the abuse (if not prevented) is commonly as
dangerous, as the use is advantagious."[56]

The first end of order in the press, *i.e.*, censorship, was conceded to
be "the advancement of wholesome knowledge," which was merely
public; but the second end, providing for the prosperity of printing
and printers, was not merely private, because this was necessary to
the accomplishment of the first. As to the first and public aim of regulation in printing, the advancement of knowledge, "The main care is
to appoint severe Examiners for the licensing of things profitable, and
suppressing of things harmfull: and the next Care is, That the endeavors of thos Examiners may not be frustrated. . . . The Stationers
therefore humbly desire to represent three things to the Parliament:
(1) That the Life of all Law consists in prosecution. (2) That in matters
of the Presse, no man can so effectually prosecute, as Stationers themselves. (3) That if Stationers at this present do not so zealously prosecute as is desired, it is to be understood, That it is partly for want of
full authority, and partly for want of true encouragement."[57]

To accomplish the second aim, the prosperity of the trade, the
company did not desire to be solely "entrusted with the Government
of the Presse," but only the power to prosecute delinquents, to be
given to "some choice Committee, nominated by the Company, and
further approved and allowed by the Parliament." What they wanted
was the power to regulate the number of presses, which, according to
the petition, had increased to unmanageable proportions within the
past four years. During that time, the petition stated, " . . . the affairs

55. I ARBER 583.
56. I ARBER 584.
57. I ARBER 585.

of the Presse have grown very scandalous and enormious, and all redresse is almost impossible, if power be not given by some binding order to reduce Presses and Apprentices to the proportion of those times which did precede these last four years. This is so farre from an Innovation, that tis the removall of a dangerous Innovation, and without this removall, the Company of Stationers being like a feeld overpestred with too much stock, must needs grow indigent, and indigence must needs make it run into trespasses, and break out into divers unlawful shifts; as Cattle use to do, when their pasture begins wholly to fail."[58] The company sought only "a modest limited power" to reduce presses and apprentices to a convenient number in order to make the reformation of the press a feasible thing.

The third point made in the petition was the necessity of copyright. The propriety of copies had been almost taken away, because "if one Stationer preferre any Complaint against another, the Complainant shall be sure to have his Copy re-Printed out of spite, and so the ruine of himself and family, is made the reward of his zeal and forwardnesse." The petition is ambiguous, and conveniently so, at this point, because it does not make clear whether the complaint is against infringers of the stationer's copyright or infringers against the patents. It is more than probable that the latter was in the mind of the draftsman, because the following sentences are devoted to justifying "propriety of Copies" against the charge of monopoly, a charge which seems never to have been made against the stationer's copyright; but the arguments in favor of copyright cover both types. Briefly, the arguments were these: (1) Books, "except *the sacred Bible*" were not a staple commodity such as food and clothing, but were items of luxury, and therefore "propriety in Books maintained amongst Stationers," was not detrimental to the public. (2) Copyright among stationers makes printing flourish, and books plentiful and cheap, whereas "Community brings in confusion, and many other disorders both to the damage of the State and the Company of Stationers also," because: (a) it results in several men printing the same book; (b) the fear of confusion will prevent many men from printing at all, to the great obstruction of learning; (c) confusion would destroy commerce

58. I ARBER 586.

among the stationers, who exchanged stocks of books with each other;
(d) community of copies would discourage authors;[59] and (e) in many
cases community of copies would cause injustice, for many families,
including orphans and widows, depended upon copies for their livelihood, "and there is no reason apparent why the production of the
Brain should not be as assignable, and their interest and possession
(being of more rare, sublime, and publike use, demeriting the highest
encouragement) held as tender in Law, as the right of any Goods or
Chattels whatsoever."[60]

The sophistry of the arguments is apparent, and it is obvious that
the company was primarily interested in the protection of its patents,[61]
and in the power to control printing. The petition concluded with the
prayer, "*That some speedy course may be taken for such a perfect
regulation of the Presse, as may procure the publike good of the State,
by the private prosperity of the Stationers' Company.*"[62]

The effect on Parliament of the arguments in the stationers' petition
is conjectural, but the Ordinance of 1643[63] gave the Company what it
had requested. One of the reasons given in the preamble for the need
of the act was that delinquents printed copies belonging to the company and other stationers. The act prohibited publication of the orders
of either House of Parliament except by order of the House, and required that books be both licensed and entered on the Stationers'
Register before printing. It protected the copies of the Company and
of individual stationers by forbidding the printing of such copies
without consent, in the first instance of the master, wardens and assistants of the company, and in the second, of the owners. The im-

---

59. "Many mens studies carry no other profit or recompence with them, but
the benefit [*copyright*] of their Copies; and if this be taken away, many Pieces
of great worth and excellence will be strangled in the womb, or never conceived
at all for the future." I ARBER 587.

60. I ARBER 587–588.

61. "And as this may be truely said in defence of Propriety, as it concerns
private men in their Interests, so much more may be said for Propriety of such
Copies as the whole Company have a Right in, the good of so many hundreds
being far more considerable then the good of any particular (which cannot be
reputed a Monopoly, though of common and universall use, become common to
the entire Profession)." I ARBER 588.

62. I ARBER 588.

63. I FIRTH & RAIT, 184–187.

portation of books printed in England was also forbidden. The traditional powers of search for unlicensed presses were given to the master and wardens of the company, and the Gentlemen Usher of the House of Lords, the Sergeant of Commons and their deputies, together with persons formerly appointed by the Committee of the House of Commons for Examinations; but the matter of unlicensed presses was apparently to be left largely to the company, as the act contained no provision for the licensing of presses, or for a limitation on the number of presses. For purposes of licensing, books were divided into nine categories: divinity; law books; physic and surgery; civil and common-law books; books of heraldry, declarations, ordinances, and other things; small pamphlets, portraits, and pictures; titles of honor and arms; books of philosophy, and the like; and books of mathematics, almanacs, and prognostication. A list of persons to license the various works was annexed, with twelve persons designated to license books of divinity.

The Ordinance of 1643 thus returned to the traditional methods of press control, with a subtle change indicating the changing basis of censorship. The persons officially named as licensers in the various decrees and proclamations until the Star Chamber Decree of 1637 had been the sovereign, the Privy Council, or ecclesiastical authorities, principally the Archbishop of Canterbury and the Bishop of London. One exception to this was the exception made for law books to be licensed by the two chief justices and chief baron, or two of them, in the Star Chamber Decree of 1586. In the Ordinance of 1643, the ecclesiastics, twelve Presbyterian ministers, were to license books of divinity only. Lawyers, doctors, members of Parliament, and one schoolmaster were the principal licensers. The clerk of the Stationers' Company was to license small pamphlets, portraits, pictures "and the like." This indicates that the primary reason for the Ordinance of 1643 was regulation of the book trade, an indication borne out by the provisions of the act itself and by later developments. In this respect, the Ordinance of 1643 was more similar to the Star Chamber Decree of 1586 than that of 1637. The Ordinance of 1647, however, begins a return to the theory of censorship manifested in the Decree of 1637.

The Ordinance of 1647 was entitled "An Ordinance against unlicensed or scandalous Pamphlets, and for the better Regulating of

Printing,"[64] and appears to have been prompted by the development of news sheets, or corantos, as they were called, which had become widespread at this time.[65] This explains why it was the first act of censorship directed as much to authors as to printers; it provided, "That what person soever shall Make, Write, Print, Publish. Sell or Utter . . . any Book, Pamphlet, Treatise, Ballad, Libel, Sheet or Sheets of News whatsoever (except the same be Licensed . . . with the name of the Author, Printer and Licenser thereunto prefixed) shall for every such Offence, suffer, pay and incur the Punishment, Fine and Penalty hereafter mentioned. . . . "[66]

The penalties imposed were: For the author, a fine of forty shillings; the printer, twenty shillings; the bookseller or stationers, ten shillings; or, in each case, imprisonment for a number of days equal to the number of shillings of the fine. Hawkers, pedlars, and ballad singers were to forfeit all their wares and be whipped as common rogues; but the penalties were not so light as these enumerations would indicate, because the Ordinance concluded with a proviso, "That the Penalties in this Ordinance expressed, shall not extend to acquit any person or persons that shall Make, Write, Print, Publish, Sell or Utter . . . any Book, Pamphlet, Treatise, Ballad, Libel, Sheet or Sheets of News that shall contain any Seditious, Treasonable or Blasphemous matter, but the Offenders in that kinde shall be liable to such farther penalties as by the Laws of this Land are provided, or by Authority of Parliament shall be adjudged according to the penalty of such Offenses."[67]

The Ordinance of 1649, "An Act against Unlicensed and Scandalous Books and Pamphlets, and for better regulating of Printing,"[68] was modeled closely on the Star Chamber Decree of 1637, although it was not nearly so detailed. The impetus for the act was "the mischiefs arising from weekly pamphlets." The former laws against spreaders of false news were to be put into execution, and the fines for unlawful

64. I FIRTH & RAIT 1021–1023.
65. See FRANK, THE BEGINNINGS OF THE ENGLISH NEWSPAPER, 1620–1660 (1961), particularly Chs. VII and VIII.
66. I FIRTH & RAIT 1022.
67. I FIRTH & RAIT 1023.
68. II FIRTH & RAIT 245–254.

books, papers, or pictures were increased to ten pounds for the author, five pounds for the printer, two pounds for the bookseller, and one pound for the buyer, if he concealed the book he bought. All books and pamphlets were to be licensed, and the Clerk of Parliament was to license news books. Treasonable matter was liable to further punishment, and the master and wardens were given the power to search for unallowed presses and books. No seditious books were to be sent by post, and printing was limited to London and the two universities, except for a press at York and Finsbury for Bibles and psalms. Printers were to enter a bond of 300 pounds. No house or room was to be let to a printer without notice to the master and wardens, and no implements of printing made, press imported, or type cast without notice to the same. The importation of books was limited to London, where they were to be viewed by the master and wardens, and no Bibles or psalms were to be imported at all.

Copyright was fully protected: "And be it further Enacted, That no person or persons whatsoever in this Commonwealth, shall hereafter print or reprint any Book, Books, or part of any Book or Books, Legally granted to the said Company of Stationers, for their relief or maintenance of their poor, without the license and consent of the Master, Wardens and Assistants of the said Company; nor any Book or Books, or part of Book or Books, now entred in the Register Book of the said Company, or which hereafter shall be duly entred in the said Register Book, for any particular member of the said Company, without the like consent of the owner or owners thereof; nor counterfeit the Name, Mark or Title of any Book or Books, belonging to the Company or particular members; nor shall any person or persons binde, stitch, or put to sale any Book or Books, upon pain of forfeiture of the same, and of Six shillings and eight pence for every Book printed or stitched, bound or put to sale contrary hereunto."[69]

For some reason, probably the rising resentment against censorship,[70] the act required offenders to be prosecuted within six months of their offense, and the act was limited by its terms to two years, to

---

69. II Firth & Rait 251.

70. The passage of the act had been preceded by a petition of the Levellers for the abolition of the licensing system, the authors of which had evidently been influenced by *Areopagitica*. See Clyde, *op. cit.*, 164–165.

expire on September 29, 1651. A similar limitation was contained in the Licensing Act, making periodic renewal necessary.

The final act of Parliament regulating printing prior to the Restoration was the Act of 1653,[71] the purpose of which was to revive the Ordinance of 1649. The only addition of significance was that printing was placed under the control of the Council of State, with directions to the officers of the Stationers' Company to observe the orders of the Council concerning printing, thereby curtailing the power of the company considerably. The Orders of the Lord Protector on August 28, 1655,[72] was the last official document to be promulgated for the regulation of printing before 1662. The document consists of orders to John Barkstead, John Dethick, and George Foxcroft to control unlawful printing and to search out violations of the Ordinances of 1647 and 1643. It is an eloquent testimony to the failure of the Puritan attempts at press control.

The Licensing Act of 1662

When Charles II returned to the throne in May 1660, the Stationers' Company sought a return to the position of power which the abolition of the Star Chamber, the Civil War, and the rule of Cromwell had destroyed. It was not, however, until two years later, in June 1662, that "An act for preventing Abuses in Printing Seditious, Treasonable and Unlicensed Books and Pamphlets, and for Regulating of Printing and Printing Presses,"[73] called the Licensing Act because of the requirement that the license be printed verbatim at the beginning of each book, went into effect. Prior government regulation of the press had been predicated on the need for safeguarding the official religion. This, of course, had political implications, but the Licensing Act of 1662 resulted from a felt need for safeguarding the government, much the same as the Ordinances of 1647 and 1649. The prime motive for enacting the act was political, with religious implications only incidental.[74] A newly restored monarch was in no mood to risk criticism,

---

71. II FIRTH & RAIT 696–699.
72. Reprinted in CLYDE, op. cit., Appendix E, 323–327.
73. 13 & 14 Car. II, c. 33.
74. See Walker, *The Censorship of the Press During the Reign of Charles II*, 35 HISTORY, n.s., 219 (1950).

and the government, without waiting for parliamentary authority, appointed Sir John Birkenhead Surveyor of the Press and issued an order in council dated June 7, 1660, instructing the Stationers' Company to seize copies of certain anti-monarchial tracts.[75]

The company, however, did not return to its former position of power in the scheme of press regulation. This task was taken over by the Surveyor of the Press. The successor to Birkenhead in this post was the notorious Sir Roger L'Estrange, who held the position from 1663 to 1688.[76] Censorship was probably never more stringent than under L'Estrange. He ". . . rigorously performed the . . . duties of his office. In October 1663, soon after assuming his post, he made midnight raids on many printing offices. . . . He regularly encouraged informers by money bribes, which he paid at his office, the Gun, in Ivy Lane. In dealing with such manuscripts as came under his supervision, he carefully excised expressions of opinion directly or indirectly obnoxious to the government or to the established church, and often modified attacks on Roman catholicism."[77]

Although L'Estrange was supposed to operate in conjunction with the Stationers' Company, the partnership was not a happy one from either viewpoint. The underlying conflict between the company's interest in the protection of property and the government's interest in censorship at last came into the open. "The Assistants hated the association with the Surveyor of the Press. . . . Even if they had worked amicably together, the control of the press was bound to be incomplete; one reason was that the Court, as it pointed out to L'Estrange in 1671, regarded its powers as inadequate, and another that the problem of printing-house supervision had grown in size and complexity since the time of Laud; a third reason was the difficulty—and delay—in getting a verdict in the courts; but the most important reason of all was that the main interest of the Court was the guarding of English Stock rights."[78]

75. *Id.* at 222–223.
76. His successors, Fraser and Bohun, held office for very short periods, "both being removed for licensing books which gave cause for public offence. . . . In this way the censorship was discredited, and the Licensing Act, together with the surveyor, came to an end in 1695." Ogg, England in the Reigns of James II and William III 511 (1955).
77. 33 Dictionary of National Biography 118, 122.
78. Blagden, The Stationers' Company 172–173 (1960).

The conflict was compounded by the interest of the patentees who now sought restitution of their former grants, and the division within the company between the booksellers and the printers. The printers were restive under the booksellers' power and sought incorporation as a separate company, which they failed to achieve.[79]

The Licensing Act was not passed until 1662, but Parliament had been aware of the press problem from the beginning of the Restoration. On August 24, 1660, complaint was made that Henry Hills and John Field had printed acts "now depending before the Parliament" without warrant; this matter was referred to a committee "to consider and advise what is fit to be done for regulating of Printing; and to peruse the several Acts and Ordinances heretofore made for that End; and to consider what is defective; and to prepare a Bill for remedying the Inconveniences of the Press for the future; inserting a Clause therein, to authorize the breaking open of Doors of any Printer, for the better Discovery of Abuses of this Nature; and to report the same to the House."[80]

Nothing came of this order, and on July 3, 1661, three persons were ordered to prepare and bring in a "Bill, for the Regulation of Printing,"[81] which was again not presented. Finally, on July 25, 1661, it was, "Ordered, That M. Sollicitor-General do bring in a Bill to impower his Majesty to regulate the Press, till it be otherwise provided for,"[82] which was presented the following day.[83]

The bill, entitled, "An Act for regulating unlicensed and disorderly Printing,"[84] was finally dropped, because the House of Lords wanted

79. *Id.* at 150–153. "Of the three parties, patentees, printers and booksellers, the first were concerned with the restoration of their interests and a protective clause in the new Act. They got this, but individuals like Norton, Atkyns, and Seymour had to fight hard in the Law Courts for their individual patents. To decide between the more general rights of the Stationers' Company and the particular copies of the Patentees was the delicate work of the Courts. The printers were left as they had been in a miserable way still sighing for freedom. They had been the first to petition against the monopolists in 1641. Their best fortune was to have no restraint on the Press at all. Hence—so the stationers said—their opposition to the new Act of 1662." KITCHIN, SIR ROGER L'ESTRANGE 103 (1913).

80. VIII H. C. JOUR. 134.

81. *Id.* at 288. The three persons were "Sir *John Maynard*, his Majesty's Serjeant at Lew, Serjeant *Keeling*, and Sir *Solomon Swale.*"

82. *Id.* at 312.

83. *Id.* at 313.

84. *Id.* at 314.

the houses of peers to be excepted from the search provisions, to which the House of Commons refused to agree. The reasons given by the House of Commons were: "1. The Bill is to prevent a general Mischief, which will not be prevented by this Exception, it being very possible, that this may be attempted chiefly in great Houses by Servants, without the Privity of their Lords, especially in Absence. 2. The Matter of some Books may be . . . Treason and Sedition, for which there neither is, nor ought to be, any Sanctuary. 3. The Matter of some Books may be tending to the Overthrow of the Religion established; which may come abroad freely, if there be a Privileged Place. 4. All Houses, as well of Commons as Peers, are equally the Castles and Proprieties of the Owners: And therefore if all the Gentry of *England* submit their Houses for publick Safety, it would look as if were prodigal of the Liberty of the Gentry, if we admit this Exception. 5. The very Exeception shews Men the Way to attempt the Servants of Peers."[85]

There the matter remained for a year, until May 2, 1662, when the House of Commons received and read for the first time an engrossed bill "sent from the Lords, to prevent the frequent Abuses in printing seditious, treasonable and unlicensed Books and Pamphlets; and for regulating Printing and Printing-Presses."[86]

The Licensing Act of 1662 is simply the Star Chamber Decree of 1637 modified in a few minor respects, with one major change, a clause that the act was to remain in force for only two years, added by the House of Commons.[87] Twenty-four clauses of the 1637 Decree were in the Licensing Act. Omitted were clauses which dealt with type-founders who were covered by the provisions on printers; those requiring the giving of bonds for good behavior, the finding of work for journeymen, and prohibiting interference with the printers at Oxford and Cambridge, although the Act made it clear that the privileges of these universities were not affected.[88] The attempts to license reprints and to make authors produce two copies of a manuscript were rejected by Commons[89] and the control of imports was lightened.[90]

85. VIII H. C. JOUR. 315.
86. VIII H. C. JOUR. 417.
87. *Id.* at 435.
88. Clause XVIII.
89. VIII H. C. JOUR. 435.
90. Clauses V–IX.

Other changes made by the Licensing Act included a clause allowing London booksellers who had served seven years to import books not formerly prohibited and books which had been printed ten years before importation,[91] and a clause protecting stallholders in Westminister who were in business on November 20, 1661.[92] The press at York was reserved, and it was not to print the Bible or English Stock books.[93] Three copies of each book were to be given to the king's library and the library at Cambridge, as well as the Bodleian Library at Oxford, which had been given this right in the 1637 Decree.[94] The powers of search were restricted to houses of men in the trade, with special warrant from the king required for any other searches.[95] Finally, the act was not to apply to royal grants,[96] or to John Streater,[97] who was then negotiating with the Atkins family for the working of the law patent.[98]

Efforts to Secure New Legislation

Even before the expiration of the Licensing Act, the company was taking measures to secure more rigorous control, but Parliament simply renewed the old act from session to session until the dissolution of the Cavalier Parliament.[99] The act was revived again for seven years in 1685[100] under the new king, James II, and was renewed for the last

91. Clause XX.
92. Clause XXI.
93. Clause XXIV.
94. Clause XVII. The addition of the other two libraries was made by 17 Car. II, c. 4. The origin of this practice is apparently an agreement made in 1610 between the Stationers' Company and Oxford University. An entry of March 14, 1610, in Court Book C reads: "Received from Oxon by the delyuery of mr Dor. Kinge Deane of Christ church & vicechauncellor of Oxon the Counterpte, vnder the vniu'sities seale, of one Indenture before sealed at mr Leaks house in Paules churcheyeard, vnder the comon seale, [15to ffebr' vlt'] for one booke of eu'ry newe Copy to be gyuen to the publique library at Oxon, And they appoynt Sr. Thomas Bodley to receiue them /." COURT BOOK C, 48–49.
95. Clause XIX. The bill from the House of Lords had provided this requirement for a search of the houses of peers. Commons added "or of any other Person or Persons, not being free of, nor using any of, the Trades in the Act before mentioned." VIII H. C. JOUR. 435. Thus, the point on which the bill of 1661 failed was resolved.
96. Clause XXII.
97. Clause XXIII.
98. BLAGDEN, THE STATIONERS' COMPANY, 154 (1960).
99. 16 Car. II, c. 8; 17 Car. II, c. 4.
100. 1 Jac. II, c. 17, sec. 15.

time in 1692.[101] When, in February 1694, the House of Commons omitted the Licensing Act from a bill for continuing certain acts,[102] the House of Lords restored it by amendment,[103] which Commons rejected.

On the same day it refused to renew the Licensing Act, the House of Commons appointed a committee to prepare and bring in a bill for better "Regulating of Printing, and Printing-Presses."[104] Shortly thereafter, on March 30, Commons received a petition from the Stationers' Company urging passage of the bill because "if their Property should not be provided for by the said Bill, not only the Petitioners, but many Widows, and others, whose whole Livelihood depends upon the Petitioners Property, will be utterly ruined."[105] The petition was without effect, because nothing came of the bill, and on April 17, the House of Commons, in stating its reasons for opposing the renewal of the Licensing Act,[106] made clear what it thought of "Petitioners' Property."

There were eighteen reasons stated. The Licensing Act, it was said, "in no-wise answered the End for which it was made;" there were no penalties for printing seditious and treasonable books, whereas "there are great and grievous Penalties imposed by that Act for Matters wherein neither Church nor State" is concerned. The act gave a property in books to patentees, whether or not the crown had any right to grant the patents, and, since books were required to be entered in the register of the Stationers' Company, the stationers "are impowered to hinder the printing all innocent and useful Books; and have an Opportunity to enter a Title to themselves, and their Friends, for what belongs to, and is the Labour and Right of, others."

The act limited the importation of books to the Port of London, except with special license, and gave the Stationers' Company and the Archbishop of Canterbury and Bishop of London the power to prevent the importation of any books for refusing to act, and there were other needless restraints on the importation of books.

The act confirmed all "Patents of Books granted and to be granted," whereby the classics, "together with a great number of the best Books, and of most general Use" were monopolized by the Stationers' Com-

101. 4 & 5 William & Mary, c. 24, sec. XIV.
102. XI H. C. Jour. 228.
103. 1 House of Lords Manuscripts, 1693–95, (n.s.), 540.
104. XI H. C. Jour. 228.
105. XI H. C. Jour. 288.
106. XI H. C. Jour. 305–306.

pany; and the act "prohibits the importing any such Books from beyond Sea; whereby the Scholars in this Kingdom are forced not only
to buy them at the extravagent Price they demand, but must be content with their ill and incorrect Editions."

The act did not provide a fee of the licenser for licensing, "by colour
whereof great Oppression may be, and has been practised." The act
restrained printers and founders of type from exercising their trade,
and compelled master printers to hire journeymen they did not need,
and it restrained all men not licensed by the Bishop, except stationers,
from selling innocent books. It prohibited "any one not only to print
Books whereof another has entered a Claim of Property" in the register
of the stationers, but also "to bind, stitch, or put them to Sale," and it
forbade any smiths to make any iron work for any printing press without notice to the stationers, under penalty of five pounds.

The act prohibited the printing and importing of all offensive books,
without defining offensive, and sanctioned searches of the houses of all
men with "a warrant under the Sign Manual, or under the Hand of one
of the Secretaries of State" upon suspicion that unlicensed books were
there, and searches of the houses of stationers on warrant from the
master or a warden of the company.

The penalties of the act were excessive; and "Lastly, There is a Proviso in that Act for *John Streater*, That he may print what he pleases,
as if the Act had never been made; when the Commons see no Cause
to distinguish him from the rest of the Subjects of *England*."[107] All of
these objections were to be taken care of in the Statute of Anne.

The expiration of the Licensing Act did not, of course, end the question of press control; but it had a decisive effect in changing the problem from one of censorship to one of property. On December 7, 1697,
the House of Commons gave leave to bring in a "Bill for Regulating
of Printing and Printing-presses,"[108] which was received on February
12, 1697 (o.s.),[109] and rejected on February 16, 1697 (o.s.).[110] There
matters remained for a year, until the House of Lords sent to Commons
a bill entitled, "An Act for the better Regulating of Printers, and

107. XI H. C. JOUR. 305–306.
108. XII H. C. JOUR. 3.
109. *Id.* at 99.
110. *Id.* at 104.

Printing-Presses," on January 31, 1698 (o.s.).[111] The bill, as it was originally drafted,[112] was a censorship act without licensing provisions, and it said nothing about copy or the property in books. Briefly, it provided for the registration of the owners of printing presses with the Court of Aldermen and the Stationers' Company and entrance of the title of works with the same, and required the name and place of habitation of the publisher and owner of the press on the title page of each printed work.

This bill censored works in an indirect way, providing that if any person printed or published anything "treasonable, seditious, atheistical, or heretical," and refused to disclose the author thereof, then the master or owner of the press would be liable to the same punishment as would have been inflicted on the author of the work. There were also provisions allowing search, prohibitions against secret presses, and the importation of unlawful books; no English book was to be printed beyond the sea or imported because "printing is, and for many years hath been, an art and manufacture of this Kingdom;" and provisions were made for insuring that journeymen printers had lawful work.

Many of these provisions were changed by amendments, which had primarily to do with omitting the provisions of censorship, but the bill is particularly interesting because, as a modified version of the Star Chamber Decree of 1637 and the Licensing Act, with no mention of copy, it illustrates the irrelevancy of the concept of copyright to censorship, and as amended, it marks the beginning of the shift of emphasis from censorship to property. But the bill was rejected by the House of Commons on February 1, 1698 (o.s.).[113]

The last attempt of the stationers to renew their monopoly through censorship laws was made in 1703, under the guise of a bill to prevent "Licentiousness of the Press," for which leave was granted on December 15, 1703.[114] The bill was received and read the first time on January 13, 1703 (o.s.),[115] and was apparently finally disposed of on January 18, 1703 (o.s.), when it was committed to a committee of the whole House.[116]

111. XII H. C. Jour. 466.
112. III House of Lords Manuscripts, 1697–1699 (n.s.), 271–276.
113. XII H. C. Jour. 468–469.
114. XIV H. C. Jour. 249.
115. XIV H. C. Jour. 278.
116. Id. at 287.

When next the stationers sought Parliamentary relief, on February 26, 1706 (o.s.),[117] they did so in the interest of "securing Property" in books. The petition presented on this occasion, by thirteen persons on behalf of themselves "and other Booksellers, and Printers," made no mention of religion or security of the state, but spoke of "many learned Men . . . who used to dispose of their copies" for valuable consideration "to be printed by the Purchasers, or have reserved some Part, for the Benefit of themselves, and Families," and the invasion of the property of purchasers "to the great Discouragement of Persons from writing Matters, that might be of great Use to the Publick."

The basic argument of the stationers for legislative support for their copies had not changed, but the tactics had, for the petition asked for leave "to bring in a Bill, for the securing Property in such Books, as have been, or shall be, purchased from, or reserved to, the Authors thereof."[118] Permission was granted, and on February 28, 1706 (o.s.), "Mr. *Topham* (according to Order) presented to the House a Bill, for the better securing the Rights of Copies of printed Books."[119] The bill made two appearances in Commons[120] before the final one on March 18, 1706 (o.s.), a report from the committee,[121] after which there is no further record of it.

On December 12, 1709, the bill that was to become the first copyright statute got its start with a petition similar to the one made in 1706.[122] The bill was received,[123] read,[124] engrossed,[125] passed, and sent to the House of Lords within the space of three months, under the title, "An Act for the Encouragement of Learning, by vesting the Copies of printed Books in the Authors, or Purchasers, of such Copies, during the Times therein mentioned."[126]

117. XV H. C. JOUR. 313.
118. *Ibid.*
119. XV H. C. JOUR. 316.
120. March 4, 1706 (o.s.), for the second reading, XV H. C. JOUR. 321; March 5, 1706 (o.s.), for an order to include a clause that "one Book may be delivered to the Library of *Syon* College, in the City of London." XV H. C. JOUR. 322.
121. XV H. C. JOUR. 346.
122. XVI H. C. JOUR. 240.
123. *Id.* at 260.
124. *Id.* at 300.
125. *Id.* at 339.
126. 8 Anne, c. 19.

7

The Statute of Anne

AUTHORSHIP CAME of age in eighteenth-century England as a respectable profession, and it would be fitting to think that the first English copyright statute was enacted in 1709 (o.s.) to benefit such authors as Pope, Swift, Addison, Steele, and Richardson. Fitting, perhaps, but hardly accurate.

The facts are less romantic. The Statute of Anne[1] was neither the first copyright act in England, nor was it intended primarily to benefit authors. It was a trade-regulation statute enacted to bring order to the chaos created in the book trade by the final lapse in 1694 of its predecessor, the Licensing Act of 1662, and to prevent a continuation of the booksellers' monopoly.

Earlier English copyright acts, the Star Chamber Decrees of 1586 and 1637, the Ordinances of 1643 and 1647, and the Licensing Act of 1662, were fundamentally censorship laws, which may explain why their relevance to the so-called first copyright act was ignored. Even so, the Statute of Anne descends directly from this earlier legislation, and just as these earlier laws functioned essentially in censorship, so the Statute of Anne was intended to function principally in regulating the book trade.

As finally enacted, the Statute of Anne provided for two copyrights —the statutory copyright for all books subsequently published, and the stationer's copyright already existing in published works, which was extended for twenty-one years—and allowed a third, the printing patent, to retain its status quo.

1. 8 Anne, c. 19.

The major question to arise in connection with the statute was the nature of the copyright for which it provided.

The statutory copyright provided in the Statute of Anne was a publisher's copyright; but the act was construed to have provided an author's copyright. The distinction between the two concepts—the one intended and the one which resulted—was fundamental. This development had little to do with the Statute of Anne itself; but because the act provided for copyright, and the statutory copyright it provided later came to be an author's copyright, the inevitable conclusion was that the statutory copyright was originally designed to be an author's copyright.

Had the concept of copyright as an author's right proved satisfactory, the Statute of Anne would be of little more than antiquarian interest today. The author's copyright, however, has not proved satisfactory, and it may be useful to see that it was not created by the Statute of Anne.

Although the Statute of Anne was enacted in 1709, it was 1774 before it finally reached the House of Lords for a definitive construction. Events and circumstances of the sixty-five years since its enactment had obscured both the background of the legislation and its antecedents. Fundamental changes had occurred between the enactment of the statute and its construction by the Courts. By 1774, the statute, in effect, had come to have an existence independent of its origins. Consequently, the statutory copyright that finally resulted bore little resemblance to the concept of copyright embodied in the statute.

The problem facing Parliament in enacting the Statute of Anne was a difficult one. Three monopolies existed in the book trade: that of the Stationers' Company itself, which purported to control the book trade generally; that of the booksellers within the company, based on their stationers' copyrights of the works of old authors; and the printing patent, by this time of little importance.

The Statute of Anne's statutory copyright was aimed at preventing future monopolies and the monopoly of the company itself; the twenty-one-year copyrights were directed at the existing monopoly of the booksellers. These copyrights would cease at the end of their term, putting the copyrighted works into the public domain. There were three other provisions, of eleven in the statute, directed to the problem of monopoly generally. Section III provided an alternative means of securing copyright by advertisement in "the Gazette," should the clerk of the Stationers' Company refuse to register a copyright as required by the statute. Section IV provided an intricate, and probably unworkable, procedure designed to prevent prices "too high and unreasonable." And Section VII provided that the act should not be construed to extend to prohibit "the Importation, Vending or Selling of any Books in *Greek, Latin,* or any other foreign Language printed beyond the Seas."

The Statute of Anne is usually thought of as having vested the copyright of works in their authors; and, superficially, the language of the statute conveys the idea that the act was especially to benefit authors. It did enable authors for the first time to acquire the copyright of their works, and to this extent, it was a benefit to them.

The radical change in the statute, however, was not that it gave authors the right to acquire a copyright—a prerogative until then limited to members of the Stationers' Company—but that it gave that right to all persons.

Except in Section XI, the term "author" in the statute was always used alternatively with the terms "purchaser of copy," "proprietor of copy," "bookseller," or "assignee." Thus, the title of the act was: "An Act for the Encouragement of Learning, by vesting the Copies of printed Books in the *Authors or Purchasers*[2] of such Copies, during the Times herein mentioned."

The preamble recites the conditions whereby booksellers and other persons have published works "without the Consent of the *Authors or Proprietors* of such Books and Writings. . . ."

Section I provides that after April 10, 1710, "the *Author* of any Book or Books already printed, who hath not transferred to any other the Copy or Copies of such Book . . . or the *Bookseller or Booksellers, Printer or Printers, or other Person or Persons*, who hath or have purchased or acquired the Copy or Copies of any Book or Books" shall have the right to the printing of the books for twenty-one years.

The act further provides that "the *Author* of any Book or Books . . . and his *Assignee or Assigns*, shall have the sole Liberty of printing and reprinting such Book and Books for the Term of fourteen Years. . . ."

2. 12 Geo. II, c. 36.

Section III provides that if the clerk of the company refused to enter the works or give a certificate therefor, "being thereunto required by the *Author* or *Proprietor* of such Copy . . ." then copyright could be secured by advertisement in the *Gazette*.

Section XI reads: "Provided always, That after the Expiration of the said Term of fourteen Years, the sole Right of printing or disposing of Copies shall return to the *Authors* thereof, if they are then living, for another Term of fourteen Years."

The author is nowhere else mentioned in the statute, and the only benefit the statute conferred on authors not available to a person who purchased the copy was the right to a renewal of the copyright. The statute, except for Section XI, thus gave the author no greater rights than any other person who was entitled to copyright by reason of the consent of the author. The only difference between an author's securing a copyright and another's securing a copyright was that the author did not have to purchase the right.

The most significant point about the statutory copyright is that it was almost certainly a codification of the stationer's copyright. The similarity of the two is too great to be coincidental. With the exception of the printing patent, the stationer's copyright was probably the only copyright familiar to Parliament. The statutory copyright showed two major changes: it was limited to a term of fourteen years, and it was made available to all persons, not just to members of the Stationers' Company. Other than that, the chief difference between the two was that the stationer's copyright was granted by the wardens of the Stationers' Company.

The method of acquiring the statutory copyright was similar to that for acquiring the stationer's copyright—registration of the title of a work prior to publication in the register books of the Stationers' Company. Moreover, the protection secured by the statute was the same protection given by the stationer's copyright—protection from the piracy of printed works. And the provisions of Section II indicate that the statutory copyright was designed, just as the stationer's copyright was, to maintain order in the book trade, as much as anything else. The right to protection given by the copyright did not arise from ownership of copy, nor did it arise from any natural rights of the author.

Section II provided: "And whereas many Persons may through Ignorance offend against this Act, unless some Provision be made, whereby the Property in every such Book, as is intended by this Act to be secured to the Proprietor or Proprietors thereof, may be ascertained, as likewise the consent of such Proprietor or Proprietors for the printing and reprinting of such Book or Books may from time to time be known . . . "the act should not be construed to subject anyone to its penalties for printing and reprinting, unless the title to the copy of books thereafter published were entered in the register books of the Stationers' Company. Thus, unless the terms of the statute were complied with, the act gave no protection. The modifications of the statutory copyright are explained as efforts to destroy the monopoly in the book trade. Making the copyright available to all was a move directed to the monopoly of the company itself; limiting the term of copyright was directed at preventing future monopolies such as the existing one of the booksellers based on old copyrights.

If it is correct that the statutory copyright was a codification of the stationer's copyright, it follows that the statutory copyright was not intended to be comprehensive of an author's interest in his works. The statutory copyright, like the stationer's copyright, was a right to which a book was subject and not the whole property interest in the book.

Emphasis on the author in the Statute of Anne implying that the statutory copyright was an author's copyright was more a matter of form than of substance. The monopolies at which the statute was aimed were too long established to be attacked without some basis for change. The most logical and natural basis for the changes was the author. Although the author had never held copyright, his interest was always promoted by the stationers as a means to their end. Their arguments had been, essentially, that without order in the trade provided by copyright, publishers would not publish books, and therefore would not pay authors for their manuscripts. The draftsmen of the Statute of Anne put these arguments to use, and the author was used primarily as a weapon against monopoly.

The second copyright in the Statute of Anne was the twenty-one-year copyright granted to holders of the stationer's copyrights in old works. The act changed the booksellers' perpetual copyrights, the basis of their monopoly, into copyrights of twenty-one years.

This extension of existing copyrights for twenty-one years is somewhat surprising, in view of the resentment against the monopoly; but it was undoubtedly the result of compromise. The booksellers had large sums of money invested in the old copyrights, and limited continuation of the copyrights would prevent the destruction of their capital investments without warning and in the end achieve the desired result. A fourteen-year copyright—or, at most, one valid for twenty-eight years—was a much less potent instrument of monopoly than one which existed in perpetuity.

When the old copyrights did expire, however, the booksellers began a relentless campaign to preserve their monopoly. The result was the famous battle of the booksellers for perpetual copyright—a battle resulting in the establishment of copyright as an author's right, rather than a publisher's right.

The third kind of copyright, the printing patent, was not mentioned in the Statute of Anne by name, but it seems clear that it was this copyright the draftsmen had in mind in section IX, which reads: "Provided, That nothing in this Act contained shall extend, or be construed to extend, either to prejudice or confirm any Right that the said Universities or any of them, or any Person or Persons have, or claim to have, to the printing or reprinting any Book or Copy already printed, or hereafter to be printed." Read literally, the language is wholly inconsistent with the other provisions of the act, and when the question of the author's copyright came before the courts in the latter part of the eighteenth century, it was argued that this section was intended to preserve the author's common-law copyright.[3] And in fact, several of the early American state copyright statutes include provisos apparently based on this section to reserve the author's common-law rights.[4]

But this interpretation was supported by neither the language of the section nor by history; the language refers to "any . . . persons," a class far too large to be restricted in scope to authors; and there was no author's copyright to preserve, apart from the statute. The best interpretation seems to be that this provision had reference to printing

3. See Mr. Justice Aston's opinion in Millar v. Taylor. "If there was not a common-law right previous to this statute, what is this clause to save?" 4 Burr. 2303, 2351, 98 Eng. Rep. 201, 227.

4. Those of Connecticut, Georgia, and New York, all discussed *infra*.

patents or privileges granted by the sovereign.[5] The clue that "any Right" in Section IX refers to patents or privileges is the phrase "either to prejudice or confirm," which indicates that Parliament was willing to leave something in status quo. The printing patent is the logical choice, and if one substitutes the words "printing patent" for "right," the section becomes perfectly intelligible. Without this provision, the statute could have been construed to nullify the royal prerogative of making the grants. The confusion and controversy that would almost surely have resulted were probably deemed not worth the effort, particularly since the prerogative was no longer being abused to the extent it had been in former times,[6] and Parliament simply took the expedient way out by remaining neutral on the topic.

That the section does in fact refer to printing patents is almost conclusively shown by a similar provision in the Licensing Act of 1662, sections XVIII and XXII, which apparently served as the basis for the Statute of Anne's Section IX. Section XVIII of the Licensing Act reads: "Provided always, That nothing in this Act contained, shall be construed to extend to the prejudice or infringing of any the just Rights and Privileges of either of the two Universities of this Realm, touching and concerning the Licensing or Printing of Books in either of the said Universities."[7]

5. Mr. Justice Aston rejected this position. "It has been said, 'that this was inserted, that the rights which the universities or others had, under letters patent, might not be affected.'

"There can be no ground for this: for, the Act does not at all meddle with letters patent, or enact a title that could either prejudice or confirm them." Millar v. Taylor, 4 Burr. 2303, 2351, 98 Eng. Rep. 201, 227.

6. John Dunton, on June 30, 1693, received a fourteen-year patent from Queen Mary for the printing of " 'The History of the Edict at Nantes, translated by several Hands.'—It was a wonderful pleasure to Queen Mary, to see this History made English, and was the only Book to which she ever granted her Royal License; and, for the rarity of it, I will here insert it: . . . " I DUNTON, THE LIFE AND ERRORS OF JOHN DUNTON, 153 (1818).

7. Section IX, it seems, originally read, "that the said two universities, or either of them," making it more nearly like section XVIII of the Licensing Act. The House of Lords amended the language by striking the word "two" and substituting "any" for "either". See XVI H. C. JOUR. 394. The reason for the change was that universities other than Oxford and Cambridge were referred to in the statute. See section VII.

Section XXII reads: "Provided also, That neither this Act, nor any thing therein contained, shall extend to prejudice the just Rights and Privileges granted to [sic; by?] his Majesty, or any of his Royall Predecessors, to any person or persons, under his Majesties Great Seal, or otherwise, but that such person or persons may exercise and use such Rights and Privileges, as aforesaid, according to their respective Grants; any thing in this Act to the contrary notwithstanding."

The Statute of Anne can thus best be understood as a trade-regulation statute directed to the problem of monopoly in various forms. It dealt with the monopoly of the Stationers' Company itself by making copyright available to all persons. It dealt with the monopoly of the booksellers by substituting a twenty-one-year copyright for the perpetual copyright. It intended to prevent future monopolies of the type of the booksellers' by limiting the term of future copyrights. And it did not disturb the printing patent, which had ceased to be a problem of monopoly. When analyzed in this way, the statute emerges as a comprehensive, intelligible scheme for regulating the book trade.

The important feature of the Statute of Anne, as matters developed, was the continuation of the old copyrights for twenty-one years. This secured the booksellers' monopoly for that time and undoubtedly delayed a judicial interpretation of the statute. When the statute was finally interpreted, copyright, primarily through the efforts of the booksellers, had ceased to be thought of as a publisher's right and had become an author's right. When the problem of copyright reached the House of Lords in 1774, the scheme of the Statute of Anne for destroying the monopoly of the Stationers' Company by making copyright available to all, and for preventing the development of future monopolies by limiting the term of copyright were no longer important for interpretative purposes. The booksellers' monopoly based on the old copyrights had continued, despite much opposition; and it was now based in theory on the author's common-law copyright—a copyright which had never existed. Since the booksellers had turned copyright into an author's right, with the help of the King's Bench in 1769, the House of Lords had no alternative in interpreting the Statute of Anne. If it was to destroy the booksellers' monopoly, it had to say that the statutory copyright was the author's sole means of protecting his books after publication.

8

Copyright in England from 1710 to 1774

IN 1710, copyright was the right of a publisher to the exclusive publication of a work, and functioned to prevent literary piracy; by 1774, copyright had come to be the right of an author, and still functioned to protect the exclusive right of publication.

The change, however, was less a boon to authors than to publishers, for it meant that copyright was to have another function. Rather than being simply the right of a publisher to be protected against piracy, copyright would henceforth be a concept embracing all the rights that an author might have in his published work. And since copyright was still available to the publisher, the change meant also that the publisher as copyright owner would have the same rights as the author.

Copyright, in short, was to become a concept to embrace all the rights to be had in connection with published works, either by the author or publisher. As such, it was to prevent a recognition of the different interests of the two and thus preclude the development of a satisfactory law to protect the interests of the author as author.

At the same time, the change made copyright monopolistic in a way the stationer's copyright had never been.

That copyright became an author's right was not the result of authors' efforts, but of the efforts of booksellers to circumvent the Statute of Anne and to perpetuate their monopoly of the book trade. The change was thus a by-product of the "Battle of the Booksellers."

In the eighteenth century, the power of the book trade had passed from the Stationers' Company to the hands of a few booksellers, called the Conger, who controlled the trade through their monopoly of copyrights. This inner circle of booksellers maintained control by strictly regulating the sale of copyrights within the book trade. Although they maintained a fiction of public sales, in practice, the catalogues of copyrights for sale were sent to a chosen few, and other persons were rigorously excluded from the auctions.[1]

The power of the booksellers depended upon their ability to control the publication of old works such as those of Shakespeare, Milton, Dryden, and Congreve. As the Statute of Anne had continued these copyrights for twenty-one years, it is not surprising that it did not have an immediate impact on the monopoly of the booksellers. And they did not intend that it have any subsequent impact, for they apparently ignored it altogether, not even bothering to enter their new copyrights in the Stationers' Registers, as the statute required.[2] Copyright, after all, was a concept with which they had long dealt, and their ideas of copyright had the long tradition of the stationer's copyright behind it. It is not likely that a mere statute would alter these ideas, especially as the new ideas affected their monopoly adversely. Thus, despite the copyright statute, "there grew up a tacit understanding among the booksellers of the eighteenth century that there should be no interference with each other's lapsed copyrights."[3]

That the author was entitled by the statute to hold the copyright of his works did not really disturb the booksellers. They simply insisted on having the copyright before they would consent to publish a work. If the author refused, he ran the risk, if the bookseller accepted at all, of having the promotion of his book ignored.[4]

The opposition to the booksellers' monopoly, however, was such

1. William Johnston testifying in the House of Commons on the Booksellers' Copyright Bill in 1774 after the decision of Donaldson v. Beckett said: "[T]he sales are open to the whole trade; but he never knew any but booksellers apply to be admitted." 17 COBBETT'S PARL. HIST. 1079 (1813). Cf. "The chief thing they all seemed to complain of was, not being admitted to the booksellers' sales . . . " Id. at 1093. See COLLINS, AUTHORSHIP IN THE DAYS OF JOHNSON 18 (1928): "When the rights of Thomson's Seasons were offered for sale in 1769, Donaldson, the intruding Scotsman, was sent a private notice that his presence was not desired."
2. 17 COBBETT'S PARL. HIST. 1085 (1813).
3. Gray, Alexander Donaldson and the Fight for Cheap Books, 2, 38 JURIDICAL REV. 180, 193 (1926).
4. " 'In general, he affirmed, where authors keep their own copyright they do not succeed, and many books have been consigned to oblivion through the inattention and mismanagement of publishers, as most of them are envious of the success

that conflict was inevitable. In May 1736, the Society for the Encouragement of Learning was formed. This organization strongly opposed the control over publication exercised by the Conger. An early account of the Society in the Diary of the first Earl of Egmont, March 17, 1735, reveals a bitter attitude toward such leading booksellers as Jacob Tonson and Knapton. Wrote the Earl:

> "I was made acquainted this day with a subscription of ten guineas a man by divers noblemen and gentlemen in favour of ingenious authors to rescue them from the tyranny of printers and booksellers, who buy their works at a small rate, and while they almost starve then make fortunes by printing their labours. Thus Jacob Tonson the bookseller got very many thousand pounds by publishing Dryden's works, who hired himself to write for a starving pay, and thus Knapton has got 10,000 £. by publishing Rapin's history in English, while he paid Dr. Tindal the translator scarce ten shillings a day for his labour. My Lord Carteret is at the head of this generous designe, the sume of which is to be at the expense of printing such works as shall be brought to them, and shall by them be approved, and having reimbursed themselves the charge, to give the authors all the remainders of the profits."[5]

The booksellers proved to be formidable adversaries in a conflict which constituted a battle of ideas about copyright. The two ideas involved were, in essence, that copyright can be conferred only by statute, and that copyright is a natural right of the author. This latter idea, if accepted, would have meant the judicial recognition of a perpetual common-law copyright in the author. And if the author had a common-law copyright, he could then convey that copyright to the bookseller, and the limitations on copyright imposed by the Statute of Anne would be circumvented. The monopoly would be safe.

The idea of the author's common-law copyright was thus the principal weapon of the booksellers. Before resorting to this idea in the courts, however, they first attempted to obtain new legislation from Parliament.

---

of such works as they do not turn to their own account. [Authors] should sell their copyrights, or be previously well acquainted with the characters of their publishers.' That some works having a poor sale while the author had the copyright, had a rapid one when it was sold, was asserted by Lackington to be indisputable; they were purposely kept back, he said, that the booksellers might obtain the copyright for a trifle from the disappointed author." COLLINS, AUTHORSHIP IN THE DAYS OF JOHNSON 43 (1928) quoting from LACKINGTON, MEMOIRS 229.

5. Printed in McKILLOP, SAMUEL RICHARDSON 309–310 (1936).

In Parliament

On March 3, 1734 (o.s.), the booksellers presented a petition to the House of Commons, alleging "That the Expence of printing and publishing learned and useful Books, frequently obliges the Authors thereof to transfer their Property therein; and that the Property of the Authors of such Books, and their Assignees, hath, of late Years, been, and still continues to be, injured by surreptitious Editions and Impressions made as well in *Great Britain* as in foreign Parts, where Paper is purchased at Half the Expence that it can be provided for in *England* . . ." and asking leave to bring in a bill to make the Statute of Anne more effectual, "and for the better preventing the surreptitious Printing or Importing thereof from foreign Parts. . . ."[6]

The Committee to which the petition was referred made its report on March 12, 1734 (o.s.),[7] and the petitioners, after establishing "the great Labours of the Authors of Books, and the Expences those Persons are at, to whom such Authors alienate or transfer their Property therein," emphasized the losses incurred by the importation of pirated works. Robert Aynsworth testified that he had compiled a *Latin Dictionary* over a twenty-year period, and sold the copy for five hundred pounds, with an additional three hundred pounds to be received upon the printing of a second edition. The bookseller's cost, "with what has been paid for the Purchase money, will arise to very near 3,000 £.,"[8] and the proposed price of the book was ten shillings, so the profit of the purchaser had to come from the second edition. The petitioners informed the committee that they were ready "to produce surreptitious and pirated Editions, printed abroad, of the Works of 29 different Authors," and they actually produced several of these.

The 173 sermons of the late Dr. Samuel Clarke, for which Knapton paid one thousand pounds, were sold for forty shillings in sheets and were undersold by an Irish edition at twenty-six shillings. Philip Miller's *The Gardener's Dictionary*, a share of which had been purchased by Charles Rivington, sold in England for twenty-five shillings; an Irish edition sold at twenty-two shillings, and other evidence was

6. XXII H. C. JOUR. 400.
7. *Id.* at 411.
8. *Id.* at 412.

offered as to Irish editions of Delaney's *Revelation examined with Candor*, Clarendon's *History of the Rebellion*, and Bishop Burnet's *History of his own Time*. Evidence of similar competition from Holland was offered as to Shaftesbury's *Characteristics*, Buckingham's *Works*, and Bishop Burnet's first part of the *History*.

The problem of the importation of pirated books was genuinely troublesome, although the problem was apparently chiefly in the provinces rather than London.[9] Aside from not having to pay for the copyright, the pirates were able to undersell English books with foreign editions because the import tax on paper, much of which was imported, was much higher than on books,[10] and the committee gave leave to bring in a bill.

But the booksellers had ignored the question of copyright in the presentation of their case, and when the bill was submitted, it apparently contained a provision for securing another twenty-one year copyright in old books. No copy of the bill has survived, but a sheet entitled, "A letter to a M. P. concerning the Bill now depending in the House of Commons," attacked the bill for containing this provision.[11]

The writer struck directly at the weakness of the booksellers. If this bill should pass, there would be equal reason for granting another twenty-one-year copyright when it expired so that its passage would " '. . . in Effect be establishing a perpetual Monopoly, a Thing deservedly odious in the Eye of the Law. . . .' "[12]

The bill passed the House of Commons on May 1, 1735, by a vote of 163 to 111,[13] but it was killed in the House of Lords by the expedient of successively postponing the second reading.[14]

On February 11, 1736 (o.s.), the House of Commons gave the

9. COLLINS, *op. cit.*, 70–71.

10. The duty on paper was more than three times that on books; the duty which on paper would amount to 18 l. 19 6 3/4, would amount to 5 l. 6 8 on the same quantity of books. " . . . including the Duties paid on Importation, the Price of Paper sold abroad is near *80 l. per Cent.* cheaper than what it can be sold for in *England*." XXII H. C. JOUR. 412.

11. See COLLINS, *op. cit.*, 71–72.

12. *Id.* at 72.

13. XXII H. C. JOUR. 482.

14. COLLINS, *op. cit.*, 73.

booksellers leave to bring in another bill to make the 1710 Act more effective,[15] which it passed by a vote of 150 to 87, under the title of "An Act for the Encouragement of Learning, by the more effectual securing the Sole Right of printing Books to the Authors thereof, their Executors, Administrators, or Assigns, during the Times therein mentioned; . . ."[16] Unfortunately—because, for the first time, it offered real protection to the author—the bill was rejected by the House of Lords.

It began with a declaration that the Statute of Anne " 'has proved ineffectual to prevent the Publication and Sale of surreptitious Editions, and Impressions of Books; and the mischief intended by the said Act to be prevented, hath, of late years, greatly increased, and many Works do daily continue to be printed and are openly sold to the great Detriment and oftentimes the utter Ruin' of booksellers and authors." It did not propose retrospective protection of books, but did propose that after June 24, 1737, an author and his assigns should have the copyright of his works " 'during his natural Life, and for the Term of eleven Years after his Death, in case such Author shall live Ten Years after the first publication, . . . and, if he shall die within Ten Years after such Publication, then for the Term of 21 Years after his Death.' " Posthumous works were to be protected for twenty-one years.[17]

Of the various provisions of the bill,[18] the most surprising was one aimed directly against the booksellers. It read, " 'Forasmuch as the true Worth of Books and Writing is in many cases not found out till a considerable Time after the Publication thereof; and Authors who are in necessity may often be tempted to sell and alienate their Right which they will hereby have to original Copies of the Books before the value thereof is known, and may thereby put it out of their Power to alter and correct their Compositions, therefore from 24th June,

15. XXII H. C. Jour. 741.
16. " . . . and to repeal an Act, passed in the Eighth Year of the Reign of her late Majesty Queen *Anne*. . . . and for the better securing the Payment of the Drawback of the Duties for Paper used in printing Books in the *Latin, Greek,* Oriental, and Northern Languages, within the Two Universities of *Oxford* and *Cambridge*, so far as the said Drawback relates to Paper made in *Great Britain*." XXII H. C. Jour. 838.
17. COLLINS, *op. cit.*, 77.
18. "The penalties against pirates were considerably stiffened, that of forfeiture and damasking of copies remained unchanged, but the fine of one penny a sheet was raised to one of five shillings, and the whole sum was recoverable by the

1737, no Author shall have the Power to sell or alienate, except by his last Will and Testament, the Copyright for any longer than Ten Years.' "[19]

This language indicates that copyright had by this time come to be thought of as embracing the whole property of a book. It is not clear to what extent the booksellers influenced the drafting of the bill, but it was no doubt considerable, and the bill probably represents the booksellers' realization that this was as near to getting a perpetual copyright statute as they could come. If this is so, the language also indicates how little fear the booksellers had of the authors' interference with their monopoly; they were willing that an author should retain a control over his works, as they were interested only in the profits from publishing.

At any rate, the bill came nearer than any other to solving the basic dilemma of copyright law: the true interest of the author as opposed to that of the publisher. Samuel Johnson recognized this dilemma when he stated: "There seems (said he,) to be in authours a stronger right of property than that by occupancy; a metaphysical right, a right, as it were, of creation, which should from its nature be perpetual; but the consent of nations is against it, and indeed reason and the interests of learning are against it; . . ."[20]

The booksellers made another try on April 24, 1738,[21] this time limiting their petition for a bill to prohibit the importation of books re-

---

author, who was also to be entitled to the full costs of his suit. In addition to these penalties it was to be enacted that, as books were often printed and sold so covertly and their vending carried on and managed so craftily 'that the Authors and Proprietors can seldom come to the Knowledge thereof, or be able to make due Proof,' these penalties could be waived, and instead an injunction filed in the Chancery for the discovery of the number and value of the piratical copies, and for an account of the profits, which were to be recovered by the owner of the copyright. There was a very detailed regulation as to registry at Stationers' Hall, and the supply of fourteen copies for the various libraries; and to distinguish a genuine book each was to have affixed to it a copy of the receipt for these fourteen copies. Security against importation was to be gained by penalties of forfeiture and fines of £ 5 and of double the value of every copy, half to go to whoever would sue and half to the Crown. Last among the more important clauses was the extension of the time within which an action must be brought from three months to three years." *Id.* at 77–78.

19. *Id.* at 80.
20. BOSWELL, THE LIFE OF SAMUEL JOHNSON 467 (Mod. Lib. Ed.).
21. XXIII H. C. JOUR. 158.

printed abroad, and to limit the prices of books. They left out the question of copyright altogether. The bill got as far as the third reading in the House of Lords and was then rejected and dropped.[22]

A year later, April 6, 1739, the booksellers brought in still another bill against the importation of books, this time with the secondary purpose of abolishing, not amending, the clause of the Statute of Anne which gave power to certain authorities to limit the excessive prices of books.[23] The bill was passed and came into force on September 29, 1739.[24] "It proved effective, and from that time the danger of invasion of rights by importation became negligible, although in later years the Irish booksellers proved somewhat troublesome."[25]

In the Courts

After failing in Parliament in their quest for perpetual copyright, the booksellers turned to the courts. Their tactic was simple: they argued that an author had a common-law copyright based on his natural rights as an author. The House of Lords finally held that the sole copyright after publication is statutory. The context of the times in which the decision was rendered made the result almost inevitable, for it was the only decision which could make the Statute of Anne effective against the booksellers' monopoly.

The significant aspect of the developments during this time, however, is not the holding of the House of Lords. It is, rather, that the booksellers, in their quest for perpetual copyright, promoted—and the courts developed—the idea that the author had a common-law copyright based upon his natural rights as author. This idea seems to be the source of the idea that copyright constitutes the author's whole property interest in his works after publication. How this idea was developed can be seen in two lines of cases, one involving authors, the other involving booksellers.

The few cases during this period involving authors were cases in which an author sought to enjoin the unpermitted publication of his

22. COLLINS, op. cit., 67.
23. XXIII H. C. JOUR. 320.
24. 12 George II, c. 36.
25. COLLINS, op. cit., 67.

manuscript. The courts had no difficulty in granting the authors relief, and while these cases did not bear directly on the question of statutory copyright, they apparently constitute the first legal recognition of an author's property interest in his works. Thus, the cases gave substance to the proposition that an author had a common-law copyright. They were cited as supporting cases both in arguments by counsel for booksellers,[26] and in opinions favoring the booksellers.[27]

The first of the cases involving the author's rights directly was *Webb v. Rose*, on May 24, 1732, in which Sir J. Jekyll, Master of the Rolls, enjoined the publication of the drafts of conveyances devised by a father to his plaintiff son. Since the drafts had never been published, Blackstone argued that the case "turned on the original and natural right which every man has in his own composition."[28]

In 1741, injunctions were granted to restrain the publication of notes of the plaintiff "gotten surreptitiously, without his consent,"[29] and to restrain the "vending of a book of letters from *Swift*, *Pope* and others."[30]

In 1758, an injunction was granted to restrain the printing of an unpublished manuscript. A copy of it had been given by a representative of the author to a person under whom defendant claimed, but not with the intention that the manuscript be published.[31] And in 1770, the plaintiff author enjoined the publication of a farce called *Love a la*

---

26. See, *e.g.*, Tonson v. Collins, 1 Black W. 321, 96 Eng. Rep. 180 (1762) (argument of Blackstone).

27. See Millar v. Taylor, 4 Burr. 2303, 98 Eng. Rep. 201 (1769) (opinion of Justice Willes).

28. 1 Black. W. 330–331, 96 Eng. Rep. 184.

29. Forrester v. Waller, 4 Burr. 2331, 98 Eng. Rep. 216.

30. Pope v. Curl, 2 Atk. 342, 26 Eng. Rep. 608 (1741). The case was on motion of the defendant to dissolve the injunction. There were two questions. Was a book of letters within the Statute of Anne? Was a book originally printed in Ireland a "lawful prize to the booksellers here?" The court answered the questions yes and no, respectively, and continued the injunctions, but "only as to those letters, which are under Mr. *Pope's* name in the book, and which are written *by him*, and not as to those which are written *to him*." On the second question, the court stated that if the answer were otherwise, "a bookseller who has got a printed copy of a book, has nothing else to do but send it over to *Ireland* to be printed, and then by pretending to reprint it only in *England*, will by this means intirely evade the act of parliament."

31. Duke of Queensberry v. Shebbeare, 2 Eden. 329, 28 Eng. Rep. 924 (1758).

Mode which defendant had transcribed from a presentation on the stage.[32]

There is, of course, a considerable difference between an author's right to prevent a publication of his manuscript without permission and the right to control his work after publication with permission. But if the author has, as Blackstone argued, an "original and natural right" in his compositions before publication, it is easy to argue that this right remains after publication.

The soundness of this position as a matter of policy, however, depends upon the content of this "original and natural right." This is where the confusion in regard to the author's common-law copyright arises. If this right entails the same rights as copyright, there would seem to be little reason for recognizing it apart from the statutory copyright. If, however, this right involves rights other than those of copyright, there may be reason for recognizing it. The difficulty is that in the early cases involving the booksellers the opinions do not clearly delineate the meaning of this right, with the result that it was apparently deemed to include the rights of copyright as it originally developed as well as other rights. It was this confusion of ideas that led to the idea of copyright as embracing the whole property interest of a work.

In the early cases involving booksellers during this period, the Chancellors apparently granted injunctions to the booksellers to restrain piracy without reference to or concern for the Statute of Anne. By 1731, the date when old books ceased to be protected by the statute, several injunctions had already been obtained; but whether even the relief in these cases was granted on the basis of the statute is conjectural. On November 9, 1722, in *Knaplock v. Curl*, Chancellor Macclesfield granted a perpetual injunction against the printing of Prideaux's *Directions to Churchwardens*, which, according to Blackstone, was independent of the statute;[33] and on December 11, 1722, in

32. Macklin v. Richardson, Amb. 694, 27 Eng. Rep. 451 (1770). The court held that a stage presentation did not constitute a gift to the public, as the right of printing was a valuable right.

33. 1 Black W. 329, 96 Eng. Rep. 183.

Tonson v. Clifton, the same chancellor granted an injunction to restrain the printing of Steele's *Conscious Lovers,* which had not been
entered in the register of the Stationers' Company; but Lord Mansfield demurred to Blackstone's contention that these cases were not
under the statute, saying that in both instances, they were.[34]

Even though there is some question as to whether the injunctions
in these and other cases were based on the Statute of Anne,[35] there are
a sufficient number of cases about which there is no question to show
that the chancellor did not consider himself bound by the statute. On
June 9, 1735, Sir J. Jekyll in *Eyre v. Walker*[36] enjoined Walker from
printing *The Whole Duty of Man,* first published in 1657; on November 28, 1735, Chancellor Talbot in *Motte v. Falkner*[37] enjoined Falkner
from printing Swift's and Pope's *Miscellanies,* which had been published in 1701, 1702, and 1708; in *Walthoe v. Walker* on January 27,
1736, Sir J. Jekyll enjoined the printing of Nelson's *Festivals,* first
published in 1704;[38] and in *Tonson v. Walker,* May 12, 1739, Chancellor Hardwicke enjoined the printing of Milton's *Paradise Lost,* first
published in 1667.[39]

Since these cases, though often cited and stated, are not reported,
it is impossible to know the reason for judgments so obviously contrary to the Statute of Anne. One reason is that the cases involved

---

34. In the first case, the books were ordered to be damasked, i.e., to be defaced.
"The court could not have ordered this, unless under the statute." As to the second,
the entry was necessary only to enable the party to bring his action for a penalty.
"But the property is given absolutely to the author, at least during the term."
1 Black. W. 330, 96 Eng. Rep. 183, 184.

35. Gulliver v. Watson, May 19, 23, 1729, enjoining publication of Pope's
Dunciad; Ballex v. Watson, December 6, 1737, enjoining publication of Gay's
Polly; Read v. Hodges, May 19, 1740, enjoining publication of abridgement of
History of Peter the Great; and Tonson v. Mitchell, enjoining the publication
of Byng's Expedition to Sicily. All these cases are cited in counsel's argument in
Donaldson v. Beckett at 2 Bro. P.C. 138, 1 Eng. Rep. 842, as being cases under the
Statute of Anne. The list also includes other cases as being under the statute
which clearly were not.

36. 1 Black. W. 331, 96 Eng. Rep. 184.

37. *Ibid.*

38. *Ibid.*

39. *Ibid.*

preliminary injunctions, without litigation of the issue.[40] There are several reasons, however, for believing that the chancellors acted on the basis of custom in the trade. Copyright had been a long-established property in which the booksellers had large sums of money invested, and literary piracy was nothing new. Thus, the bias, if anywhere, would be in favor of the offended booksellers; but more important, it seems that the chancellors felt that they were actually protecting the property interests of authors. In *Gyles v. Wilcox*,[41] a bill was brought to enjoin the printing of a book alleged to be an infringement of Hale's *Pleas of the Crown*. In the opinion, the Lord Chancellor said (in reference to the contention that the Statute of Anne was a monopoly and ought to receive a strict construction), "I am quite of a different opinion, and that it ought to receive a liberal construction, for it is very far from being a monopoly, as it is intended to secure the property of books in the authors themselves, or the purchasers of the copy, as some recompence for their pains and labour in such works as may be of use to the learned world."[42]

The chancellors also seemed to have considered themselves as having a proprietary control over books. In *Burnett v. Chetwood*,[43] the action was to enjoin the printing of a work in English translated from the original Latin. The chancellor said that a translation was not within the prohibition of the Statute of Anne, but the book "contained notions, intended by the author to be concealed from the vulgar in the Latin language." Consequently, he granted an injunction prohibiting the publishing of it in English. He looked upon it "that this Court

40. "The causes which have come before the court of Chancery since the statute, I find to be 17 in number. Of these eight were founded on the statute right; in two or three, the question was, whether the book was a fair abridgement; and all the rest were injunctions granted *ex parte*, upon filing the bill, with an affidavit annexed. In these cases the defendant is not so much as heard; and can I imagine, that so many illustrious men, who presided in the court of Chancery, would, without a single argument, have determined so great and copious a question, and which has taken up so much of your lordships time? In fact, none of them wished to have it said he had formed any opinion on the subject." Lord Chief Justice De Grey in Donaldson v. Beckett, 17 COBBETT'S PARL. HIST. 953, at 989–990 (1813).

41. 2 Atk. 141, 26 Eng. Rep. 489 (1740).

42. Atk. 143, 26 Eng. Rep. 490.

43. 2 Mer. 441, 35 Eng. Rep. 1008 (1720 ?).

had a superintendency over all books, and might in a summary way restrain the printing or publishing any that contained reflections on religion or morality."[44]

It was not until around 1750 that doubts as to the propriety of granting injunctions in favor of the booksellers began to appear. The judicial bias which had existed in favor of the booksellers began to turn in 1750, with *Millar v. Kincaid*.[45] The case was instituted in 1743 in the Court of Sessions by seventeen booksellers of London against twenty-four booksellers of Edinburgh and Glasgow for offenses under the Statute of Anne and 12 George II, c. 36, seeking penalties, an injunction, and damages. The plaintiffs restrained their demand to an account of profits by way of damages for two or three books only, and the case was argued several times. The court at first found " 'that there lies no action of damages in this case.' " On petition for rehearing, the plaintiffs insisted that the Statute of Anne gave an additional security by penalties, during a limited time, to a property which existed before, and chancery had always so understood and given relief on the basis of common-law property. The court found " 'that an action of damage lies, to the extent of the profits made by the defendants, on such of the books libelled, as have been entered in the Stationers Hall and reprinted in Britain.' " The defenders asked for a review, and the court ordered re-argument directed to the question of " 'whether, by the laws of Scotland, an action lay, at the instance of an author or proprietor of a book, before the statute.' " On re-argument, both sides avoided the question upon the common law, and the court gave no opinion as to the common law, but found " 'that no action lies on the statute, for offenses against the same, except when it is brought within three months after the committing such offence; and that no action lies, except for such books as have been entered in Stationers Hall in terms of the Statute,' " and " 'that no action of damages lies on the statute.' " The plaintiffs objected to the ambiguity of the proposition " 'that no action of damages lies on the statute,' " because they did not contend this, and asked for a review. The court found " 'that no action of damages does lie upon or in consequence of the statute, but only for the penalties.' " The plaintiffs appealed to the House of

44. *Id.* at 1009.
45. 4 Burr. 2319, 98 Eng. Rep. 210.

Lords, which finally concluded that the action " 'was improperly and inconsistently brought, by demanding at the same time a discovery and account of the profits . . . and also the penalties of the Acts of Parliament . . . and also by joining several pursuers, claiming distinct and independent rights in different books, in the same action. . . . ' "

Millar v. Kincaid was a technical setback for the booksellers, and except for *Millar v. Taylor*, they did not again achieve any satisfactory results in the courts. The second case of *Tonson v. Walker* in 1752,[46] in which Tonson again enjoined Walker from printing *Paradise Lost*, was only a technical victory, and the case contained portents of unhappy developments for the booksellers. Tonson won because the edition in question contained notes of a Dr. Newton, which came within the terms of the Statute of Anne, although the poem did not. The solicitor-general made two points: at common law, authors have a right to their productions independent of the Statute of Anne; and the act accumulated remedies to secure a prior right violated, and not to take it away. Lord Chancellor Hardwicke said that if the case came to be heard, "I shall be inclined to send a case to the judges, that the point of law may be finally settled," but since Dr. Newton's notes came within the Act, the only question was how far and to what extent to grant the injunction, because "in waste, not a clear right, but probability of right, may be, and is, a ground for an injunction."[47] The chancellor conceded that "Arguments from public utility may be urged on both sides," but because Walker had no right to print Dr. Newton's notes, he enjoined the publication of *Paradise Lost* or the *Life of John Milton* or the notes of the various authors on the said poem compiled by Dr. Thomas Newton until the hearing of the case. The relief was granted, but the chancellor relied on the Statute of Anne, which was directly contra to the aims of the booksellers.

The doubt manifested in *Tonson v. Walker* indicated that the problem of copyright was coming to a conclusion in the English courts, as it was also in the public mind. After the institution of *Millar v. Kin-*

46. 3 Swans. 672, 36 Eng. Rep. 1017.
47. 3 Swans. 679, 36 Eng. Rep. 1020. The case was sent "to law. It was there twice argued, but never certified." Lord Mansfield, in Tonson v. Collins. 1 Black. W. 311, 96 Eng. Rep. 173.

caid in 1743, the question of literary property "came more and more before the public." Many pamphlets were written about it, and opinion was considerably divided.[48] The booksellers apparently became desperate for a satisfactory precedent in their favor, and they may have been aware that the tide of public opinion was building up against them. In 1758 they resorted to the extreme of a collusive action at law, in *Tonson v. Collins*,[49] argued twice before the King's Bench and appealed to the Exchequer Chamber before being dismissed for collusion. The action was on the case for selling *Spectators*, first published in 1711, without the consent of the proprietors of the copy, and the jury in a special verdict assessed the damages at five pounds, should the court adjudge the defendant liable.

In the first argument of the case, plaintiff's counsel, Wedderburn, clearly delineated the concept of copyright as it was envisioned by the booksellers, and indeed, understood by all at the time. The right of the plaintiff, if any, he conceded, must be found at common law, for the case was quite out of the Statute of Anne, and he based his case squarely on the right of the authors. "The right of authors in general is now to be determined; not of any particular bookseller."[50] The author's industry resulted in a profit to somebody. "I contend it belongs to the author; and when I speak of the right of property, *I mean in the profits of his book, not in the sentiments, style, &c.*"[51]

Wedderburn argued two points: the right of an author to the profits of his book is as well-founded as any other; and this was recognized by the laws of England.

On the first point, he based the property on the ground of invention. "While a work is in manuscript, the author has entire dominion over it. . . . If, instead of copying by clerks, an author prints for the use of his friends, he gives them no right over the copies. Proceed one step further: if he publishes by subscription, and no books are delivered but to subscribers, they have no right over the copies, but only to use them. This leads us to a general publication: there also

48. COLLINS, *op. cit.*, 85.
49. 1 Black. W. 301, 321, 96 Eng. Rep. 169, 180 (1761).
50. 1 Black. W. 301, 302, 96 Eng. Rep. 169.
51. *Ibid.* (Emphasis added).

every purchaser has a right to use, but nothing further. The profits of the sale must go to somebody. The printer and other mechanic artists concerned in the impression are paid for their parts; the author who is the first mover ought in justice to be paid too."[52]

On the second point, Wedderburn relied on the history of press control and printing patents. The most interesting point he made, because it reveals the contention of plaintiff that copyright was solely an author's right, was in regard to printing patents. In speaking of the law patent, he said, "It confines the author of a law book to print with a particular person. It does not take away any copy-right."[53]

Thurlow, for defendant, responded with arguments as to monopoly. "The establishment of copy-right may tend to the advantage of authors; not of the public. When a perpetual monopoly is established, printers who purchase copies will print in the vilest and cheapest manner; which will make the curious resort to foreign countries. The Act of Parliament therefore wisely gives a limited monopoly, and not a perpetual."[54] Moreover, "Publications by subscription shew, that there is a method, by which an author may gain a profit for his works, without resorting to any copy-right."[55]

Lord Mansfield ordered the case to stand over for further argument, and Blackstone argued for the plaintiff the second time. "I contend, that by law, (independent of Stat. 8 Anne) 'every author hath in himself the sole exclusive right of multiplying the copies of his literary productions;' which right is, by assignment, now vested in the plaintiffs."[56] Blackstone relied on, first, the natural foundation and commencement of property, invention, and labor; second, the end of establishing and protecting property, its utility to mankind; and third, the right as supported by law.

Yates, later to render the dissenting opinion in *Millar v. Taylor,* argued for the defendant. "I allow," he said, "that the author has a property in his sentiments till he publishes them. He may keep them

---

52. 1 Black. W. 301, 302–303, 96 Eng. Rep. 169, 170.
53. 1 Black. W. 301, 305, 96 Eng. Rep. 169, 171.
54. 1 Black. W. 301, 306–307, 96 Eng. Rep. 169, 171.
55. 1 Black. W. 301, 307, 96 Eng. Rep. 169, 171.
56. 1 Black. W. 321, 96 Eng. Rep. 180.

in his closet; he may give them away; if stolen from him, he has a remedy; he may sell them to a bookseller, and give him a title to publish them. But from the moment of publication, they are thrown into a state of universal communion."[57]

After these two arguments, the case was adjourned into the Exchequer Chamber, and the court, so far as they had formed an opinion, inclined to the plaintiff, but they refused to proceed because the defendant was nominal only and the whole expense was paid by the plaintiff.[58]

While *Tonson v. Collins* was before the courts, the booksellers took it upon themselves to resort to extralegal methods to secure their ends. They established a fund to finance prosecutions against all booksellers who, after May 1, 1759, sold any books the London booksellers claimed. Booksellers in the provinces were invited to subscribe and cooperate, and promise was made that proprietors of the copies would buy up pirated editions of them in possession of booksellers who did join; a total of 3,150 pounds was subscribed, and Tonson headed the list with a contribution of 500 pounds. Anyone who refused to sign the agreement was to be excluded from all trade sales.[59]

The booksellers of London found their nemesis in Alexander Donaldson, an Edinburgh bookseller. In 1763, James Boswell wrote, "Mr. Alexander Donaldson, bookseller, of Edinburgh, had for some time opened a shop in London, and sold his cheap editions of the most popular English books in defiance of the supposed common law right of Literary Property."[60] Donaldson was prepared for battle. In addition to selling cheap editions, he engaged in propaganda "altogether more forcible and to the point than the other side produced,"[61] and in 1765 came the first clear defeat of the booksellers in the courts at his

---

57. 1 Black. W. 321, 333, 96 Eng. Rep. 180, 185.

58. Note, at 96 Eng. Rep. 191, quoting from Willes, J. at 4 Burr. 2327. The name of Collins as defendant was not "the most conducive to belief in the bona-fide nature of this action, when we remember that in these years Collins was himself laying out considerable sums in the acquisition of shares in copyright." COLLINS, *op. cit.*, 89.

59. See COLLINS, *op. cit.*, 91; 17 COBBETT'S PARL. HIST. 1086.

60. BOSWELL, THE LIFE OF SAMUEL JOHNSON 265 (Mod. Lib. Ed.).

61. *Ibid.*

hands. On July 1, 1765, in *Osborne v. Donaldson* and *Millar v. Donaldson*,[62] Lord Northington dissolved injunctions obtained by the assignee of an author after the expiration of the two terms allowed by the Statute of Anne.[63] The stage was now set for the two landmark cases in copyright law, *Millar v. Taylor* and *Donaldson v. Beckett*.

Millar v. Taylor

In 1767, Andrew Millar, a bookseller, brought an action in the Court of King's Bench against Robert Taylor for printing a work by James Thomson called "The Seasons," which Millar had purchased from the author in 1729. The plaintiff had duly entered his copy in the Stationers' Register, but the period of protection granted by the Statute of Anne had expired, and there were two questions in the case: Did the author of a book have a copyright at common law after publication? Was this right taken away by the Statute of Anne?

The court, faced with a case of first impression, answered the questions yes and no, respectively, in a three-to-one decision, and the plaintiff in *Millar v. Taylor*[64] won his case. The defendant brought a writ of error, but "suffered himself to be nonpros'd," and in 1774, the House of Lords overturned this historic decision in *Donaldson v. Beckett*,[65] deciding that the Statute of Anne had taken away the common-law copyright of authors.

The most striking aspect of the *Millar* case is that all of the four opinions were concerned with the common-law copyright of the author, but there was no author in the case. The reason for this, of course, was that the plaintiff bookseller was relying upon rights derived from the author, and it was the author's rights which were de-

---

62. 2 Eden. 328, 28 Eng. Rep. 924.

63. The Lord Chancellor "said his reasons were, that it was a new question (none of the cases being precedents in point, being orders made before the expiration of the fourteen years given by the statute). That it was a point of so much difficulty and consequence, that he should not determine it at the hearing, but should send it to law for the opinion of the judges. . . . He desired to be understood as giving no opinion on the subject, but observed that it might be dangerous to determine that the author has a perpetual property in his books, for such a property would give him not only a right to publish, but to suppress too." 2 Eden. 328, 28 Eng. Rep. 924.

64. 4 Burr. 2303, 98 Eng. Rep. 201 (1769).

65. 4 Burr. 2408, 98 Eng. Rep. 257, 2 Bro. P.C. 129, 1 Eng. Rep. 837 (1774).

terminative of the issue. The issues in the case, as stated by Mr. Justice Willes, were:

> If the copy of the book belonged to the author, there is no doubt but that he might transfer it to the plaintiff. And if the plaintiff, by the transfer, is become the proprietor of the copy, there is as little doubt that the defendant has done him an injury, and violated his right: for which, this action is the proper remedy.
>
> But the term of years secured by 8 Ann. c. 19, is expired. Therefore the author's title to the copy depends upon two questions—
>
> 1st. Whether the copy of a book, or literary composition, belongs to the author, by the common law:
>
> 2d. Whether the common-law-right of authors to the copies of their own works is taken away by 8 Ann. c. 19.[66]

The way in which the issue was presented made it necessary that the judges treat copyright as essentially and fundamentally a right of the author. This, of course, was what the booksellers desired. Although the basis of the monopoly in the trade was perpetual copyright, the booksellers and not the authors were the monopolists. By focussing the court's attention on the rights of the authors and securing those rights, the booksellers would achieve their aims and avoid the problem of having to defend their monopoly. The importance of the *Millar* case is that it is the first case in which the problem of the meaning of copyright was judicially delineated. Because the court was concerned with the copyright of authors, it was almost inevitable that thereafter copyright should be treated as an author's right.

The significant question about the *Millar* case involves the meaning the judges attributed to copyright. The answer to the question is found in two places: the definition the judges gave to copyright; and the reasons they gave for affirming, or, in the opinion of Mr. Justice Yates, for rejecting the common-law copyright.

Insofar as the technical meaning of the term "copyright" is concerned, all four of the judges used its traditional meaning—"to signify the sole right of printing, publishing, and selling." Three of the judges concluded that the author had this right at common law, and they relied on two principal grounds—the stationer's copyright and the natural rights of the author.

---

66. 4 Burr. 2303, 2311, 98 Eng. Rep. 201, 206.

Mr. Justice Willes, in particular, relied on the charter and by-laws of the Stationers' Company, the various Star Chamber Decrees regulating the press, the ordinances passed by Parliament during the Interregnum, and the Licensing Act of 1662. The fault in the use of this evidence, as Mr. Justice Yates, dissenting, pointed out, was that it was irrelevant. None of these matters provided any protection for the author, and since the stationer's copyright was limited to members of the company, the author was not even qualified to have the copyright. Even so, this judicial tying in of the stationer's copyright with the author undoubtedly helped to promote the idea of copyright as an author's right.

It is, however, the other reasons for supporting the common-law copyright that are most interesting. These reasons had primarily to do with the natural right of a man in property he creates. On this point, the opinions of Mr. Justice Aston and Lord Mansfield are particularly interesting. Mr. Justice Aston, after discussing the concept of property, concluded, "That a man may have property in his body, life, fame, labours, and the like; and, in short, in anything that can be called his."[67] Later, he commented, "I do not know, nor can I comprehend any property more emphatically a man's own, nay, more incapable of being mistaken, than his literary works."[68] This language indicates that the concept of copyright which Mr. Justice Aston had in mind was the complete property interest in a work. What this interest consisted of was indicated by Lord Mansfield. In speaking of the author's common-law copyright before publication, he said that the right is not found in custom or precedent, but is drawn "From this argument—because it is just, that an author should reap the pecuniary profits of his own ingenuity and labour. It is just, that another should not use his name, without his consent. It is fit that he should judge when to publish, or whether he ever will publish. It is fit he should not only choose the time, but the manner of publication; how many; what volume; what print. It is fit, he should choose to whose care he will trust the accuracy and correctness of the impression; in whose honesty

67. 4 Burr. 2303, 2338, 98 Eng. Rep. 201, 220.
68. 4 Burr. 2303, 2345; 98 Eng. Rep. 201, 224.

he will confide, not to foist in additions: with other reasonings of the same effect."[69]

These were sufficient reasons to protect the copy before publication, and the same reasons apply after the author has published. If he does not retain the copyright after publication, "The author may not only be deprived of any profit, but lose the expense he has been at. He is no more master of the use of his own name. He has no control over the correctness of his own work. He can not prevent additions. He can not retract errors. He can not amend; or cancel a faulty edition. Any one may print, pirate, and perpetuate the imperfections, to the disgrace and against the will of the author; may propagate sentiments under his name, which he disapproves, repents and is ashamed of. He can exercise no discretion as to the manner in which, or the persons by whom his work shall be published."[70] Lord Mansfield's argument was best summed up in the following statement. "His (an author's) name ought not to be used, against his will. It is an injury, by a faulty, ignorant and incorrect edition, to disgrace his work and mislead the reader."[71]

The two opinions of Mr. Justice Aston and Lord Mansfield say, in effect, that copyright contains two basic rights of the author, a right to the rewards of his labor, and a right to protect his fame. Mr. Justice Aston states as much, and Lord Mansfield elucidates this proposition when he speaks of the right of an author to profits and the right not to be disgraced by the publishing of his works. Thus, in *Millar v. Taylor*, the concept of copyright was clearly understood as embracing the author's whole property interest in his works.

Mr. Justice Yates, in his dissenting opinion, apparently agreed with this concept of copyright. He contended that there was no common-law copyright of the author, because one cannot have a property "in the style and ideas of his work" at common law. The only copyright, he said, was the statutory copyright under the Statute of Anne. "The Legislature indeed may make a new right. The Statute of Queen Ann. has vested a new right in authors, for a limited time: and whilst that right

69. 4 Burr. 2303, 2398; 98 Eng. Rep. 201, 252.
70. 4 Burr. 2303, 2398, 98 Eng. Rep. 201, 252.
71. 4 Burr. 2303, 2405, 98 Eng. Rep. 201, 256.

exists, they will be established in the possession of their property."[72]

The four opinions in the *Millar* case thus treat copyright as an author's right. The opinion so thoroughly discussed the point that it is easy to understand why copyright was subsequently treated as an author's right embracing the entire property interest of a work. Yet, in the light of the earlier history of copyright, all of the opinions missed the basic point that copyright was essentially a publisher's right, with the development of which the author had nothing to do.

Donaldson v. Beckett

Millar v. Taylor was not appealed, and it lasted as a precedent for only five years. Millar himself died in June 1768, while his case was pending, and the executors of his estate sold his copies at auction on June 13, 1769. Thomas Beckett and fourteen partners purchased in shares the copyrights of several poems by James Thomson for 505 pounds.

The works of Thomson had proved to be a profitable investment for Millar, who had purchased the copyrights for a total of 242 pounds many years earlier and had presumably gained much profit from their publication. His first purchase from the author, on January 16, 1729, consisted of a tragedy called "Sophonisba" and a poem entitled "Spring," and cost him 137 pounds and ten shillings. The second purchase, on June 16, 1738, from John Millan, another bookseller, consisted of poems entitled "Summer," "Autumn," "Winter," "Britannia," and "Hymn on the Succession of the Seasons," and an "Essay on Descriptive Poetry," for 105 pounds. This was the sum which Millan had paid the author on July 28, 1729, some nine years before, for the same works.

Under the Statute of Anne, the copyrights of these works, all of which had been first published no later than 1729, had expired at the latest in 1757, and Alexander Donaldson, who had been excluded from the sale of Millar's copyrights, claimed the right to publish the works involved free of charge. In November 1772, Beckett and his partners received, on the authority of *Millar v. Taylor*, a perpetual injunction to restrain Donaldson, who was alleged to have sold several thousand

---

72. 4 Burr. 2303, 2386; 98 Eng. Rep. 201, 245.

copies of *The Seasons* printed in Edinburgh, and Donaldson appealed to the House of Lords. The result was the landmark case of copyright law, *Donaldson v. Beckett*.[73]

Donaldson v. Beckett is generally cited for the proposition that it abolished the author's common-law copyright, and thus limited the author's rights in connection with his published works to rights granted by statute. The correctness of this conclusion, however, depends upon the meaning of copyright the House of Lords had in mind at the time it rendered its decision, and the concept as used by the judges was not so broad as to make the author dependent solely on statutory rights.

It is true that at the time of the decision the term "copy" or "copyright" was commonly thought of as embracing the whole of the property in a literary work; the best illustration of this is *Millar v. Taylor*. The judges in the House of Lords, however, did not use either the term "copy" or "copyright," but spoke in terms of the right of "printing and publishing for sale." In doing this, they avoided the error which the judges in *Millar v. Taylor* committed by the use of the term "copy."

When Justice Willes framed the issue in the Millar case as "Whether the copy of a book, or literary composition, belongs to the author, by the common law," he had either to deny all common-law rights to the author, or to recognize his common-law rights without limitation, because of the inclusive meaning the word "copy" had taken on. He chose to do the latter, and thus gave judicial approbation to the booksellers' monopoly by reason of the effect the ruling had on the provisions of the Statute of Anne.

The judges in the House of Lords, however, employed the terminology of the Statute of Anne, and by so doing, limited the scope of their decision to the problem at which the statute was aimed, the monopoly of the booksellers. In effect, the House of Lords in the *Donaldson*

73. 2 Bro. P.C. 129, 1 Eng. Rep. 837; 4 Burr. 2408, 98 Eng. Rep. 257 (1774). The Court of Session rendered a decision, Hinton v. Donaldson, in Scotland in point with Donaldson v. Beckett on July 27, 1773, some six months prior to the House of Lords Decision. "The general question was, whether authors have, at common law, a perpetual and exclusive property in their works after publication?" 35 THE SCOTS MAGAZINE 497 (1773). Thirteen judges voted 12 to 1 (Lord Monboddo, the one) against a perpetual property in books. *Id.* at 498.

case returned to the concept of copyright as developed by the Stationers' Company, and avoided the question of author's rights except as those rights were directly related to the monopolistic practices of the booksellers.

The judges probably did not intend by the framing of their questions in fundamental terms of copyright to avoid the problem of an author's interest other than copyright in his works. It was simply that the problem was not before them, as shown by the terms of the various contracts involved in the case. When Thomson sold the copyrights of certain of his works to Millar in 1729, the language of the contract indicates that he assigned only the right to publish them as he had written them. He "did assign to Millar, his executors, administrators and assigns, the true copies of the said tragedy and poem, and the sole and exclusive right and property of printing the said copies for his and their sole use and benefit, and also all benefit of all additions, corrections, and amendments which should be afterwards made in the said copies."[74] The conveyance by the author to Millan in 1729 was of like import,[75] and it is not likely that Thomson was conveying the benefits of "additions, corrections, and amendments" the copyright holders should make. By way of contrast to the wording of the conveyance from the author, the conveyance from Millan to Millar, *i.e.*, bookseller to bookseller, in 1738, included "all the right, title, interest, property, claim, and demand of the said John Millan to or in the said copies."[76] By virtue of these agreements, "Andrew Millar became lawfully entitled to all the profits arising by the printing and publishing of the several poems . . . and to all the sole and exclusive property and right of printing copies of them, and of vending and disposing of the same."[77]

The actual holding of the *Donaldson* case is that the author's common-law right to the sole printing, publishing, and vending of his works, a right which he could assign in perpetuity, is taken away and supplanted by the Statute of Anne. The case did not hold that the author's rights at common law consisted *only* of the right of printing, publishing, and vending his works, and for present purposes, it is

74. Donaldson v. Beckett, 2 Bro. P.C. 129, 1 Eng. Rep. 837, 838 (1774).
75. *Ibid.*
76. *Ibid.*
77. *Ibid.*

irrelevant whether the author's common-law rights actually were so limited. The point is that the *Donaldson* case did not so hold, a point of considerable importance, because it was this case which implemented the Statute of Anne. If the House of Lords did hold that the Statute of Anne abrogated all of the author's common-law rights, this issue properly became a closed matter. If it did not so hold, the question of the author's common-law rights, other than that of publishing and vending his works, at least remained an open issue, to be decided in a proper case.

There are two principal reasons for the misunderstanding of the *Donaldson* case. First, of course, is *Millar v. Taylor*, in which the various judges in their opinions had used copyright to embrace the whole of the author's interest in his property. More important, however, was the fact that the form of the questions put to the judges in the *Donaldson* case left the impression, unsupported by substance, that the author's common-law rights did consist only of the rights of publishing and vending his works.

There were five questions directed to the judges in *Donaldson v. Beckett:*

1. Whether an author of a book or literary composition had at common law "the sole right of first printing and publishing the same for sale," and a right of action against a person printing, publishing, and selling without his consent. Held, yes by a vote of 10 to 1.

2. If the author had such a right, did the law take it away upon his publishing the book or literary composition; and might any person thereafter be free to reprint and sell the work? Held, no by a vote of 7 to 4.

3. Assuming the right of common law, was it taken away by the Statute of Anne, and is an author limited to the terms and conditions of that statute for his remedy? Held, yes by a vote of 6 to 5.

4. Whether an author of any literary composition and his assigns have the sole right of printing and publishing the same in perpetuity by the common law? Held, yes by a vote of 7 to 4.

5. Whether this right was restrained or taken away by the Statute of Anne? Held, yes by a vote of 6 to 5.[78]

---

78. 4 Burr. 2408–2409, 98 Eng. Rep. 257–258.

The questions fall into two categories. The first three were phrased in terms of the author only; the last two were phrased in terms of the author and his assigns, the terminology of the Statute of Anne. Thus, analytically, the first three questions were directed to the rights of the author, the latter two to the rights of the booksellers.

There is nothing in the wording of the first two questions to imply that the sole right of publishing his work constituted the whole of the author's rights. The problem, however, is more subtle than mere wording. The affirmation of a right—and the rights stated in the first two questions were both affirmed—tends to be exclusive, while the denial of a right tends to be inclusive, unless the denial is limited. Both the rights here involved, after having both affirmed as existing at common law, were denied by the answer to the third question, that the Statute of Anne took them away. Because of this, the questions were unfairly weighted against the author. The affirmation of the right was to print and sell; the denial of the right resulted in a denial of "every remedy except of the foundation of the said statute (of Anne) and on the terms and conditions prescribed thereby."[79]

If the author no longer had the common-law right to publish, and was denied common-law remedies, the conclusion that he had no rights except those provided by the statute is almost self-evident. The fallacy in this conclusion, of course, is that the court and the Statute of Anne did not purport to deal with anything more than the copyright in its most limited form. But the fallacy was obscured by the conclusion that, except when the author complied with the terms of the statute, publication resulted in a gift of the work to the public. As long as the relationship was between the author and publisher—that is, a two-dimensional affair—it was fairly easy to say that the author retained certain rights upon selling the copy. The making of a gift of the work to the public, however, resulted in the inference of an abdication of all rights.

The fourth question directed to the judges, when compared with the second question, shows an implicit distinction between the author's copyright and the publisher's copyright.[80] Since the second question

79. 4 Burr. 2408, 98 Eng. Rep. 258.
80. It is, perhaps, significant that the fourth and fifth questions were posed at the suggestion of Lord Camden, who was bitterly opposed to the stationers' monopoly. Donaldson v. Beckett, 17 COBBETT'S PARL. HIST. 953, at 971 (1813).

had to do with the author's copyright, the fourth question is merely redundant if it too is concerned only with the author's copyright. The question purports to concern the duration of the author's copyright, *i.e.*, whether it existed in perpetuity. But obviously the author could not exist in perpetuity, and if his copyright was not lost upon publication, as indicated by the answer to the second question, it follows that he retained the copyright until his death, unless he conveyed it. Question four has to do with the copyright of the author upon conveyance— that is, the publisher's copyright—for this was the only copyright that could, theoretically, exist in perpetuity.

The second question was not even necessary to the disposition of the case. But the appeal had been brought "to obtain a final determination of this great question of literary property,"[81] and to do this, the judges found it necessary to make the two-fold distinction between copyright on the basis of ownership. Logically, it was not necessary to say that the author had had a common-law copyright in order to say that copyright was purely a statutory matter. But the judges were faced with the *Millar* case, which had established a common-law copyright of the author in perpetuity, independent of the statute. Unless they dealt with the particular point, they ran the risk of permitting the booksellers to continue their claim to perpetual copyright. The *Millar* case thus made it mandatory on the House of Lords to deal with the question of the author's common-law copyright in order to deal effectively with the problem of monopoly.

But the author's right in his property, "the right of creation," as Johnson called it, was not an aspect of the monopoly problem, and it was the second question which was the biggest factor in the *Donaldson* case. This might not have been so, except that in the *Millar* case Mr. Justice Aston and Lord Mansfield in elucidating the concept of copyright made the concept inclusive of all the author's rights, and the *Millar* case was thought to be a particularly valuable annotation of the *Donaldson* case because Justices Willes and Aston participated in the *Donaldson* decision.

Given the context of the *Donaldson* case, the monopoly of the booksellers, the decision could hardly have been otherwise. It was the only decision which would destroy the monopoly of the booksellers, and

81. 2 Bro. P.C. 132, 1 Eng. Rep. 839.

there is little question that the decision was directly aimed at that monopoly. "All our learning," said Lord Camden, "will be looked up in the hands of the Tonsons and Lintons of the age, who will set what price upon it their avarice chuses to demand, till the public become as much their slaves, as their own hackney compilers are."[82] Unfortunately, the decision does not seem to have been properly understood because of the confusion surrounding the author's so-called common-law copyright. The issue was a completely false one, and Lord Chief Justice De Grey's statement about it makes the point well:

> The truth is, the idea of a common-law right in perpetuity was not taken up till after that failure (of the booksellers) in procuring a new statute for an enlargement of the term. If (say the parties concerned) the legislature will not do it for us, we will do it without their assistance; and then we begin to hear of this new doctrine, the common-law right, which, upon the whole, I am of opinion, cannot be supported upon any rules or principles of the common law of this kingdom.[83]

The decision in the *Donaldson* case was widely approved at the time of its rendering, except by the few monopolists whom it affected directly, and who once again turned to Parliament for relief, contending that in reliance on the *Millar* case they had invested thousands of pounds in the purchase of old copyrights not protected by statute.[84] The claims of economic ruin were sufficient to get a bill before the House of Commons,[85] but there was widespread opposition both inside and outside of Parliament. The authors did not support the booksellers,[86] and there were many counter-petitions opposing the claims of the booksellers.[87] The most effective opposition was probably that of various booksellers who "stated that only a few of the London booksellers were affected by the decision" of the *Donaldson* case.[88]

82. Donaldson v. Beckett, 17 COBBETT'S PARL. HIST. 953, 1000 (1813).
83. Donaldson v. Beckett, 17 COBBETT'S PARL. HIST. 953, 992 (1813).
84. 17 COBBETT'S PAR. HIST. 1078 (1813).
85. XXXIV H.C. JOUR. 100.
86. COLLINS, *op. cit.*, 102.
87. "We find petitions of the booksellers and printers of Edinburgh; of sundry booksellers in London and Westminster on behalf of themselves and their brethren in the country; of the printers and booksellers of the city and University of Glasgow; of the Committee of the Royal Boroughs of Scotland; of the booksellers, printers, and bookbinders of York; and of Donaldson himself." COLLINS, *op. cit.*, 100.
88. *Ibid.*

There is no copy of the bill presented in April 1774, but Mr. Dempster in the House of Commons charged, "That this Bill was not meant to restore the law concerning copyright as it formerly stood, but as the individual booksellers of London thought it stood; . . . "[89] In spite of strong opposition, the bill passed the House of Commons and was sent to the House of Lords.

Opposition to the bill by the Lords was indeed bitter. Lord Denbigh stated "that the very principle of the Bill was totally inadmissible, and that it was not necessary to call witnesses, or to make any inquiry into a Bill that violated the rights of individuals, and affronted that House." The Lord Chancellor said "that the booksellers never could imagine that they had a common-law right, . . . that the monopoly was supported among them by oppression and combination, and that there were none of their allegations nor any part of the Bill, required any further enquiry." Lord Camden said "that the monopolizing booksellers had robbed others of their property; for that printing was a lawful trade, and, without all manner of doubt, therefore they had property in it; consequently thus to deprive printers of the subject on which they might lawfully exercise their trade, was robbing them of their property; that they had maintained this monopoly by most iniquitous oppressions, and exercised it to the disgrace of printing; that they were monopolists, and if the line of justice and equity were drawn, it would be, that those who had deprived others of their right for a series of years, should make compensation to all those they had injured by such conduct."[90] It hardly need be added that the bill was rejected.

So, late in the eighteenth century, the Battle of the Booksellers ended. Copyright had ceased to be a publisher's right and had become an author's right. And it was as an author's right that it was received into the new American nation only a very few years later.

89. 17 COBBETT'S PARL. HIST. 1090 (1813).
90. 17 COBBETT'S PARL. HIST. 1400–1402.

9

The Early American Copyright

IN THE United States, copyright was the subject of widespread legislation almost as soon as the new nation was founded. The absence of an author class makes this unusual activity in regard to the writing and publishing of books—when one considers the problems involved in establishing a new nation—a remarkable tribute to the intellectual quality of the leaders of the day. And perhaps, also, it is a measure of the intellectual ferment that characterized the young United States.

More remarkable than that, even, is that four stages, each dominated by a different idea of the function of copyright, can be discerned in the development of early American copyright. The stages are the state copyright statutes, the constitutional provision, the federal copyright act of 1790, and the landmark case of American copyright law, *Wheaton v. Peters*, decided in 1834.

These phases are, to some extent, artificial. They spanned only half a century, from 1783 to 1834; and the lawmaking agency in each stage was a different one—the state legislatures, the Constitutional Convention, Congress, and the Supreme Court.

The rapid development of copyright in America, of course, is explained in part by the creation of a new nation; but it was also due to the fact that all of the ideas originated in the English history of copyright. The state acts and the federal act were based on the Statute of Anne, and the issues in the *Wheaton* case were very similar to the issues in the leading English cases, *Donaldson v. Beckett* and *Millar v. Taylor*.

Moreover, no stage in the American development of copyright presents a fully developed concept of copyright. The constitutional provision was not intended to, and the state copyright statutes apparently never became operative. And the last two stages—the federal copyright act of 1790 and the *Wheaton* case—can be viewed as only two aspects of the same stage of development.

Because copyright is so conceptual in nature, it may help to understand the development of American copyright law to consider the four developments separately for the ideas of copyright they contained. A remarkably clear pattern emerges from those ideas which could have—and those ideas which did—shape the final concept of copyright.

Running parallel to the four stages of development of early American copyright were four basic ideas as to the purpose of copyright during this period. They were: that copyright is to protect the author's rights; that copyright is to promote learning; that copyright is to provide order in the book trade as a government grant; and that copyright is to prevent harmful monopoly.

The idea that copyright is primarily for the benefit of the author was central to the state statutes; that copyright is necessary for learning was central to the constitutional provision; that copyright is a government grant (or statutory privilege) was central to the first federal copyright act; and that copyright was to prevent monopoly was central to the *Wheaton* case.

All of these ideas were present in varying degrees in all four stages, and the relative importance of each in the various stages can be seen in the following analysis:

I. The State Copyright Statutes: (1) To secure the author's right; (2) to promote learning; (3) to provide order in the book trade by government grant (statutory privilege); (4) to prevent monopoly.

II. The Constitutional Provision: (1) To promote learning; (2) to secure the author's right; (3) to provide order in the book trade by government grant (statutory privilege); (4) to prevent monopoly.

III. The Federal Act: (1) To provide order in the book trade by government grant (statutory privilege); (2) to promote learning; (3) to secure the author's right; (4) to prevent monopoly.

IV. The *Wheaton* Case: (1) To prevent monopoly; (2) to provide order in the book trade by government grant (statutory privilege); (3) to promote learning; (4) to secure the author's rights.

As indicated above, all of the ideas were present in the four stages, but the point here is that, in each of the stages, one idea tended to predominate. It was the predominant idea which manifested the basic purpose of copyright in each stage and determined the relative importance of the other ideas. A caveat is here appropriate: the relative importance of the ideas has been inferred from the materials. With a few exceptions, neither the ideas nor their importance is explicitly stated. And as the stages of development are not all of equal consequence, the shift in the prominence of the ideas can be attributed in part to the natural biases of the various lawmaking groups involved. Even so, the scheme appears to reflect an accurate representation of the various ideas of copyright in the early United States and the way those ideas changed. The change can be seen by noting that the relationship of the ideas in the state statutes and in the *Wheaton* case are exactly reversed.

The effect of the transition can be illustrated by constructing definitions of copyright on the basis of the ideas as arranged above. Under the first ranking—the state statutes—copyright is a right to protect the author's interest, given to promote learning and secured by statute so as to maintain order in the book trade, but limited, to prevent the growth of a harmful monopoly.

The definition to be constructed from the second ranking, the constitutional provision, does not vary too much. Under it, copyright is a device to promote learning by giving protection to the author under a statute so as to maintain order in the book trade, but limited, to prevent the growth of a harmful monopoly.

Under the third ranking, the federal statute, the change in definition becomes more pronounced: copyright here is a statutory privilege for the purpose of maintaining order in the book trade and of promoting learning, given to authors for a limited time to prevent harmful monopoly.

The fourth ranking of the ideas, under the *Wheaton* case, changes the definition completely: copyright is granted by statute for the purpose of preventing harmful monopoly, maintaining order in the book trade, and promoting learning by rewarding authors to encourage them to produce.

The fourth definition requires an approach to copyright completely different from that required by the first. If the primary purpose of copyright is to protect the author's interest, the ideas that it also promotes learning, that it is a statutory grant to maintain order in the trade, and that it is to prevent monopoly will be subordinated to the primary purpose.

On the other hand, if copyright is thought of as a device for the prevention of a harmful monopoly, the idea of its being a statutory grant to maintain order in the trade and to promote learning by rewarding the author will be subordinated to this purpose. Thus, under the first definition, the statute providing for copyright is to be given a liberal construction in favor of the author; under the fourth definition, the statute is to be given a strict and technical construction to guard against monopoly.

The following material on the early history of American copyright treats, generally at two levels, the state statutes, the constitutional provision, the first federal copyright act, and *Wheaton v. Peters*. It is presented in some detail because of general unfamiliarity with these aspects of the development of copyright in America.

The State Copyright Statutes

Copyright was not secured by law in colonial America,[1] but the new nation immediately recognized the importance of providing a means of protecting published books. On May 2, 1783, the Continental Congress passed a resolution "recommending the several States to secure to the Authors or Publishers of New Books the Copyright of such Books."[2] The recommendation was obviously based on the Statute of Anne. The copyright recommended was to be granted to the authors or publishers, for a "certain time not less than fourteen years," with a similar renewal term to authors, "if they shall survive the term first mentioned," and the right to be secured was the "right of printing, publishing, and vending." Three states—Connecticut, Massachusetts, and Maryland—had already enacted copyright statutes shortly before the date of the resolution, and the remaining states, except Delaware,

1. I THOMAS, THE HISTORY OF PRINTING IN AMERICA, 150, n. 1 (2d ed. 1874).

2. U.S. COPYRIGHT OFFICE, COPYRIGHT LAWS OF THE UNITED STATES OF AMERICA, 1783–1862, 1 (1962). Hereafter referred to as COPYRIGHT LAWS.

subsequently complied, New York being the last to do so, on April 29, 1786.[3]

The state acts fall into two broad categories, those more or less patterned after the English act, and those not so patterned. In the latter group are the statutes of Massachusetts, New Hampshire, Rhode Island, and Virginia. The Massachusetts act,[4] March 17, 1783, copied by the New Hampshire and Rhode Island legislatures, gave the author "the sole property" of his works if the name of the author were printed in the published work; it provided a penalty not to exceed 3,000 pounds or be less than five pounds, for the printing, publishing, or selling of a copyrighted work without the consent of the author or his assigns. As a condition of suing for the penalty, two copies of every printed book were to be presented to "the library of the University of Cambridge." The term of the copyright was twenty-one years from the date of first publication.[5]

The Virginia Act, October 17, 1785,[6] gave a copyright of twenty-one years for "the printing and re-printing" of any book or pamphlet upon the registration of the title of the work with "the clerk of the council," and provided penalties "double the value of all the copies" against anyone who printed, reprinted, imported, published, or sold a copyrighted work without the consent of the author or proprietor.

Of the remaining acts, those of Maryland, New Jersey, Pennsylvania, and North Carolina can be classed together. The Maryland statute, April 21, 1783,[7] gave the "author of any book or books, writing or writings" and his "executors, administrators, or assigns . . . the sole liberty of printing and reprinting such" for a term of fourteen years. Offenders were to forfeit twopence for every sheet in their custody, if the title of the work were registered. At the expiration of

---

3. See COPYRIGHT LAWS, 1–21.

4. Id. at 4.

5. The New Hampshire Act, November 7, 1783, COPYRIGHT LAWS, 8, gave a term of twenty years and provided a penalty of five to 1,000 pounds; the Rhode Island Act, December 1783, COPYRIGHT LAWS, 9, followed the Massachusetts act in this respect. Both the New Hampshire and Rhode Island acts, of course, omitted the provision of copies to be given to the university.

6. COPYRIGHT LAWS, 14.

7. Id. at 5.

the first term, "the sole right of printing or disposing of the copies shall return to the authors thereof, if they are then living, for another term of fourteen years." The New Jersey statute, May 27, 1783,[8] gave "the author of any book or pamphlet . . . and his heirs and assigns" the "exclusive right of printing, publishing, and vending" his work for fourteen years; provided a penalty for infringers double the value of the infringed copies, required registration, and gave a renewal term of fourteen years to the author if living at the end of the first term.

The Pennsylvania act,[9] January 1784, contained similar provisions, but, like the Maryland statute, is characterized by direct copying of the language of the Statute of Anne. The North Carolina statute, November 19, 1785,[10] is somewhat different from the above acts. It gave "the author of any book, map or chart . . . and his heirs and assigns . . . the sole liberty of printing, publishing, and vending the same . . . " for a term of fourteen years, with no renewal term. The penalty for offenders was a sum double the value of the infringing articles (plus forfeiture), with one half of the sum recovered to go to the state, the other half to the person who should sue. The statute also contained a price-control provision, and provided that no protection was to be extended to authors or publishers of "books, maps, or charts which may be dangerous to civil liberty, or to the peace or morals of society."

The South Carolina statute,[11] March 26, 1784, was the longest and most comprehensive of the state acts and followed the Statute of Anne in language and substance more closely than any of the other acts. It provided that "the author of any book or books . . . and his assignee or assigns, shall have the sole liberty of printing and reprinting such books" for a term of fourteen years, with the usual renewal term. Offenders were to forfeit the offending works to the proprietor of the copy "who shall forthwith damask and make waste paper of them," and were to forfeit one shilling per sheet, one half of which sum was to go to the state, the other half to the person suing. Registration was required, and the act was not to be construed as prohibiting the importation of books in a foreign language printed be-

---

8. *Id.* at 6.
9. *Id.* at 10.
10. *Id.* at 15.
11. *Id.* at 11.

yond the seas. A price-control provision was included, and the "inventors of useful machines" were given "a like exclusive privilege of making or vending their machines for the like term of fourteen years, under the same privileges and restrictions hereby granted to, and imposed on, the authors of books."

The Connecticut statute,[12] January 1783, served as a model for the Georgia,[13] February 3, 1786, and New York,[14] April 29, 1786, acts. These acts provided that "the author of any book or pamphlet . . . or of any map or chart, . . . and his heirs and assigns shall have the sole liberty of printing, publishing, and vending the same." The fourteen-year term, with a renewal term to the author, registration, and penalty double the value of the infringing copies were provided. A price-control provision was included, and there were two provisions not found in the other acts. One of these gave the author or proprietor of any unpublished manuscript a right of action against one printing or publishing of it without consent; the other provided, "that nothing in this act shall extend to affect, prejudice or confirm the rights which any person may have to the printing or publishing of any book, pamphlet, map or chart at common law, in cases not mentioned in this act." There was also a proviso that nothing in the act should protect persons who had printed or published works that were "prophane, treasonable, defamatory, or injurious to government, morals or religion."

The preambles to the state statutes deserve special attention because eight of them[15] state the purpose of copyright, the reason for it, and the legal theory upon which it was based. The purpose of copyright, according to these preambles, was to secure profits to the author; the reason for it was to encourage authors to produce and thus to improve learning; and the theory upon which it was based was that of the natural rights of the author.

The Connecticut preamble provided, "Whereas it is perfectly agreeable to the principles of natural equity and justice, that every author should be secured in receiving the profits that may arise from the sale

---

12. *Id.* at 1.
13. *Id.* at 17.
14. *Id.* at 19.
15. Those of Connecticut, Georgia, New York, Massachusetts, New Jersey, New Hampshire, North Carolina, and Rhode Island.

of his works, and such security may encourage men of learning and genius to publish their writings; which may do honor to their country, and service to mankind."[16] The preambles to the Georgia and New York statutes were substantially the same.

The Massachusetts preamble, copied in the New Hampshire and Rhode Island acts, stated that, "Whereas the improvement of knowledge, the progress of civilization, the public weal of the community, and the advancement of human happiness, greatly depend on the efforts of learned and ingenious persons in the various arts and sciences: As the principal encouragement such persons can have to make great and beneficial exertions of this nature, must exist in the legal security of the fruits of their study and industry to themselves; and as such security is one of the natural rights of all men, there being no property more peculiarly a man's own than that which is produced by the labour of his mind: . . . "[17]

The New Jersey preamble stated: "Whereas learning tends to the embellishment of human nature, the honour of the nation, and the general good of mankind; and as it is perfectly agreeable to the principles of equity, that men of learning who devote their time and talents to the preparing treatises for publication, should have the profits that may arise from the sale of their works secured to them: . . . "[18]

The North Carolina preamble provided: "Whereas nothing is more strictly a man's own than the fruit of his study, and it is proper that men should be encouraged to pursue useful knowledge by the hope of reward; and as the security of literary property must greatly tend to encourage genius, to promote useful discoveries, and to the general extension of arts and commerce: . . . "[19]

The preambles of the state copyright statutes appear to be the only place where the purpose, reason, and legal theory of copyright were expressed in copyright statutes. The ideas expressed in the preambles are particularly valuable as an aid in interpreting the statutes to determine the concept of copyright held in mind by the draftsmen of the statutes. Since these statutes existed for less than a decade before

16. COPYRIGHT LAWS, 1.
17. *Id.* at 4.
18. *Id.* at 6–7.
19. *Id.* at 15.

being supplanted by the federal copyright act, and since some of them by their own terms never became operative, the copyright they provided for apparently never came into existence. At least, it seems fairly certain that there was no opportunity for courts to interpret the acts. How the courts would have construed them, had they been litigated, must remain a matter of conjecture. Even so, it is possible to infer the theory of copyright underlying them, and the theory arrived at would be considerably different had the preambles not been written.

The dominant idea of copyright underlying the state statutes was the idea of copyright as an author's right. More to the point, however, the state lawmakers must have been aware of the choice of making copyright an author's right or a publisher's right. The title of the Statute of Anne was "An act for the encouragement of learning, by vesting copies of printed books in the authors *or* purchasers of such copies . . . " and the resolution of the Continental Congress had recommended the states to secure copyright to "authors *or* publishers."

With the exception of the South Carolina and Virginia statutes, not one of the state copyright acts specifically provided a copyright for the purchaser of copy, or publisher. The person who was entitled to copyright was the author and his heirs and assigns, and in one instance (Maryland), his executors and administrators or assigns. The language is characteristic of language used in the conveyance of real property, and it seems justified to say that copyright was given only to the author. This is further indicated by the language of the provisions for renewal terms which was, in five of the seven statutes providing for renewal terms, "shall return to the author thereof, if then living, and his heirs and assigns."[20] However, they granted copyright to persons who had purchased the copy or shares thereof, "in order to print or re-print the same," from the author prior to the date of the statute. Thus, the two statutes are not really exceptions as to the copyright for books published after the act became effective.

The other three ideas—that copyright is to promote learning, that it is a government grant, and that it is to prevent monopoly—were

20. The Maryland and South Carolina statutes provided, "shall return to the authors thereof." Five statutes, Massachusetts, Rhode Island, New Hampshire, North Carolina, and Virginia, contained no renewal term. Four of them gave a single term of twenty-one years. The North Carolina statute gave a single term of fourteen years.

also present in the state statutes. The most prominent of the ideas after the idea of copyright as an author's right was that the purpose of copyright is to encourage learning. The idea of copyright as a statutory grant is implicit in the existence of the statutes and is indicated by the provision that no one could take the benefit of the act unless he duly register the title,[21] or have the book published with the author's name.[22] As to monopoly, all of the statutes limited the term of copyright, and five of them—Connecticut, South Carolina, North Carolina, Georgia, and New York—contained price-control provisions because it was necessary "for the encouragement of learning, that the inhabitants of this State be furnished with useful books, &c., at reasonable prices."[23]

The main problem in analyzing the statutes is to explain how the three other ideas can be accommodated to the idea of copyright as an author's right in order to achieve a satisfactory law of copyright and literary property. Before dealing with the main problem, however, there are two questions which must first be answered: Precisely what were the rights copyright in the state statutes entailed? Was that copyright merely an affirmation of part of the author's rights, or did it create and include all of the author's rights?

The preambles state the purpose of securing to the author the profit of his works. The right was to print, publish, and sell, with the corollary that no one else print the copyrighted work without permission. Most important, however, three of the statutes—those of Connecticut, Georgia, and New York—specifically provided: "That nothing in this act shall extend to affect, prejudice, or confirm the rights which any person may have to the printing or publishing of any book, pamphlet, map, or chart, at common law, in cases not mentioned in this act . . . " The provision is not well phrased, and was apparently based on section IX of the Statute of Anne, which was intended to preserve the printing patents. Even so, it is indicative of a recognition that the author might have rights at common law not protected by the statute. And finally, the right of the author to be secured in his profits was based on the idea of natural rights.

---

21. Connecticut, New Jersey, Pennsylvania, Maryland, Virginia, North Carolina, South Carolina, Georgia, and New York.
22. Massachusetts, New Hampshire, Rhode Island.
23. Connecticut, Georgia, New York.

The next question, before dealing with the main problem of accommodating the four ideas, is why should the state copyright have entailed only protection for part of the author's rights when later the copyright granted by federal statute, containing substantially the same provisions, was held to be otherwise? The answer here is twofold. First, the dominant idea of the state copyright was protection for the author, and was based on the author's natural rights. So long as the dominant idea of copyright is that it is an author's natural right, it is only logical to construe that right so that it will not interfere with other rights the author might have. If copyright embraced all the rights of the author, there was the real possibility that he would be wholly dependent upon the statute for protection, without recourse to the common law to protect possible rights not provided for in the statute.

Second, the reason given in the preambles for providing copyright was to benefit society by encouraging authors to produce. On a pragmatic level, however, the reason was simply to prevent the piracy of printed works and provide a means of order for the book trade. The right to publish a work is an intangible right which is peculiarly susceptible to violation by others. Notwithstanding the use of natural rights as the basis of copyright by the lawmakers, the efficacy of this right without protection secured by statute was at least doubtful. The nature of the right involved made the need for protection immediate: a new nation could not leave the establishment of the right to be secure against piracy to the slow, deliberative processes of the common law. Somewhat inconclusively, however, the problem of what rights of the author should be recognized, in addition to the exclusive right of publication, could be left for common-law determination.

Because the state copyright was limited in scope, it is possible to relate the four basic ideas in the statutes in a harmonious fashion.

The idea of promoting learning was consistent with copyright as an author's right limited in scope for three reasons: (1) The author's statutory right is limited to the right to print, publish, and sell. Thus, the published work is available for any proper use a reader wishes to make of it, not inconsistent with the right of the author to his profits. (2) The author, even though he assigns the copyright, retains an interest to protect the integrity of his work, which is beneficial to learning because there is a right to prevent corrupt editions. (3) And, of course, the protection granted by copyright encourages publication.

The idea of copyright as a statutory grant was consistent with copyright as an author's right because it is simply a means of providing protection for published works. The type of interest involved makes statutory protection appropriate, and so long as the idea of protecting the author remains dominant, the provisions of the state are directory only, not mandatory.

Finally, the idea of copyright as an author's right was not inconsistent with the statutory limitations to prevent monopoly. Even though the copyright was based on the idea of natural rights, those rights must give way in the face of conflict with a paramount interest of society. Thus, it is reasonable to limit the term of copyright to prevent monopoly, even though an author has a natural right to his profits. The point that it is the perpetual copyright which is monopolistic has been discussed earlier, in connection with the history of copyright in England. However, the right of an author to protect his reputation does not present a problem of monopoly, and thus, even after the expiration of copyright, he should have this right.

The key to the above scheme is the limited scope of the copyright, and the result is really two bodies of law, a statutory law of copyright and a (potential) common law of literary property. If the four basic ideas of copyright are to be harmoniously related, it is essential that copyright be limited in scope, whether it is called an author's right or a publisher's right. Otherwise, since copyright provides only for the right of printing, publishing, and selling, there is a large area of the author's interest which is not covered by copyright and which cannot be protected after publication at common law because of copyright. If, for example, the author assigns his copyright, as is often the case, he no longer has any interest at all in his works. The above-stated result is, of course, what eventually happened in American copyright law, and one reason is that copyright ceased to be limited in scope and became the entire property interest of the author in his works after publication.

The relationship of the four basic ideas suggested above provides a basis for a theory of copyright to be inferred from the state acts. That theory is that copyright is a right to protect the author in securing his profits from the publication of his works by giving him the exclusive right of printing, publishing, and selling his works for a limited time, which right can be assigned to a publisher. It is a right which affirms and protects only those rights of the author pertaining to his economic interests. As such, it is a right to which a given work is subject, and neither confirms nor denies other rights of the author which might be appropriately recognized at common law.

Although the copyright of the American states' statutes was an author's right, and the English stationer's copyright was a publisher's right, there is a strong resemblance between them. The similarity is in the limited scope of both copyrights, which were rights to which a given work was subject, and did not constitute the whole property of a work. The analogy extends further: Both were the first copyrights to exist in their respective countries; and both were ignored, in the subsequent development of copyright, to the extent that they became historical curiosities for the purposes of copyright law.

The Constitutional Provision

The various state statutes on copyright made obvious the need for a power in Congress to provide for copyright. The state statutes varied in procedural detail; some of them provided that the act would not come into force until all states had enacted similar laws; and the majority of them extended protection to residents of other states only on the basis of reciprocity. As Madison said, writing in No. 43 of the Federalist Papers, "The states cannot separately make effectual provision for" copyright, and there was good reason for the framers of the Constitution to include the power to confer copyright in the miscellaneous powers granted to the legislative branch of the government.

The Constitutional Convention convened in May 1787, and its work was completed by September 17, but August 18 is the first date in the records with any reference to copyright. On that date, James Madison and Charles Pinckney each submitted lists of powers "as proper to be added to those of the general legislature."[24] The list submitted by Madison included three powers of particular interest: "To secure to literary authors their copyrights for a limited time. To establish a university. To encourage, by premiums and provisions, the advancement of useful knowledge and discoveries."[25]

24. V ELLIOT, DEBATES ON THE ADOPTION OF THE FEDERAL CONSTITUTION (2d ed.) 439–440 (1836), hereafter referred to as ELLIOT. Cf. I ELLIOT 247.
25. Id. at 440.

The list submitted by Pinckney included the power "To establish seminaries for the promotion of literature, and the arts and sciences. . . . To grant patents for useful inventions. To secure to authors exclusive rights for a limited time."[26]

Both proposals were unanimously "referred to the committee of detail which had prepared the report."[27] On September 5, "Mr. Brearly, from the committee of eleven" made a further report, which included a proposal that Congress be empowered " 'To promote the progress of science and the useful arts, by securing for limited times, to authors and inventors, the exclusive right to their respective writings and discoveries.' "[28] The provision was agreed to without debate,[29] and the copyright clause of the Constitution was created.

The four basic ideas pertaining to copyright which were prevalent at the time are all present in the federal copyright clause. Congress was empowered "To promote the progress of science and useful arts (learning), by securing (government grant) for limited times (monopoly), to authors. . . . the exclusive right (author's right) to their respective writings . . . "

The dominant idea in the minds of the framers of the Constitution appears to have been the promotion of learning. The proposals submitted by Madison and Pinckney, apparently arrived at independently, are instructive on this point. Both manifest an interest in having the federal government promote knowledge, and both provide for the author's copyright in addition to other provisions for this specific purpose—Madison by "premiums and provisions," and Pinckney by establishing seminaries.

The idea next in importance seems to have been protection for the author. The language used by both Madison and Pinckney indicates that copyright was to be statutory protection for a recognized right. Madison recommended the power "To secure to literary authors their copyrights for a limited time." Pinckney recommended the power "To secure to authors exclusive rights for a limited time." Madison's language implies the recognition of copyright as a pre-existing right, and Pinckney's language implies a limited concept of copyright apart from

26. *Ibid.*
27. *Ibid.*
28. V ELLIOT 511, *cf.* I ELLIOTT 285.
29. *Id.* at 512.

an author's general property interest. Madison's language in particular indicates that he thought the author had a common-law copyright; writing in No. 43 of the Federalist Papers, he made the point explicit, saying, "The copyright of authors has been solemnly adjudged, in Great Britain, to be a right of common law."

The idea of statutory privilege was obviously in the minds of the framers, because the clause gave Congress the power to enact a copyright statute. The use of the word "securing" indicates that the statutory copyright was to affirm and protect an existing right, not create one. And the language of Pinckney's recommendations, "To grant patents . . . " and "To secure to authors . . . " indicates that the choice of words was made advisedly.

The idea of monopoly is manifested in the phrase "limited times," but there is little other indication of how significant the founding fathers considered the danger of monopoly to be. The limited term of copyright had come to be so accepted that it may be the framers gave little thought to the idea of monopoly, simply accepting the fact that all statutory copyrights had been limited.

The constitution does not, of course, tell what copyright Congress was empowered to secure, and does not even use the word *copyright*. The copyright clause, however, is one of the few clauses, and probably the only one, which gave Congress a power to enact a statute of the kind twelve of the thirteen states had already enacted. It seems safe to assume that all the members of the Constitutional Convention were familiar with at least some of the state acts, and the copyright itself is consistent with the provisions of those acts. The emphasis in the state acts on securing the author's profits almost certainly did not escape attention, and it seems probable that the members of the convention had in mind a copyright limited in scope, which would affirm and protect only the author's economic right. The "exclusive right," as they undoubtedly understood it, was the right to print, publish, and sell. This right had to be exclusive, because copyright was to prevent the piracy of published works. Thus, the phrase "exclusive right" does not imply that the right was to be exclusive of any other rights the author might have.

The point that makes it difficult to infer the nature of the copyright the framers of the constitution had in mind is that the copyright clause also provides for patents. Yet, the history of patents and copyright indicates that this combination of the two meant that copyright was to be a right, limited in scope, and designed to protect the author's economic right.

Pinckney had recommended to the Convention that Congress be given the power "To *grant* patents for useful inventions," and the power "To *secure* to authors exclusive rights for a limited time."[30] This distinction between *grant* and *secure* takes on particular significance against the historical background of patents and copyrights. An inventor in England was never conceded to have the common-law right to a monopoly of manufacture by reason of his invention. The exclusive right of manufacture based on a new invention was derived solely from the prerogative of the sovereign, and was made statutory by the Statute of Monopolies. This was not true of copyright. The right of an author to the property in his works was recognized almost from the beginning; even when the "copy right" was granted by letters patent, the patentee was not relieved from the obligation of paying the author. By 1600, more than one hundred years before the Statute of Anne, the evidence on this point is beyond question, and whether Pinckney's choice of terms in connection with patents and copyrights was fortuitous or not, it is consistent with history.

The inclusion of copyrights and patents in the same clause can be explained on the basis that the right in both instances was an economic one. This is the only point at which the legal rights regarding writings and inventions coincided historically. When Madison said in No. 43 of the Federalist Papers, "The copyright of authors has been solemnly adjudged, in Great Britain, to be a right of common law. The right to useful inventions seems with equal reason to belong to the inventors," he was merely stating that the economic right of authors embodied in copyright was also appropriate for inventors.

The Constitution's copyright clause is so general that it is impossible to infer any one theory of copyright alone from the language. The fact that the clause contains the four basic ideas of copyright means that it will support, to some degree, four different theories of copyright, according to the importance attached to the various ideas. Thus,

---

30. Emphasis added.

if the dominant idea is the promotion of learning, the primary purpose of copyright is to promote learning, and the rights of the author are recognized only as an aid in furtherance of this purpose. The interest of the public is paramount, and copyright is only a statutory privilege, limited in time to prevent monopoly. If the dominant idea is the protection of the author, this purpose becomes paramount, and to the extent that copyright can be used to promote learning, it is so used, but not at the expense of protection for the author. As a statutory privilege, it simply affirms rights of the author, and the so-called monopoly of copyright is accepted, but limited in time.

When the dominant idea is that copyright is a statutory privilege, it is a device which creates rights for the author, but these rights are wholly subject to the statutory provisions, which are construed to prevent monopoly, to promote learning, and, almost incidentally, to protect the rights of the author.

Finally, if copyright is thought of as a device for preventing harmful monopoly, the result is similar to that achieved when the dominant idea is that copyright is a statutory privilege: the statute will be strictly construed in the interest of the public, and the author's rights become almost incidental.

The essential point here is that, regardless of which idea is dominant, the effect and importance of the ideas is determined by whether copyright is thought of as embracing only rights to which a work is subject or whether it constitutes the whole property interest of a work. If copyright is deemed to embrace the whole property interest of a work, regardless of which idea is dominant, the development of a common law of literary property is almost certainly foreclosed. On the other hand, if copyright is deemed to be only a right to which a given work is subject, no matter which idea is dominant, there is the possibility of developing a common law of literary property in conjunction with copyright. It is this point which makes the change of copyright from a publisher's right into an author's right so significant. It was this change which led to the idea of copyright's constituting the whole property interest of a work. One of the most important results of the change was that it led to the conclusion that statutory copyright under the Constitution does not affirm part of the author's right, but actually creates all of them.

The Copyright Act of 1790

The first federal copyright act, passed by the First Congress at its second session in 1790, was entitled, "An act for the encouragement of learning, by securing the copies of maps, charts, and books, to the authors and proprietors of such copies, during the times therein mentioned."[31] The statute contained only seven sections.

Section 1 provided for two copyrights, the copyright for maps, charts, and books already printed in the United States, and for maps, books, and charts to be printed or published. For books already printed, the persons entitled to copyright were the author and authors, being citizens or residents of the United States, who had not transferred the copyright, "his or their executors, administrators or assigns," and any person who was a citizen or resident of the United States, who had purchased the copyright "in order to print, reprint, publish or vend the same." The term was fourteen years. For maps, charts, and books not printed or published, the author, being a citizen or resident of the United States, "and his . . . executors, administrators or assigns" was entitled to "the sole right and liberty of printing, reprinting, publishing and vending" for the term of fourteen years. A like renewal term was provided for an author living, and a citizen or resident of the United States, at the expiration of the first term and his "executors, administrators, or assigns."

Section 2 indicates that the purpose of copyright was to protect printed works from piracy. There were three ways of infringing copyright: (1) to print, reprint, or publish a copyrighted work; (2) to import copies of copyrighted works; and (3) to sell a work which infringed a copyright, with knowledge that the work was an infringing copy. None of these acts was unlawful if the consent of the "author or proprietor thereof" was obtained in writing, "signed in the presence of two or more credible witnesses." An offender was to forfeit all the infringing works to the author or proprietor of copyright "who shall forth with destroy the same," and be fined fifty cents for every infringing sheet found in his possession, to be recovered in an action of debt. One half of the sum recovered was to go to the United States, the other to the copyright owner. Such actions were to be commenced

---

31. 1 Stat. 124.

"within one year after the cause of action shall arise, and not after-wards."

The method for acquiring copyright was provided in Section 3. It required that a printed copy of the title be deposited "in the clerk's office of the district court where the author or proprietor shall reside." Within two months from the date thereof, a copy of the record was to be published "in one or more of the newspapers printed in the United States, for the space of four weeks."

Under the provisions of Section 4, the author or proprietor of copy-right was, within six months after publication, to deliver a copy of the work to the Secretary of State.

Section 5 permitted the pirating of foreign works. It provided: "That nothing in this act shall be construed to extend to prohibit the im-portation or vending, reprinting, or publishing within the United States, of any map, chart, book or books, written, printed, or pub-lished by any person not a citizen of the United States, in foreign parts or places without the jurisdiction of the United States."

Section 6 provided protection for manuscripts. Any person who pub-lished any manuscript without consent of the author or proprietor thereof "(if such author or proprietor be a citizen of or resident in these United States) shall be liable to suffer and pay to the said author or proprietor all damages occasioned by such injury . . ."[32]

The four basic ideas of copyright—author's right, promotion of learning, government grant, and monopoly—are all present in the statute. But the tone of the federal act is completely different from that of the state acts and the constitutional provision. The ideas of pro-tecting the author and promoting learning have become subordinated to the ideas that copyright is a government grant and a monopoly. Only the title of the act mentions learning, and as in the Statute of Anne, the proprietor of copyright is given almost equal billing with the author.

The idea that pervades the statute is that copyright is a govern-ment grant, a statutory privilege—not a right. This idea is apparent in the most striking aspect of the statute, the limitation of its benefits

---

32. Section 7 allowed a defendant to "plead the general issue, and give the special matter in evidence" in any action under the statute.

to citizens or residents of the United States. This theme is carried throughout the act—only persons who are citizens and residents of "these United States" can acquire copyright; only authors who are citizens or residents at the expiration of the first term of copyright are entitled to the renewal term; no work copyrighted under the act can be imported without the consent of the author or proprietor thereof; but the statute did not prohibit the importation, selling, reprinting, or publishing "within the United States" any work "written, printed, or published by any person not a citizen of the United States, in foreign parts or places without the jurisdiction of the United States"; and even the protection for unpublished manuscripts is limited to manuscripts of those who were citizens or residents of "these United States."

Why the statute should have been so restrictive in application is something of a mystery. The source of the idea that, to acquire copyright, a person had to be a citizen or resident of the United States was apparently the state statutes. Only two of those statutes, those of Maryland and South Carolina, did not require that the author be a citizen, inhabitant, or resident of the United States to obtain copyright. There was good reason for this provision in the state acts, because it made clear that copyright was available for citizens and residents of all the states, not merely those of the state of the statute in question. The source of the idea of preventing the importation of copyrighted works seems also to be the state statutes. Only three of the state acts, those of Massachusetts, New Hampshire, and New Jersey, did not contain similar provisions. Again, there was good reason for this prohibition; it was necessary to insure complete protection because of state lines, and a similar need may have been felt by a new nation, intending to protect itself against the established trade in England.

The source of the idea of permitting the importation, reprinting, and publishing of foreign works not eligible for copyright under the statute was apparently section VII of the Statute of Anne. That section, however, was aimed at the monopoly of the English booksellers and the Stationers' Company, and did not legalize piracy of foreign works; it simply provided that the act should not be construed to prohibit "the importation, vending, or selling" of books in a foreign language printed beyond the sea.

While the idea of monopoly is not explicit in the statute, *e.g.*, there are no price-control provisions, it is implicit in the restrictive nature of the whole act. And when one considers the restrictive limitations in the statute, the limiting of its benefits to citizens and residents of the United States, the one-year limitation for bringing actions, and the legalizing of piracy, it is difficult to come to any conclusion except that the copyright provided for was wholly statutory, without any reliance upon natural rights of the author. The conclusion that inevitably follows is that the copyright under the federal act did not, as did the copyright under the state acts, merely affirm and protect rights of the author; it created them.

The federal statute indicates not only the power of ideas, but the importance of understanding ideas in context. If the copyright under the statute is thought of as creating all the rights of the author after publication, it is because of the idea that copyright is a statutory privilege, granted at the will of the government. This is a complete reversal of ideas from a recognition of natural rights in the author in the state statutes. So complete a change in so short a time is almost impossible to explain satisfactorily. The earliest state statute, Connecticut's, was enacted in 1783, only seven years before the federal act, and the last, New York's, was enacted in 1786, only four years before the federal act. Moreover, this was the era of natural rights, the Rights of Man, the Declaration of Independence, and the Bill of Rights. The only explanation is a confusion of ideas, and there is indication of such a confusion.

Two sections of the federal act—Section 5, permitting the piracy of foreign works, and Section 6, protecting unpublished manuscripts—are apparently based on a misunderstanding of two provisions, Sections VII and IX, of the Statute of Anne. Section VII of the Statute of Anne was directed at the monopoly of the booksellers and the Stationers' Company. It was to allow books to be imported, not to be pirated, as under Section 5. One reason for including that provision in the Statute of Anne was undoubtedly because of the restrictions on importation of books under the acts of censorship. Section IX of the Statute of Anne was merely to save copyrights granted by the printing patents, and was picked up in three of the state acts, those of Connecticut, Georgia, and New York, as a basis for protecting common-

law rights. In the federal act, protection was given simply for unpublished manuscripts. The implication is that there was no such
right at common law, but the right of the author to prevent publication
of his manuscript without permission was the one right of the author
which had been clearly recognized at common law.

Had the dominant idea in the federal act, that copyright is only a
statutory grant, been related to the natural rights of the author, it is
probable that copyright would not have been held to be the only
source of the author's rights after publication. Even without the idea
of natural rights, had copyright not become an author's right, probably rights of the author not inconsistent with the terms of the statute
would have been recognized. The rights under copyright granted by the
statute were not essentially different from those under the stationer's
copyright, except, of course, for the limited term. The right granted
was "the sole right and liberty of printing, reprinting, publishing, and
vending." There were three ways of infringing copyright: to print
a copyrighted work, to import copies of a copyrighted work, and to
sell infringing copies with knowledge that they were infringing copies.
Thus, functionally, the American copyright was still a right to which
a given work was subject. But because it was thought of as an author's
right, and was a statutory grant, it became the exclusive source of the
author's protection after publication.

Before the question of copyright and literary property was brought
to the Supreme Court in 1834, the 1790 statute had been amended in
1802,[33] and was replaced by the first general revision of the U.S. copyright laws in 1831.[34] There was another amendment in 1834.[35] The
principal changes made by the 1802 amendment were to require that
the mandatory newspaper advertisement of the 1790 act be inserted
in the title page or on the page immediately following the title page
of all copyrighted books, and to provide copyright protection for prints.
The 1831 revision extended copyright protection to musical compositions, extended the term of copyright to twenty-eight years, and permitted a living widow or children of a deceased author to acquire the
renewal term. There were technical changes, but the most significant

33. 2 Stat. 171.
34. 4 Stat. 436.
35. 4 Stat. 728.

change was in Section 11, which made it unlawful for any person to falsify notice of copyright on a work without having acquired the copyright.

The 1834 act provided that assignments of copyright, "being proved or acknowledged in such as deed for the conveyances of land," could be recorded in the office where the original copyright was recorded and deposited.

This continued legislative activity only enhanced the idea that rights in a published work were granted solely by statute, and supported the dominant idea in the *Wheaton* case, that copyright was a means to prevent monopoly.

10

The *Wheaton* Case

IN JUNE 1828, Richard Peters, who had succeeded Henry Wheaton as reporter for the United States Supreme Court the previous year, sent out a circular entitled "Proposals for publishing, by subscription, the cases decided in the Supreme Court of the United States, from its organization to the close of January term, 1827."[1]

So began the case of *Wheaton v. Peters*,[2] the American analogue to *Donaldson v. Beckett*.

Peters's plan, to publish in six volumes decisions contained in the twenty-five volumes published by his three predecessors—four by Alexander Dallas, nine by William Cranch, and twelve by Wheaton—was an ominous one for the former reporters, particularly for Wheaton. The early custom was for the court reporters to be compensated for their work by the sale of their reports of the court's decisions, published at their own expense. Dallas and Cranch had received no pay, but Wheaton, after a year as reporter, prevailed upon Congress to provide him with an annual salary of $1,000. In return, he was to publish the decisions within six months after they were rendered and deliver eighty copies to the Secretary of State for use by various government officials.[3]

Wheaton had arranged for Matthew Carey & Sons of Philadelphia to publish his reports, but the sale of the first volume, published in 1816, was so small that before the publication of the second volume in 1817, Carey had assigned his rights as publisher to Robert Donald-

1. HICKS, MEN AND BOOKS FAMOUS IN THE LAW 205 (1921).
2. 33 U.S. (8 Pet.) 591 (1834).
3. Act of Feb. 3, 1817, c. 63, 3 Stat. 376.

son of New York. The assignment gave Donaldson the right to publish an edition of from 1,000 to 1,500 copies of each subsequent volume.

Peters's circular announcing his plan of publication brought a letter from Cranch, saying that Cranch must protect his legal rights, since he was still out of pocket by $1,000 for the publication of the last three volumes of his report,[4] but only Wheaton took legal action. Although the sale of his reports had not been large, "there was prospect of a growing and continuous sale," and Wheaton's *Reports* were made particularly valuable "not only on account of the nature and importance of the decisions, but also because of the manner in which they are reported and the extensive supplementary material added by Wheaton."[5]

Despite a plea from Donaldson, Wheaton's publisher, not to proceed, Peters went ahead with his plan of publishing *Condensed Reports of Cases in the Supreme Court of the United States* in six volumes. In February 1831, he published his third volume, which included the first volume of Wheaton's Reports.

In May 1831, Wheaton and Donaldson, claiming a copyright under both the Copyright Act and the common law, filed a bill in the Circuit Court in Pennsylvania against Peters and his publisher, John Grigg, seeking an injunction and an accounting.

The complaint alleged that Peters had published in his *Condensed Reports* "without any material abbreviation or alteration, all the reports of cases in the said first volume of Wheaton's reports. . . . "[6] Peters denied that the *Condensed Reports* was in violation of complainant's rights in Wheaton's *Reports* because (1) the requisites of the Copyright Act had not been complied with; (2) there was no common-law copyright in the United States, and (3) Wheaton's *Reports* was not a work entitled to copyright, either statutory or common-law. There were four opinions rendered in the case—one in the circuit court; and three, the majority and two dissenting opinions, in the Supreme Court.

The opinion of Judge Joseph Hopkinson in the circuit court[7] dealt

4. HICKS, *op. cit.*, 207.
5. *Id.* at 202.
6. 33 U.S. (8 Pet.) 591, 594.
7. Wheaton v. Peters, 29 Fed. Cas. 862 (No. 17486) (C.C.E.D. Pa. 1832).

first with the claim of a copyright under the statute. The alleged de-
fect in Wheaton's statutory copyright was his failure to deliver to the
Secretary of State a copy of the book within six months of its publication, as required by the fourth section of the Act of 1790. The question was whether this was essential for the acquisition of copyright.
After concluding as a matter of fact that complainants had failed to
prove delivery of the book (although eighty copies of the work had
been delivered to the Secretary of State under another statute), Judge
Hopkinson concluded that such delivery was essential to secure a
copyright.

In construing the copyright statute, Judge Hopkinson's basic premise was that copyright was a grant from the government, a privilege,
not a right. From this, it followed that all of the statutory requirements had to be strictly complied with in order to obtain copyright.
"When a statute creates a right, confers a benefit, a privilege on any
individual," he said, "and at the same time . . . enjoins upon him to do
certain things in relation to the right or privilege granted, can we
separate them . . . ?"[8] The grantee, he reasoned, has a duty which is
as much a part of the creation as the grant to which it relates. This
was because "The public, the citizens of a community, acting by their
representatives, confer upon an author certain privileges or rights for
his exclusive benefit; and to protect him in the enjoyment of them, they
impose certain penalties or give certain remedies against any person
who shall violate these rights. But some protection is due on the other
side, that innocent and ignorant invaders of the privilege may not be
involved in suits and penalties, by the want to accessible means of
information of the subject and extent of the grant."[9] Consequently,
the delivery of a copy to the Secretary of State was "an essential part
of the scheme for the encouragement of authors, so as not to bring
others innocently into trouble or, it may be, ruin."[10]

To Judge Hopkinson, the claims of a copyright to be had under a
statute and at common law were wholly inconsistent. Since the passing
of the statute, he said, the claim was put under the common law.
"These are technical refinements which would occur only to the learned

8. 29 Fed. Cas. 862, 866–867.
9. *Id.* at 867.
10. *Ibid.*

ingenuity."[11] The author had forfeited his claim to the remedies of the statute, by virtue of which he claimed the right, because he did not obey the injunctions of the statute. But he was still claiming the right, to be enforced in another way, "notwithstanding such a disobedience of the injunctions of the statute as have forfeited its remedies."[12]

On the question of the common-law copyright generally, Judge Hopkinson first concluded that there was no federal common law, and that one must look to the states for this law. Even the states, however, did not adopt the whole of English common law, and he concluded that the asserted common-law copyright of England had never been adopted by any "one of the United States."

The very existence of a common-law copyright in England was doubtful. "What is its history—its judicial history? It is wrapt in obscurity and uncertainty."[13] He discussed briefly the *Millar* and *Donaldson* cases, and concluded that to recognize the common-law copyright as co-existing with the statutory copyright would produce "uncertainty and inconvenience." Who, he asked, would take for a limited period under the statute what he could enjoy in perpetuity by the common law? What is there to prevent an author, he wondered, from using the statutory copyright and then going back to the common-law right? Judge Hopkinson resolved the problem simply: "We shall keep ourselves free from such embarrassments . . . by resting the protection of authors upon the statutes expressly enacted for that purpose, and in believing that our legislature has done that which is just to them, and without inconvenience and danger to the public."[14] He dissolved the injunction and dismissed the bill.

The case came before the Supreme Court in the January term, 1834. The members of the court were Chief Justice John Marshall, and Associate Justices Henry Baldwin, Gabriel Duval, John McLean, Joseph Story, and Smith Thompson. Justice William Johnson was absent "from indisposition during the whole term."

The justices could not have looked to their task with much pleasure, for their relationships with the former court reporter and his successor

11. *Id.* at 868.
12. *Ibid.*
13. *Id.* at 871.
14. *Id.* at 872.

must have been characterized by a degree of intimacy which made the dispute a personally distasteful one. And they may well have looked to the larger issue of the "great question of literary property" as a means of rising above the personal bitterness the dispute had engendered. They had an almost clean slate, for only two American decisions had been rendered on copyright during the forty-four-year period from 1790 to 1834,[15] and they were assisted by able lawyers. Counsel for Wheaton were Daniel Webster and Elijah Paine, and for Peters, Thomas Sergeant and J. R. Ingersoll, all giants of the American bar.

The members of the court split, four to two, and the majority and dissenting justices agreed on only one limited point, that opinions of the Court could not be copyrighted. The majority opinion concluded with the statement: "It may be proper to remark, that the court are unanimously of opinion, that no reporter has or can have any copyright in the written opinions delivered by this court; and that the judges thereof cannot confer on any reporter any such right."[16] However, "the marginal notes, or syllabus of the cases and points decided, the abstract of the record and evidence, and the index to the several

---

15. The first case, Nichols v. Ruggles, 3 Day 145 (Conn. 1808), was an action of debt in the Supreme Court of Errors of Connecticut by a printer for charges including a sum for printing part of a book entitled THE FEDERAL CALCULATOR. The defense was that the contract for the printing was void, as the printing infringed another's copyright; but there was no proof that the copyright owner had published the title of his book in a newspaper or delivered a copy of the work to the Secretary of State as required by statute. The Court held that these provisions were merely directory, "and constitute no part of the essential requisites for securing the copyright," 3 Day at 157, and upheld the copyright. The second case, Ewer v. Coxe, 8 Fed. Cas. 917 (No. 4584) (C.C.E.D. Pa. 1824), was an action in federal court for the infringement of the copyright of a book entitled THE PHARMACOPOEIA OF THE UNITED STATES OF AMERICA by defendants who published a work entitled THE AMERICAN DISPENSATORY. The plaintiff had deposited copy of the title of the work in the clerk's office of the District Court of Massachusetts, but had neither published notice in the paper nor sent a copy to the Secretary of State. Justice Washington was of the opinion that under the Act of 1790, the depositing of the title of the work was sufficient to secure the copyright; but the amendment to that act, passed in 1802, required the publishing of a copy of the record of title in the copyrighted work. The language in this amendment, referring to the requirements of the 1790 act, was held to make all of the steps essential to copyright.

16. 33 U.S. (8 Pet.) 591, 668.

volumes"[17] were subject to copyright, and since it was not denied that this material was freely copied, the fact that the decisions themselves could not be copyrighted did not dispose of the controversy between the parties.

There were two main points in the case. The first was: Does an author have a common-law copyright in his work after publication? Subsidiary to this point were the questions of whether a federal common law existed; whether the common-law copyright existed in England; and whether, assuming its existence, Pennsylvania incorporated the common-law copyright in its common law. The majority held that no federal common law existed; the dissenters took the position that this was irrelevant to the case, as the law of Pennsylvania applied. As to the existence of the common-law copyright in England, the majority thought this was much in doubt, and the dissenters argued that it existed without question. The majority did not think that Pennsylvania, assuming the existence of a common-law copyright in England, had incorporated that right into its common law; and the dissenters took the opposite view.

The second main point of the case was the question whether the requirements of the Copyright Act for securing copyright had to be strictly complied with. Subsidiary to this point were the questions of whether these requirements were mandatory or merely directory, and whether the complainants in the case had complied with them. The majority held that all the requirements of the act were mandatory, and the dissenters thought part of them merely directory. As to whether the complainants had complied with the requirements, the majority was not satisfied with the circuit court's finding on this point, and remanded the case for a determination of fact by a jury. The dissenters did not discuss this point.

Apart from the subsidiary issues in the case, it is apparent that *Wheaton v. Peters* was a decision based on policy involving considerations other than the meaning of statutory language. The varying interpretations (all within the limits of reason) of the same historical material given in the three opinions are indicative of this, and if one accepts the basic premise of any of the opinions, he cannot fault its

17. 33 U.S. (8 Pet.) 591, 698g (Brightly's 3rd ed.).

reasoning. Thus, the most important factor in analyzing the opinions is to determine the basic premises on which they were predicated.

The basic premise of the majority opinion was simply that copyright is a monopoly. Justice John McLean, writing for the majority, said that there can be no doubt that an author at common law has a property in his manuscript, and can obtain redress against anyone who improperly obtains a copy and publishes it; "but this is a very different right from that which asserts a perpetual and exclusive property in the future publication of the work, after the author shall have published it to the world."[18] The author, he said, is entitled to the fruits of his labor, and he realizes them by the transfer of his manuscript, or the sale of his work when first published. "A book is valuable on account of the matter it contains, the ideas it communicates, the instruction or entertainment it affords. Does the author hold a perpetual property in these? Is there an implied contract by every purchaser of his book, that he may realize whatever instruction or entertainment which the reading of it shall give, but shall not write out or print its contents?"[19]

With this view of copyright, it would be difficult indeed to recognize a common-law copyright, particularly when its existence was so much in doubt, and it is not surprising that Justice McLean concluded that Congress, in enacting the copyright statute, did not legislate in reference to existing rights. "Congress, then, by this act, instead of sanctioning an existing right, as contended for, created it."[20] Nor is it surprising that Justice McLean gave the copyright statute a strict construction. As to the requirements for securing copyright, the depositing of a title of the work in the clerk's office of the district court, the publishing of the clerk's record in the book, public notice in the newspapers, and the depositing of a copy of the book with the Secretary of State, it was contended that only the first two were essential. Justice McLean disagreed. He agreed that the right accrued when the clerk made a record and it was published in the book, and that the other two conditions were in the nature of conditions subsequent. "But the inquiry is made, shall the nonperformance of these subsequent condi-

18. 33 U.S. (8 Pet.) at 658.
19. Ibid.
20. 33 U.S. (8 Pet.) at 660–661.

tions operate as a forfeiture of the right? The answer is, that this is not a technical grant on precedent and subsequent conditions. All the conditions are important; the law requires them to be performed; and, consequently, their performance is essential to a perfect title."[21]

The basic premise of the dissenting opinions is that an author, as the creator of a work, is entitled to be protected in and to enjoy his property as a matter of justice and equity. Justice Smith Thompson entertained no doubts as to the existence of the common-law copyright, and said that "Every one should enjoy the reward of his labor, the harvest where he has sown, or the fruit of the tree which he has planted. . . . [L]iterary property is . . . it seems founded upon the same principle of general utility to society, which is the basis of all other moral rights and obligations. Thus considered, an author's copyright ought to be esteemed an invaluable right, established in sound reason and abstract morality."[22]

From this, it followed that the Copyright Act did not create a new right, but protected an existing one, and it gave "cumulative security or protection," which attached from the recording of the title of the book in the clerk's office. Thus, even "if the statute should be considered as creating a new right, that right vests upon recording the title. This is the only prerequisite, or condition precedent, to the vesting of the right."[23] But, Justice Thompson said, even if the complainants have not made out a complete right under the Copyright Act, the term for which the copyright is secured had not expired. "[A]nd according to the admitted and settled doctrine in England, under the Statute of Anne, the common-law remedy exists during that period."[24]

Justice Henry Baldwin thought the complainants entitled to an injunction on the basis of their long-continued peaceable and quiet possession of the copyright. But as the other justices did not agree with him, he proceeded to other issues in the case. Except for this point, he seems to have fully concurred with his fellow dissenter. He held the common-law right to exist, and said that, "So far from any act of Congress having impaired this common-law right, they seem to me to

21. *Id.* at 664–665.
22. *Id.* at 671.
23. *Id.* at 692.
24. *Id.* at 698.

recognize its existence, and to have been intended to afford it additional security."[25] But assuming no copyright independent of the statute, he would have construed the statute liberally in its requirements for the securing of copyright. "I cannot believe," he said, "that it was ever intended by Congress, that any publication in a paper, or delivery of the book, should be indispensable to the vesting, as well as the enjoyment of the right."[26]

The striking point about the premises of the majority and the dissenters is that they are polar, one proceeding from the interest of the public, the other from the interest of the individual creator. This is not to say that both views did not take into account the interest of both the public and the individual author; it is to say that their premises brought the justices to different conclusions as to how best to resolve the conflict between the public's interest in learning and the author's interest in his property. The majority, viewing copyright as a monopoly, were content to protect the author's property for a limited period under the conditions prescribed by the statute. To do otherwise would be contrary to the public interest. The dissenters, on the other hand, seemed to think that the best way to protect the public interest would be to give unlimited protection to the author's property.

Judge Hopkinson's decision dissolving the injunction was reversed, and the case was remanded to the circuit court to determine whether the copyright statute had been complied with; but the battle was over. The concept of copyright—the statutory grant of a monopoly for the benefit of the author—was settled.

Wheaton took his loss bitterly. He charged that Judge Hopkinson had corresponded with Justice Joseph Story about the case, and that Story had agreed "to confirm above" what Hopkinson decided below, and that Hopkinson had taken advantage of Justice Henry Baldwin's absence because of illness to dissolve the injunction in the Circuit Court.[27] Wheaton's former friendship with Story was destroyed, and he explained Chief Justice Marshall's actions on the ground that he never studied the cause. "He pinned his faith on the sleeve of his prevaricating brother, believing that, if the latter had any leaning it

25. 33 U.S. 698*m* (Brightly's 3rd ed.).
26. 33 U.S. 698*z* (Brightly's 3rd. ed.).
27. BAKER, HENRY WHEATON 127 (1937).

was toward me on the friendship the hypocrite once professed—and which doubtless still continued to pour into that venerable man's ear."[28]

The regret, however, was not all on one side. Justice Story, in a letter to Chancellor James Kent of New York, dated May 17, 1834, wrote:

I am sorry for the controversy between Mr. Wheaton and Peters, and did all I could to prevent a public discussion of the delicate subject of copyright . . . The strict construction of the statute of Congress we adopted with vast reluctance, but after turning it fully and freely to our minds, the majority of the Court did not see how they could give any other construction to it. I wish Congress would make some additional provision on the subject to protect authors, of whom I think no one more meritorious than Mr. Wheaton. You, as a Judge, have frequently had occasion to know how many bitter cups we are not at liberty to pass by. . . .[29]

28. *Id.* at 131.
29. WARREN, THE SUPREME COURT IN UNITED STATES HISTORY 786–787 (1926).

11

The Continuing Discontent

THE *Wheaton* DECISION remains the bedrock case of American copyright law. The concept of copyright it laid down—a statutory grant of a monopoly for the benefit of the author—continues as basic doctrine. Yet, the body of law based upon this concept has proved to be unsatisfactory from the beginning. The discontent has continued.

Justice Joseph Story, the leading expositor of American copyright law in the first half of the nineteenth century, gave expression to this discontent when he lamented the fact that it was not possible to "lay down any general principles applicable" to all copyright cases.[1] A few years later, Justice John McLean, author of the majority opinion in the *Wheaton* case, echoed this sentiment when he said, "On the subject of copyright, there is a painful uncertainty in the authorities, and indeed there is an inconsistency in some of them."[2]

The discontent was also manifested in Congress. The copyright of 1790 was followed by three general revisions, in 1831,[3] 1870,[4] and 1909.[5] In 1904, by which time more than two hundred copyright bills had been introduced in Congress—almost two a year—the Register of Copyrights wrote, "The [copyright] laws as they stand fail to give the protection required, are difficult of interpretation, application, and administration, leading to misapprehension and misunderstanding, and

1. Folsom v. Marsh, 9 Fed. Cas. 342, 344 (No. 4901) C.C.D. Mass. 1841).
2. Story's Executors v. Holcomb, 23 Fed. Cas. 171, 172 (No. 13497) (C.C.D. Ohio 1847).
3. Act of Feb. 3, 1831, c. 16, 4 Stat. 463.
4. Act of July 8, 1870, c. 230, 16 Stat. 198.
5. Act of March 4, 1909, c. 320, 35 Stat. 1075, 17 U.S.C. § 1 *et. seq.*

in some directions are open to abuses."[6] The Copyright Act of 1909, to which the above comments were a prelude, has served for almost sixty years—but not well; and once again, after a study of some ten years, Congress is considering a revision of the copyright statute.

The case law confirms the continuing discontent, for Henry Wheaton was not the only author who suffered bitter personal defeats under the copyright statutes. To mention only a few examples, Harriet Beecher Stowe failed in an action for copyright infringement against a defendant who translated *Uncle Tom's Cabin* into German.[7] The translation was not a copy. Oliver Wendell Holmes, the father of Justice Holmes, lost his copyright to *Autocrat of the Breakfast Table*[8] and *Professor at the Breakfast Table*[9] because they were published serially in the *Atlantic Monthly* without copyright before being published and copyrighted in book form. And the author of two copyrighted songs, "Little Cotton Dolly" and "Kentucky Babe Schottische," failed in an action for infringement against a defendant who transscribed the songs on piano rolls for mechanical pianos.[10] The piano rolls were not copies. Yet, an advertising poster for a circus was protected against copyright infringement[11] as, more recently, was a lampbase statuette.[12]

The continuation of the inconsistency of which Justice McLean spoke can be explained in part by the fact that technology outpaced the law. The continued absence of general principles of which Justice Story spoke, however, has remained, and requires a more fundamental explanation.

The starting point is the concept of copyright laid down in the *Wheaton* case—the statutory grant of a monopoly for the benefit of the author. Monopoly is, by and large, an opprobrious term in American law, and the statutory grant of a monopoly required strong reasons. The reasons were two: The grant of a monopoly to authors was neces-

6. U.S. Copyright Office Bulletin No. 8, *Copyright in Congress 1789–1904* 7 (1904).

7. Stowe v. Thomas, 23 Fed. Cas. 201 (No. 13514) (C.C.E.D. Pa. 1853).

8. Holmes v. Hurst, 174 U.S. 82 (1899).

9. Miffin v. R. H. White Co., 190 U.S. 260 (1903).

10. White-Smith Music Publishing Co. v. Apollo Co., 209 U.S. 1 (1908).

11. Bleistein v. Donaldson Lithographing Co., 158 U.S. 239 (1903).

12. Mazer v. Stein, 347 U.S. 201 (1954).

sary to "promote science and useful arts," as stated in the Constitution, or for "the encouragement of learning" as stated in the preamble to the English Statute of Anne; and the author, as creator of a work, was entitled to economic rewards, or, as the Supreme Court stated in 1954, "Sacrificial days devoted to . . . creative activities deserve rewards commensurate with the services rendered."[13]

The rationalization was supported by two factors: a practical need to protect published books from piracy, and by history. The idea that copyright was a monopoly was not only accepted; it was obvious. The reasoning, however, did not take into account the presence of another idea, less obvious, that was to affect the development of copyright— the idea that copyright was also a legal affirmation of a natural right of the author. The presence of this idea in conjunction with the idea that copyright was a monopoly created a conceptual dilemma. The dilemma, however, went unrecognized, because both the monopoly and the natural rights of the author were limited. The monopoly was the exclusive right to reproduce the work for sale; the natural right of the author was thought of as only the economic right to profits from his works.

The two ideas, however, did not remain limited; they expanded. The term "monopoly," in connection with copyright, first meant the exclusive right to reproduce a work for sale; and in this limited sense, it protected the form of the work. Gradually, however, it came to protect the content of the work, as well. In terms of copyright, this meant that protection came to be against plagiarism as well as piracy.

The superficial distinction between piracy and plagiarism is that when one pirates a work, he reproduces it for sale without permission, perhaps with due credit to the author; when he plagiarizes, he adopts another's work as his own. The fundamental distinction between protecting a work against piracy and protecting it against plagiarism, however, is the difference between protecting the form of a work and protecting its content, between protecting the particular form of expression of ideas and protecting the ideas themselves.

To give one the exclusive right to reproduce a given work is to give him one kind of monopoly; to give him the exclusive right to the use

13. Mazer v. Stein, 347 U.S. 201, 219.

of ideas is to give him another, clearly less compatible with the public interest. And it is in the protection of ideas that the monopoly of copyright has broadened so measureably.

The idea that copyright is a natural right of the author was a major factor not always recognized in this process of the expansion of copyright. Since copyright was the sole protection available to the author after publication, it was almost inevitable that the scope of protection enlarge, in view of the fact that authors' rights were viewed as natural rights. The idea that copyright was an objectionable monopoly was difficult to maintain in the absence of any monopoly of the book trade like that which had occurred in England and in the face of the idea that copyright was an author's right protecting his natural rights. "Sacrificial days devoted to . . . creative activities," as the Supreme Court had said, "deserve rewards commensurate with the services rendered." Thus, the fear of monopoly abated, with a consequent expansion in the scope of copyright supported by the socially acceptable aim of protecting the author.

Another major factor in this development was the absence of any consideration of the role of the publisher in the law of copyright itself. One of the ironies of copyright history is that, although copyright began as a publisher's right, consideration of the publisher's interest in copyright as such disappeared altogether, after copyright came to be considered an author's right. The explanation may be in the assumption that the publisher's rights were derived from the author and thus, in dealing with copyright, only the author's rights need be considered. If this is so, the assumption was wrong. The rights of copyright never came from the author; at first, they were granted by the Stationer's Company; they then came from the copyright statutes. The right to acquire copyright, of course, came from the author. But this was entirely different from the rights to be had by virtue of the copyright itself. Once the copyright was acquired, there was no distinction between the author and the publisher insofar as the rights were concerned.

The ignoring of the publisher's interest in copyright led to the facile assumption that copyright was concerned with only two major interests, those of the author and the public. The fact that the publisher was ignored did not change the fact that copyright is concerned with three major interests, those of the author, the publisher, and the public, instead of only two. It did, however, lead the lawmakers to treat a three-dimensional problem in a two-dimensional context. They thereby precluded themselves from effectively dealing with the two problems— monopoly and author's rights—each on its own terms, for they viewed them as one.

To deal with the two problems, each on its own terms, required a recognition of two factors: the source of the monopoly problem, and the nature of the author's rights.

The source of the monopoly problem was not the author, but the publisher. The control of a given work, whether by the publisher or the author, of course, is a monopoly of that work. The difference in the danger, however, is in the source of control and, thus, in the number of works each may control. The publisher's source is contract with the author; the author's control results from the fact of his creation. It is one thing for a publisher to have a monopoly of the works he acquires from a number of authors and another for an author to have a monopoly of the work he creates. Yet, because copyright was deemed to be wholly an author's right, even though it was available as well to the publisher, the lawmakers did not make the necessary distinctions between the publisher's interest and the author's interest which would have enabled them to deal directly with the danger of monopoly. Consequently, they attempted to deal with it indirectly, by limiting the author's rights—an attempt which failed because the idea of the author's natural rights led to an expansion of the monopoly of copyright.

Despite this development, the lawmakers seem to have directed no efforts toward determining what the rights of the author are or should be. The assumption, inherited from history, was that the rights were only economic rights. An author, however, has more than an economic interest in his work. He also has a creative interest.

The creative interest is the interest of the author as creator in maintaining the integrity of his work and his reputation in connection with it. Lord Mansfield, perhaps the greatest of the common-law judges in England, recognized this creative interest in his opinion in *Millar v. Taylor* when he said, "His [an author's] name ought not be used, against his will. It is an injury, by a faulty, ignorant incorrect edition, to disgrace his work and mislead the reader."[14] Justice Smith Thompson, dissenting in the *Wheaton* case, acknowledged the author's creative interest when he said, "An author's copyright ought to be esteemed an invaluable right, established in sound reason and abstract morality."[15] And Justice Oliver Wendell Holmes gave expression to the reason for recognizing the author's creative right: "Personality always contains something unique. It expresses its irregularity even in handwriting, and a very modest grade of art has in it something irreducible, which is one man's alone."[16]

Yet, the common law has never recognized the creative interest of the author as such. And Congress, in weighing the present copyright bill, considered but omitted statutory recognition for the author's creative interest as a moral right, the name by which it is called in civil-law countries.[17]

Had the draftsmen of the present bill considered the history of copyright more carefully, they might have reached a different conclusion. Despite the failure of the law to give explicit recognition to the author's creative interest in his work, that interest has played a major but unsuspected role in the law of copyright. What Congress failed to do directly, the courts did indirectly. The creative interest is a natural right of the author, and it was the desire to protect the author's natural right that was a major force in enlarging the scope of copyright. While that natural right was deemed to be the economic interest of the author, it was not so limited. The result is that copyright has come to encompass in fact the author's creative interest without explicit statutory sanction. Copyright gives the author absolute control of his work, and thus enables him to protect both the integrity of the work and his reputation in connection with it. The situation, however, is not as salutary as it may seem, for the protection is not given

14. Millar v. Taylor, 4 Burr. 2303, 2405, 98 Eng. Rep. 203, 256.
15. 33 U.S. (8 Pet.) 591, 671.
16. Bleistein v. Donaldson Lithographing Co., 188 U.S. 239, 250 (1903).
17. Staff of Senate Comm. on the Judiciary, 86th Cong., 1st Sess., *Studies on Copyright Law Revision*, Study No. 4, William Strauss, "The Moral Right of the Author," (Comm. Print 1960).

specifically to the author, but rather to the copyright owner. And the copyright owner, more often than not, is the publisher rather than the author.

To give explicit recognition to the author's creative interest would aid in placing other ideas of copyright in proper perspective. This is the primary lesson of history. The two most important of these ideas—that copyright is a monopoly, and that it is a natural right—both assumed undue significance in copyright development and obscured the basic point that copyright is fundamentally a trade-regulation device to protect intellectual property, necessary because of the uniqueness of that property. The question is not what rights copyright protects in the light of history, but what rights it should protect in view of its purpose and function.

The starting point for ascertaining the incidents appropriate to copyright is the author. What kind of interests does he, as creator, have in his works? To what extent, and in what manner, may these interests be protected, consistent with the interests of the publisher and society? The author's interests are of two types, economic and creative.

The basic interest is economic—an interest which the author shares with the publisher—and the principal function of copyright is to protect this interest. The protection of the economic interest, however, does not require that the copyright owner have absolute control of a work. It requires only that he have sufficient rights to protect his property against competitors. The publisher thus requires protection against other publishers (and economic competitors), not against the author or the individual user.

The author, however, may appropriately be given broader protection than the publisher for the purpose of protecting his creative interest. This interest is unique and appropriate for the author alone, and it should be recognized as a personal right, which is inalienable.

The development of the author's creative interest should be left to the federal courts. Congress has long pre-empted the field of copyright; indeed, the early experience of the state copyright statutes proves that the subject is one which requires a national rather than a local law, a fact brought home with greater force today, when modern communications serve to obliterate state lines.

Yet, the federal legislation deals only with copyright as an economic property, and leaves untouched the personal and creative interests of the author. This leaves it to the courts to develop a federal common law to recognize and give appropriate protection to these interests.

The existence of a federal common law is beyond question. True, the misnamed federal common law was struck down by Justice Louis D. Brandeis in *Erie Railroad* v. *Tompkins;*[18] but on the same day, a true federal common law was announced and applied in an interstate case.[19] The necessity and appropriateness of such a law has been excellently demonstrated by Judge Henry J. Friendly of the Court of Appeals for the Second Circuit.[20]

The problem of the author's creative interest is a delicate subject which, by its very nature, can best be developed by judges in the case-by-case method of the common law, for its development will require perceptive analysis and careful distinction. Yet, if properly done, it offers an escape from the continuing discontent with copyright law.

There is little doubt that a recognition of authors' creative rights could reshape American copyright law, not by changing fundamental ideas, but by bringing those ideas into proper recognition and perspective, and doing so consistently with the copyright statute. The existence of the author's creative rights would preclude the copyright owner from claiming absolute control of a copyrighted work, and yet would not preclude the protection of rights granted to him by statute. The division of rights resulting from a recognition of the separate natures of the creative interest and the economic interest would serve to inhibit the monopolistic nature of the copyright given to a particular work. At the same time, it would provide a basis for enabling the author to protect himself against unjustified uses amounting to an abuse of the work or the author himself.

The value of recognizing the author's creative interest, then, is that such a recognition would serve as a moderating influence to the danger of monopoly on the one hand and the danger of undue interference with an author's work on the other. To recognize the author's creative

18. Erie Railroad Co. v. Tompkins, 304 U.S. 64 (1938).

19. Hinderlider v. La Plata River & Cherry Creek Ditch Co., 304 U.S. 92 (1938).

20. Friendly, *In Praise of Erie and of the New Federal Common Law,* 19 THE RECORD OF THE ASSOCIATION OF THE BAR OF THE CITY OF NEW YORK 64 (1964).

interest is not, of course, to solve the many and increasingly complex problems of copyright; it will, however, tend to bring into proper perspective all the interests with which the law of copyright is concerned and will enable the courts to deal with the problems directly rather than indirectly. It is the failure to do this in the past that has been a major factor in the continuing discontent with the law of copyright.

12

Copyright in Historical Perspective

COPYRIGHT CAN most usefully be viewed as a legal concept—a series of ideas formulated and directed to a common end. The ideas vary in their degree of definiteness, ranging from the general to the specific, for they manifest both the ends to be achieved and the means of achieving those ends. The general ideas are principles expressing the ends to be achieved; the specific ideas are rules, expressing the means of achieving those ends. The principles are directed to the purposes to be served, the rules are directed to the resolution of problems in order to achieve those purposes. Legal concepts are thus ideally formulated in terms of purposes to be achieved and problems to be resolved.

The purposes, however, are not always clearly defined, and the problems are not always agreed upon. As the history of copyright illustrates, purposes and problems vary according to whose interest is being served. Moreover, they change with new developments. The changes, however, do not necessarily result in the appropriate development of rules. Almost certainly they do not if principles have not been properly formulated, for of the two groups of ideas, principles and rules, principles are by far the more important. It is the choice of principles that determines whether a legal concept is to have the degree of consistency necessary for a unified whole, or whether it is to consist primarily of a series of fragmented rules.

The concept of copyright is more nearly of the latter than the former category, for there is no set of clearly defined principles for copyright. Our ideas of copyright are a heritage of history—few modern statutes are based on an English statute enacted in 1709; fewer still have a direct lineage that goes back to a Star Chamber Decree of 1586. And familiarity with ideas often breeds confidence in their soundness that investigation would undermine: that which is historically sound is not always logically defensible.

Herein lies the value of a historical perspective. The historical context removes obstacles—long-continued acceptance of certain ideas, self-interest, and the pressing need to resolve immediate problems—which may be present when analysis occurs in a wholly contemporary context. And it yields a basis for employing the logic of experience. The historical perspective thus provides the opportunity to compare the ideas of copyright and the problems to which those ideas were directed in origin and development with the ideas of the concept and the problems of today. A brief summary brings into focus the early problems.

Copyright began in the sixteenth century as a device for maintaining order among members of the book trade organized as the Stationers' Company. Supported by laws of press control and censorship, it developed and existed as the private concern of these guild members for a hundred and fifty years. As such, it was the basis of a monopoly in the book trade.

With the demise of censorship, the private copyright of the members of the book trade, no longer supported by governmental sanctions, failed in its purpose of protecting published works. To restore order to the trade, Parliament was finally prevailed upon to enact a copyright statute, modelled on the stationer's copyright, but without its two most objectionable features, its limitation to members of the company, and its perpetual existence. The statutory copyright was available to anyone, and it was limited to two terms of fourteen years each. Instead of an instrument of monopoly, as the stationer's copyright had been, the statutory copyright was intended to be a trade-regulation device.

The developments following the enactment of the statute created the principle source of discontent for copyright. This was the ill-considered transformation of a protection for publishers created by the Stationers' Company into a corresponding right for the author created by law. This change of a copyright to protect members of a guild into an author's legal right was a consequence of the booksellers' efforts to continue their monopoly. Their efforts resulted in a misunderstanding of the Statute of Anne and at the same time they sowed the seeds of the idea that copyright was a natural right of the author.

They almost succeeded, because they framed their issues in the courts so as to preclude the judges from distinguishing the several interests involved: the interests of the author, the publisher, and the public. In this respect, the booksellers were aided by the fact that the courts had no role in the early development of copyright. The common-law courts were thus at a disadvantage because they were dealing in a common-law context with a statute based on a concept developed by a group of private individuals. The courts accepted the ideas presented by the booksellers and applied them, but not as the booksellers desired. The result, not surprisingly, was a confusion of ideas.

In its origin and development, then, there were two fundamental problems to which copyright was directed. In origin, the problem was to provide order in the book trade for the members of a guild organization which had a monopoly of the trade. In development, the problem came to be to destroy the monopoly of the book trade subsequently developed by a small group of men controlling copyrights.

Today, the problem of copyright has taken on new dimensions. The United States of the twentieth century bears little resemblance to England of the sixteenth and eighteenth centuries. In relation to copyright, the basic difference is freedom of the press and speech rather than press control and censorship. Copyright is no longer an instrument used to control and suppress ideas for the benefit of the government; nor is it an instrument used by a private group of monopolists to control the book trade; it is used to protect the expression of ideas for profit. The modern context thus creates a fundamental contradiction for copyright law. A society which has freedom of expression as a basic principle of liberty restricts that freedom to the extent that it vests ideas with legally protected property interests. The contradiction arises from sound, although competing, policies—to enable the author to benefit from his work and to make publication feasible, thereby promoting learning. And the resolution of the conflicts created by the competing policies requires a careful delineation of the rights to be had in connection with published works in terms of principles rather than merely in terms of rules. Thus, the problem of copyright today is how best to reconcile the interests of three groups—authors, who give expression to ideas; publishers, who disseminate ideas; and the members of the public, who use the ideas.

The contradiction of protecting ideas as private property in a society devoted to freedom of expression has been rationalized away with assurances that copyright does not protect ideas, but only the expression of ideas. The rationalization, however, will not stand up in light of the concept of copyright as it exists today. While in origin copyright was a publisher's right giving the publisher protection against the piracy of his manufactured work, it has today developed so as to give protection to the content of the work as well. Here is another irony of copyright law—in a society where there was no freedom of ideas, copyright protected only against piracy; in a society where there is freedom of ideas, copyright protects against plagiarism. Copyright, begun as protection for the publisher only, has come to be protection for the work itself.

The development is due in no small measure to the confusion of ideas resulting from the events in eighteenth-century England, and the confusion has continued. The ideas—that copyright is a monopoly; that copyright is primarily an author's right; that the author has natural rights in his works which must be limited by statute—once stated by the courts, became a fixed part of the heritage of copyright. They were taken over in this country and used almost indiscriminately. And they served as an inadequate substitute for analysis of the several interests in published works and a consideration of how to deal with them appropriately. The emphasis of the lawmakers, both judges and legislators, on copyright as a monopoly and as an author's right and the issues created by this emphasis have hindered a clear-cut analysis of copyright ideas. Copyright history thus gives us reason to pause: Is the concept as presently constituted best suited to resolve the fundamental problems of reconciling the interests, conflicting in some respects, compatible in others, of the author, the publisher, and society?

There are three ideas of copyright relevant to the modern concept that the history of copyright crystallizes. The first has to do with monopoly, an idea which had its origins in the booksellers' control of the book trade in eighteenth-century England. In dealing with the monopoly problem of copyright, the real source of the monopoly danger is generally ignored. That source, of course, is not the author, but the publishers. It is the publisher, not the author, who would control the book trade; and it is the publisher, not the author, who desires protection against economic competition. Yet, the problem has been obscured because the availability of the copyright to the publisher is screened behind the idea of copyright as only an author's right.

This fact raises the second problem which history develops. Is copyright an appropriate concept to accommodate the interest of both the publisher and the author? The development of copyright implies not. Copyright changed from a publisher's right to an author's right for reasons that had little to do with the interest of the author. The change, brought about by publishers in an effort to perpetuate their monopoly, has continually obscured the difference between the interest of the publisher and the interest of the author in the author's work.

The interests of the author and the publisher, of course, coincide in the economic benefit to be derived from the publication of the work. Beyond this point, however, their interests may well conflict. The author, as creator of his work, has an interest in maintaining its integrity and protecting his personality and reputation, a creative interest which the publisher does not share. Yet, apart from copyright, the common law offers little protection for the creative interest.

The legal recognition of such interest in the author is neither logically unsound nor undesirable; it is only historically precluded. The booksellers in eighteenth-century England prevailed upon the courts to accept the idea that all rights of copyright are derived from the author. The courts, however, upon accepting the idea that the rights of the publisher conferred by copyright were derived from the author, limited the rights to those defined by statute. In so doing, they not only limited the rights of the author—they left no basis for distinguishing between the interest of the author and that of the publisher. The judges did not suggest what more careful analysis might have made apparent: to recognize common-law rights of the author would not necessarily have been inconsistent with the limitation of the rights of publishers.

If the author invariably retained the copyright, there would be fewer problems, for copyright gives the owner complete protection. But the author does not, invariably—indeed, he seldom retains the copyright.

And the subtle irony is that the scope of copyright, supposedly broadened in the author's interest, may very well serve to defeat that interest. Yet, the courts have here overlooked a basic point. Since the statutes have dealt with the economic aspect of copyright, they have left to the courts the power, as yet unused, to deal with the creative interest as justice requires.

Finally, there is a third idea of copyright which has been given little explicit consideration, an idea that was irrelevant when copyright was first developed by the Stationers' Company in the time of censorship and press control. This is the interest of the individual user and thus of society. The interest of society in copyright has now long been acknowledged—the Statute of Anne was "An act for the encouragement of learning," and the Constitution empowers Congress to establish copyright "to promote science and useful arts." But these ideas have traditionally been applied so that society is an indirect rather than a direct beneficiary. The exclusive rights conferred on the copyright owner have served to limit the rights of the individual, although pleas for copyright protection, so that, ostensibly, the public will not be deprived of an adequate supply of books, go back to the seventeenth century.

From a legal standpoint, the individual's right to use a copyrighted work is minimal. By and large, when he purchases a book, it is his chattel and no more; the work itself is owned by the copyright owner. And only the nebulous and uncertain doctrine of fair use, the idea that one may reproduce a small part of a copyrighted work for a limited purpose, protects the individual who wishes to extend his use of the work beyond the reading of it.

This problem has lately taken on enlarged significance. The limited ability of the individual a few years ago to reproduce a book has been changed by the availability of high-speed copying machines. The change has made copyright owners—that is, publishers—look to the long-continued concept of monopoly in the guise of property rights to protect their interest. A more subtle and significant point is overlooked. However slight the danger, the failure to recognize the individual user's right results in a limitation upon the freedom of expression. The copyright owner's complete control of his work, based on the notion of the expression of ideas for profit, allows him to control that work completely. A vestige of the heritage of censorship in the law of copyright remains in the interest of profit.

These three ideas—the danger of monopoly from the publisher rather than the author, the differing interests of the publisher and the author, and the rights of the individual user—are the forgotten ideas of copyright. But simple as they are, they are fundamental, and they are the basis for the principles necessary for an integrated concept of copyright.

From the fact that the danger of the monopoly of copyright is the monopoly of the publisher rather than the author, it follows that the basic function of copyright is to protect the publisher—not against the author or the individual user, but against other publishers. This suggests that copyright should be limited again to its traditional function of protecting the entrepreneur, not the work itself. Thus, the first basic principle of copyright is that a copyright owner has a right as against an economic competitor to the exclusive reproduction of a work in its original or derivative form.

To the extent that copyright protects the publisher, it also protects the author. But there is little reason to limit the author's protection to that of the publisher. Indeed, to provide the author additional protection would be effectively to limit the monopoly of the publisher's copyright. And herein lies the essential value of recognizing the author's creative interest in his works. The second principle of copyright, then, should be that an author retains an inalienable right to protect the integrity of his work and his reputation in connection therewith.

And, finally, the limitation of the publisher's protection against economic competitors would constitute a recognition of the right of the individual to make whatever use of a copyrighted work he desires, except for competing profits. The third principle of copyright is that the right of individuals to the use of a copyrighted work for personal, private, or reasonable uses shall not be impaired.

The interrelationship of these ideas suggests a major reason for the unsatisfactory law of copyright and at the same time a reason for the way in which it developed. The characteristic is a rigidity in dealing with copyright problems resulting from the application of rules without guiding principles. Copyright is a concept used to deal with exceedingly complex issues, issues which require careful distinctions based upon a perceptive awareness of the problems, an understanding of purpose, and an appreciation of function.

The distinctions were not made, the purposes not clearly understood, and the functions not appreciated. Copyright was dealt with in absolute, not relative terms.

The reason can be found in the history of copyright. Copyright was developed as a private concept by a private group; subsequently, it was embodied in a statute. When copyright problems were finally brought to the common-law courts, the task of the courts was not to develop a law, but to construe a statute, and to construe a statute for a particular purpose: to destroy an opprobrious monopoly.

In this country, from the beginning, copyright was a statutory concept, not one of common law. And the judges in copyright cases felt themselves bound by the language of the statutes. There was, in the light of history as they understood it, little room to make careful distinctions, analyze problems, and define function. Their task was to resolve disputes under the statute, not to formulate guiding principles.

The implication is clear. Copyright is too complex a matter, too delicate a subject, to be dealt with by statutes alone. Copyright statutes have provided rules, not principles, and if the principles necessary to a sound body of copyright law are to be formulated, the judges must accomplish the task. History shows the consequences to be expected if they fail. More important, however, history gives them an adequate basis upon which to proceed, to recognize the limited function of copyright, to protect the author's creative interest, and to give due regard to the rights of the individual's use of a copyrighted work.

Examples of Printing Patents

The following printing patents, to William Seres and John Day, are transcribed in II ARBER 60, 61.

LETTERS PATENTS TO WILLIAM SERES, 3 JUNE 1559.*

ELIZABETH by the grace of GOD &c To all printers bookesellers and Stationers and to all other our Subiectes, gretinge knowe ye that where we be duly informed how our louyng Subiect William Seres of our Citie of London Stationer and bookeseller had by the graunt of our late deare brother of worthie memorie kyng EDWARD the SIXT licence to printe all maner of *prymers* that then were and from thensfurth should be Sett forth agreable to the booke of Common prayer at the same tyme established And in the tyme of our late deare Syster Quene MARY was not onlie defeated [*i. e. deprived of the feat or art of printing this privilege*] therof to his great losse but was also imprisoned long tyme and depriued of gre[a]t multitude of the said *primers* and also of other great nombres of bookes which tended to his vtter v[n]doyng. We be pleased to gyue this graunte and by theis presentes for vs our heyres and Successours do of our speciall grace mere mocion and certeyn knowledge gyue and graunte full power and aucthoritie priuiledge and licence vnto our said louyng Subiect wylliam Seres and to his assignes for and during the tearme of his naturall life to imprinte or cause to be imprinted aswell all manner of *bookes of pryuate prayers* vsuallie and comonlie called or taken for *primers* as also of *Psalters* both in great volumes and in small in Latine or Englishe which nowe be or at any tyme herafter, shalbe sett fourth and permitted by vs our heyres and Successours or by any other persons therto aucthorised by vs to be hadd re[a]dd vsed and taught of our louyng Subiectes

---

* Cf. the date in the body of the document, "iij day of July." The latter date is apparently the correct one. See I ARBER 15.

thorough owt all our Realmes and domynyons duryng the said terme of his naturall life Any other priuiledge or any other order hertofore graunted or taken to the contarie notwithstanding Straightlie inhibiting and forbidding all other our Subiectes to printe vtter or sell or cause to be prynted vttered or solde any other *booke* or *bookes of priuate prayers prymers* or *psalters* than such as shalbe by the said William Seres or his assignes prynted or caused to be printed according to the true meanyng of this our present priuiledge vpon payne of forfaiture of all such bookes as they shalle imprinte vtter or sell contrarie to the meanyng herof. Wherfor we will and commaunde all our officers and subiectes as thei tender our fauour and will auoyde our displeasure that they and euery of them if nede requyre do ayde and assist the said Wylliam Seres and his assignes in the due execucyon of this our licence

In witnesse herof &c Witnesse our Self at Westminster the iij day of July [1559]

per ipsam Reginam

[*Patent Roll. (No. 941.) 1 Eliz. Part. 4. 26(7).*]

LICENSE TO JOHN DAY, 11 NOVEMBER 1559.

A lycence graunted to John Day to prynte all 'the *Cosmograficall glasse* compyled by WYLLIAM CONINGHAM' amongest other thinges./.

ELIZABETH by the grace of GOD Quene of Englond Ffraunce and Ireland defendor of the faithe &c. To all maner of Printers Bookesellers and other our officers ministers and Subiectes greatinge We do you [to] vnderstande that of our grace especiall We haue graunted and giuen Priuiledge and lycence and by theis presentes for vs our heires and successors do graunte and geve pryveledge and lycence vnto our welbeloued subiect John Daye of the Citie of London Printer and Stacyoner and to his assignes for the terme of his lyfe to imprint or cause to be imprinted aswell *the Cosmographicall glasse* compiled by WILLIAM CUNINGHAM doctor in Physicke as also duringe the tyme of seven yeares all suche bookes and Workes as he hath Imprinted or hereafter shall imprinte beinge deuysed compiled or set oute by any learned man at the payemente costes and Charges onely of the saide John Daye So that no suche booke or bookes be repugnaunt to the holye Scripture or to the lawes and orders of our Realme. PROVYDED ALWAY that none of the Sayd bookes be any of oure Copie or Copies parteyninge by office frome tyme to tyme vnto our Printer or Prynters nor yet that thei be derogatory to anye suche as haue alredie at their costes and chardges ymprinted anye booke or bookes vpon especiall licence graunted by vs or our late de[a]re father Brother or Syster. Also that everie booke and Worke which he shall imprynt and Sell or cause to be imprynted and sold by vertue of this our Priviledge be perused and allowed before it be put to prynte in suche maner and forme as by our late *Iniunccons* is prouided and ordeyned or otherwyse to be forfayted and this licence to ce[a]sse and be vtterly voyde Straitely forbidding and comaundinge by theis presentes all and Singuler our subiectes aswell Printers and bookesellers as all other persons wythin our Realmes and Domynions whatsoeuer they be, in any maner of wyse to imprinte or cause to be imprinted any of the aforesaide bookes that the sayd John Daye shall by aucthoritie of this our licence ymprinte or cause to be imprynted or anye parte of them but onely the sayde John Daye and his assignes vpon payne of our highe indignacon and that euery offendor therin shall forfaicte to oure vse fortie Shillinges of laufull money of Englond for euery suche booke or bookes at any tyme so printed contrarye to the true me[a]ninge of this our present Licence and Priuiledge ouer and besydes all suche booke or bookes so Prynted to be forfaited to whomsoeuer shall susteigne the chardges and seu the sayde forfaiture in our behalfe Willinge thereforo and comaundinge all our officers and Mynisters as they tender our favour and will avoid our displeasure and indignacon for the contrarye that they and euery of theym yf nede shall require to aide and assyste the sayd John Daye and his assignes in due exercisinge and execucon of this our present licence and Priuiledge wyth effect accordinge to the true meaninge of the same That expresse mencon &c

In Wytnes whereof &c. Witnes the quene at Westminster the xj of November [1559]

Per breve de priuato sigillo

[Patent Roll. (No. 938) 1 Eliz. 1st Part. 24(7).]

The Star Chamber Decrees of 1586 and 1637

The Court of Star Chamber, so-called because its sessions were held in a "starred-chamber" at Westminster, originated from the exercise of judicial functions by the King's Council. Its official style was "The Lords of the Council sitting in the Star Chamber." Primarily a court of criminal jurisdiction, one of its functions was the enforcement of royal proclamations and the adjudication of their breach. It was apparently this jurisdiction which was the basis for the Star Chamber Decrees regulating printers and printing. Under James I and Charles I, the Star Chamber became a hated instrument of despotism and was abolished by the Long Parliament in 1640. The decrees of 1586 and 1637, which follow, are transcribed in II ARBER 807–812, and IV ARBER 528–536.

The newe Decrees of the Starre Chamber for orders in printinge./

Vicesimo Tertio Die Jvnij Anno Domini 1586./ Annoque Regni Regin[a]e Elizabeth [æ] vicesimo octauo./

WHEREAS sondrye Decrees and Ordynaunces haue vpon grave aduice and deliberacon been heretofore made and published, for the repressinge of suche greate enormyties and abuses as of late, more then in tyme paste, haue been commonlye vsed and practised by dyvers contentyous and disorderlye persons professinge the arte or mysterye of Pryntinge or sellinge of bookes And yet notwithstandinge the saide Abuses and enormyties are nothinge abated:

but (as it is found by experience) doe rather daylye more and more encrease
to the wilfull and manifeste breache and contempte of the said ordinances
and decrees to the great dyspleasure and offence of the Quenes most excellent maiestie by reason whereof sondrye intollerable offences and troubles
and disturbances haue happened aswell in the Churche, as in the Civill governement of the state and common wealthe of this Realme, whiche seeme to
haue growen because the paynes and penaltyes conteyned and sett downe in
the said ordynaunces and decrees haue been to lighte and small for the cor-
rectyon and punishement of soe greivous haynous offences, and soe the of-
endors and malefactors in that behalf haue not been so severelye punished as
the qualytye of their offences haue deserved Her maiestie therefore of her
most godlye and gracyous disposytion, being carefull that spedye and due ref-
ormacon be had of the abuses and disorders aforesaid; And that all. persons
vsinge or professinge the arte, trade or misterye of pryntinge or sellinge of
bookes, should from henceforth be ruled and directed therein by some certayne and knowen rules and ordynaunces whiche should be invyolabie kepte
and observed, and the breakers and offendors of the same to be severelye and
sharpelye punished and corrected hathe straightlye charged and required
the moste Reverend in GOD the Archebysshop of CANTERBURY and the righte
honorable the Lordes and others of her highenes pryvye Councell, to see her
maiestye said moste gracyous and godly intencon and purpose to be duelye
and effectuallye executed and accomplished./ Wherevpon the said moste
reverend father and the wholle presence sittinge in the honorable Courte
this xxiij^{th} daye of June in the eighte and twentieth yere of her maiesties
reigne vpon grave and mature deliberacon, haue ordayned and decreed that
the ordynaunces, constitucons, rules and artycles here after followinge from-
henceforth by all persons be dulye and invyolablye kepte and observed,
accordinge to the tenour purporte and true intent and meaninge of the same,
as they tender her maiesties highe displeasure, and as they will answere to ye
contrarye at their vttermoste perill. *Viz.*

/.1./

Against the   *Inprimis* that everye Prynter and other person or persons
havinge of any   whatsoever which at this tyme presente hathe erected or
printinge presse   sett vp, or hereafter shall erecte, sett vp, keepe, maine-
or other Instru-   tayne or haue any pryntinge presse, Rowle or other In-
mentes withoute   strument for ympryntinge of bookes, Chartes, ballades,
notefyinge to the   portraictures, paper called Damaske paper, or any suche
master and   matters or thinges whatsoever, Shall bringe a true note or
wardens./   certificate of the said Presses or other pryntinge instru-
                     mentes alreadye erected, within Tenne dayes next com-

mynge after the publicacon hereof. And of the said presses
or other printinge ynstrumentes hereafter to be erected or
sett vp from tyme to tyme, within Ten dayes nexte after
the erectinge or settinge vp thereof vnto the maister and
wardens of the Cumpanye of Staconers of the Cyttye of
London for the tyme beinge, vppon payne, That everye

Pœna duplex.

person faylinge or offendinge herein, shall haue all and
everye of the said Presses and other Instrumentes vtterly
defaced and made vnserviceable for ympryntinge forever
And shall alsoe suffer Twelve monethes ymprysonment
without Bayle or maynepryse./

/.2./

Against printinge in any place savinge London and the twooe vniuersityes.

Item that noe Prynter of Bookes, nor any other person or
persons whatsoever shall sett vp, keepe, or mayneteyne any
Presse or Presses, or anye other Instrument or Instrumentes
for ympryntinge of Bookes, ballades, Chartes, Portraictures, or any other thinge or thinges whatsoever, But onelye

London. Oxford. and Cambridge

in the Cyttie of London, or the Subburbes thereof, and ex-
cepte one presse in the vniuersitye of Cambridge, and another presse in the vnyuersytie of Oxforde, and noe moe,
And that noe person shall hereafter erecte, sett vp, or
mayneteyne in anye secrett or obscure corner or place any
suche presse or instrument before expressed, but that the
same shalbe in suche open place or places in his or their
house or howses, as the wardens of the said Cumpanye of
the Staconers for the tyme beinge or suche other person or
persons as by the said wardens shall be therevnto appoynted, maye from tyme to tyme haue readye accesse
vnto, to searche for and viewe the same / And that noe

Resisting the search.

prynter or other person or persons shall at any time or
times hereafter withstand or make resystance to or in any

Concealing of Presses.

suche viewe or searche nor denye or keepe secrett any
suche presse or other instrument for ymprintinge, Vpon
payne that everye person offendinge in any thinge contrarye to this artycle, shall haue all the said presses and
other printinge instrumentes defaced and made vnservice-

Punishment

able for ympryntinge forever, and shall alsoe suffer ymprisonment one wholle yere without bayle or mayneprise,
and to be disabled forever to keepe any printinge presse
or other instrument for pryntinge, or to be master of any
pryntinge house, or to haue anye benefytt therebye, other
then only to worke as a Journeyman for wages./

3.

Against the
erecting of
Presses.

To diminish the
excessiue nomber
of Prynters.

In whose Judge-
ment it lyeth to
haue more
Presses erected./

Chosing of a
Prynter.

The Electors
of a newe
Prynter.

The presentment
of the elected
Prynter to the
Commissioners

Admission of
the Prynter
elected.

Item that no Prynter, nor other person or persons what-soever, that hath sett vp any presse or Instrument for ymprintinge within Six monethes last past, shall hereafter vse or occupye the same, nor any person or persons shall hereafter erect or sett vp any presse or other instrument of pryntinge, tyll the excessiue multytude of Prynters hauinge presses already sett vp, be abated, dyminished, and by death gyvinge over, or otherwyse brought to so small a number of maisters or owners of pryntinge houses, beinge of abylity and good behauyour, As the Archbishop of CANTERBURY and Bishop of LONDON for the tyme being shall therevpon thinck requisyte and convenyent for the good service of the Realme, to haue somme more presses or ynstrumentes for pryntinge, erected and sett vp. And that when and as often as the sayd Archbishop and Byshop for the tyme beinge shall so thinck yt requisyte and con-venyent, and shall signifye the same to the said master and wardens of the sayd Cumpanye of Staconers for the tyme beinge./ That then and so often the sayd master and wardens shall within convenyent tyme after, call the As-sistantes of the same Cumpany before them, and shall make choice of one or more (as, by the opynion of the sayd Archbishop and Bishop for the tyme beinge, need shall requier) of such persons being free Staconers, as for their skyll, abylity, and good behauiour shall be thought by the sayd master wardens and Assistantes or the more part of them, meet to haue the charge and governement of a Presse or prynting howse / And that with in xiiij. daies next after suche eleccon and choice, The sayd master war-dens and ffoure other at the least of the Assistantes of the said Cumpanye shall present before the high Commis-sioners in cause Ecclesiasticall or Six or more of them, whereof the Archbishop of CANTERBURY or Bishop of LONDON to be one, the person and persons so chosen and elected / And that vpon such choice and presentment so made, yt shallbe laufull to and for the sayd Commissioners or any Six or moe of them, whereof the sayd Archbishop to be one, to allowe and admytt euery such person soe chosen and presented to be master and governour of a presse and pryntinge howse, accordinge to the same electyon and presentment, vpon payne, that every person offendinge contrary to the entent of this Artycle, shall

Penaltye./

haue his Presse and other Instrumentes for Pryntinge, defaced and made vnserviceable and also suffer ymprysonment by the space of One whole yeare without bayle or
maynepryse. Provyded alwayes that this artycle or any
thinge therein conteyned shall not extend to the office of
the Quenes maiesties Prynter for the service of the Realme
/ But that the sayd Office and Officer shalbe and contynew
at the pleasure and dysposicon of her maiestie her heires
and successors at all tymes vpon the death of her highnes
Prynter or otherwyse./

Liberty for the
Queenes Prynter.

4.

Against prynting
of Bookes with-
out authoritye/

Allowinge of
Bookes.

Exception for
the Queenes
Prynter.

Printinge without
Licence./

Penaltyes by
defacing of
Presses.

Item that no person or persons shall ymprynt or cawse
to be ymprinted, or suffer by any meanes to his knowledge
his presse, letters [*type*], or other Instrumentes to be oc-
cupyed in pryntinge of any booke, work, coppye, matter, or
thinge whatsoever, Except the same book, woork, coppye,
matter, or any other thinge, hath been heeretofore allowed,
or hereafter shall be allowed before the ymprintinge thereof, accordinge to th[e]order appoynted by the Queenes
maiesties *Iniunctyons*, And been first seen and pervsed by
the Archbishop of CANTERBURY and Bishop of LONDON for
the tyme beinge or any one of them (The Queenes maiesties
Prynter for somme speciall service by her maiestie, or by
somme of her highnes pryvie Councell therevnto appoynted, and such as are or shalbe pryviledged to prynte
the bookes of the *Common Lawe* of this Realme, for such
of the same bookes as shalbe allowed of by the Twoo
Chief Justices, and Chief Baron for the tyme beinge, or
any twoo of them onely excepted) Nor shall ymprynt or
cause to be ymprinted any book, work or coppie against
the fourme and meaninge of any Restraynt or ordonnaunce
conteyned or to be conteyned in any statute or lawes of
this Realme, or in any Iniunctyon made, or sett foorth by
her maiestie, or her highnes pryvye Councell, or against
the true intent and meaninge of any Letters patentes, Com-
missions or prohibicons vnder the great seale of England,
or contrary to any allowed ordynaunce sett Downe for the
good governaunce of the Cumpany of Staconers within the
Cyttie of London, vppon payne to haue all such presses,
letters, and instrumentes as in or about the pryntinge of
any such bookes or copyes shalbe employed or vsed, to
be defaced and made vnserviceable for ymprintinge for-

ever. And vppon payne also that euery offendour and
offendours contrarye to this present Artycle or ordynaunce
shalbe dishabled (after any such offence) to vse or exercise
or take benefytt by vsinge or exercisinge of the art or feat
of ympryntinge./ And shall moreover sustayne ymprysonment Six moneths without Bayle or mayneprise /

Dismissing from printing

Imprisonment.

5./

Item that every such person or persons as sell, vtter, or
putt to sale, wyttingly bynd, stitch or sowe, or wyttingly
cause to be sould, vttered, putt to sale, bound, stitched, or
sowed any bookes or Coppies whatsoever prynted contrary
to th[e]intent and true meaninge of any ordynaunce or
Artycle afore sayd, shall suffer three monethes ymphryson-
ment for his or their offence./

Binders offending punishable by ymprysonment.

6.

Item that yt shalbe lawfull for the wardens of the sayd
Cumpany for the tyme beinge, or any twoo of the sayd
Cumpanye therevnto Deputed by the sayd wardens, to
make serch in all woorkhowses, shops, warehowses of
prynters, bookesellers, bookebynders, or where they shall
haue reasonable cause of suspicion / And all bookes,
Coppies, matters and thynges prynted, or to be prynted
contrarye to th[e]intent and meaninge of theis present
ordonaunces, to seize and take to her maiesties vse, and
the same carry to the Staconers hall in London / And the
partie or partyes offendinge in pryntinge, sellinge, vtter-
inge, byndinge, stytchinge, or sowinge any such bookes,
coppyes, matters or thinges, to arrest bringe and present
before the sayd highe Comissioners in causes Ecclesyasty-
call or some Three or more of them, whereof the sayd
Archbishop of CANTERBURY or Bishop of LONDON for the
tyme beinge to be one./

Search.

Seizing of Bookes.

Offendors to be presented before the highe Com-missioners.

7.

Item that yt shalbe lawfull to and for the sayd wardens
for the tyme beinge, or any twoo by them appointed, without lett or interrupcon of any person or persons whatsoeuer,
to enter into any howse, workehowse, warehowse, shop,
or other place or places, and to search take and carry away
all presses, letters, and other pryntinge instruments sett vp,

Taking of Presses vppon offences.

vsed or employed, or to be sett vp, vsed, or employed, contrary to th[e]intent and meaninge hereof, to be defaced and made vnserviceable as aforesayd / And that the sayd wardens shall so often as need shall requier, call the Assystantes of their sayd Cumpany, or the more parte of them into their sayd hall, And there take order for the Defacinge, burninge, breaking, and destroyinge of all the sayd letters; presses, and other pryntinge Instrumentes aforesayd. And therevpon shall cause all such pryntinge presses and other Instrumentes of ymprintinge to be Defaced, melted, sawed in peeces, broken, or battered at the smythes forge, or otherwyse to be made vnserviceable / And the stuffe of the same so defaced shall redelyver to the owners thereof againe within three monethes next after the takinge or seizinge thereof as aforesayd./

Defacing and making of printing stuffe vnseruiceable.

Sawing of Presses./

8./

Item that for the avoydinge of the excessyve number of Prynters within this Realme, yt shall not be lawfull for any person or persons beinge free of the Cumpany of Staconers, or vsinge the trade or mistery of pryntinge, booksellinge, or bookebyndinge, to haue take and keepe hereafter at one tyme any greater nomber of Apprentices then shalbe hereafter expressed, that is to saye / Everye person that hath been or shalbe master or vpper warden of the Cumpanye whereof he is free to keepe three apprentices at one tyme, and not aboue / And everye person that is or shalbe vnder warden or of the Lyvery of the Cumpanye whereof he is free, to keepe twoo Apprentices, and not aboue / And euery person that is or shalbe of the y[e]omanry of the Cumpanye whereof he is or shalbe free, to keepe one apprentice (yf he himself be not a Journeyman) and not aboue./

Against the excessiue nomber of Prynters.

Nomber of Apprentices lymited.

Provyded always that this ordinaunce shall not extend to the Quenes Maiesties prynter for the tyme beinge for the service of her maiestie and the Realme./ But that he be at liberty to keepe and haue apprentices to the number of Sixe at one tyme./

An exception for the Queenes Printer.

9./

Item that none of the Prynters in Cambridge or Oxford for the tyme beinge shalbe suffered to haue any more ap-

Oxford and Cambridge.

A lyberty to
retayne
Journeymen
free of
London./

prentices then one at one tyme at the most / But yt is and shalbe lawfull to and for the sayd Prynters and eyther of them and their Successors to haue and vse the helpe of any Journeyman beinge freeman of the cyttye of London without contradiccon / Any Lawe, statute, or Commaundment contrarye in the meaninge and due execucon of these Ordynaunces or any of them in any wyse notwithstandinge /.

Fynis./

A
DECREE OF STARRE-CHAMBER,
Concerning Printing,
Made the eleuenth day of July last past. 1637.

⁋ Imprinted at London by Robert Barker
Printer to the Kings most Excellent
Maiestie : And by the Assignes
of Iohn Bill. 1637.

In Camera Stellata coram Concilio ibidem, vndecimo die Iulij, Anno decimo tertio Caroli Regis.

THIS day Sir IOHN BANKES Knight, His Maiesties Attourney Generall, produced in Court a Decree drawn and penned by the advice of the Right Honourable the LORD KEEPER of the great Seale of England, the most Reuerend Father in God the Lord ARCH-BISHOP OF CANTERBURY HIS GRACE, the Right Honorable and Right Reuerend Father in God the Lord BISHOP OF LONDON LORD HIGH TREASURER OF ENGLAND, the LORD CHIEFE IUSTICES, and the LORD CHIEFE BARON, touching the regulating of Printers and Founders of letters, whereof the Court hauing consideration, the said Decree was directed and ordered to be here Recorded, and to the end the same may be publique, and that every one whom it may concerne may take notice thereof, The Court hath now also ordered, That the said Decree shall speedily be Printed, and that the same be sent to His MAIESTIES Printer for that purpose. Whereas the three and twentieth day of Iune in the eight and twentieth yere of the reigne of the late Queene ELIZABETH, and before, diuers Decrees and Ordinances haue beene made for the better gouernment and regulating of Printers and Printing, which Orders and Decrees haue beene found by experience to be defectiue in some particulars ; And diuers abuses haue sithence arisen, and beene practised by the craft and malice of wicked and euill disposed persons, to the preiudice of the publike ; And diuers libellous, seditious, and mutinous bookes haue been vnduly printed, and other bookes and papers without licence, to the disturbance of the peace of the Church and State : For preuention whereof in time to come, It is now Ordered and Decreed, That the said former Decrees and Ordinances shall stand in force with these Additions, Explanations, and Alterations following, viz.

IN CAMERA STELLATA

coram Concilio ibidem, vndecimo die Iulii, Anno decimo
tertio Caroli Regis.

IMPRIMIS, That no person or persons whatsoeuer shall presume to print, or
cause to bee printed, either in the parts beyond the Seas, or in this Realme,
or other his Maiesties Dominions, any seditious, scismaticall, or offensive
Bookes or Pamphlets, to the scandall of Religion, or the Church, or the
Government, or Governours of the Church or State, or Commonwealth, or
of any Corporation, or particular person or persons whatsoeuer, nor shall
import any such Booke or Bookes, nor sell or dispose of them, or any of
them, nor cause any such to be bound, stitched, or sowed, vpon paine that
he or they so offending, shall loose all such Bookes and Pamphlets, and also
haue, and suffer such correction, and severe punishment, either by Fine,
imprisonment, or other corporall punishment, or otherwise, as by this Court,
or by His Maiesties Commissioners for causes Ecclesiasticall in the high Commission Court, respectiuely, as the several causes shall require, shall be
thought fit to be inflicted upon him, or them, for such their offence and
contempt.

II. *Item*, That no person or persons whatsoeuer, shall at any time print
or cause to be imprinted, any Booke or Pamphlet whatsoever, vnlesse the
same Booke or Pamphlet, and also all and euery the Titles, Epistles, Prefaces,
Proems, Preambles, Introductions, Tables, Dedications, and other matters
and things whatsoeuer thereunto annexed, or therewith imprinted, shall be
first lawfully licenced and authorized onely by such person and persons as
are hereafter expressed, and by no other, and shall be also first entred into
the Registers Booke of the Company of Stationers ; vpon paine that euery
Printer offending therein, shall be for euer hereafter disabled to use or exercise the Art or Mysterie of Printing, and receiue such further punishment,
as by this Court or the high Commission Court respectiuely, as the severall
causes shall require, shall be thought fitting

III. *Item*, That all Bookes concerning the common Lawes of this Realme
shall be printed by the especiall allowance of the Lords chiefe Iustices, and
the Lord chiefe Baron for the time being, or one or more of them, or by
their appointment ; And that all Books of History, belonging to this State,
and present times, or any other Booke of State affaires, shall be licenced
by the principall Secretaries of State, or one of them, or by their appointment ; And that all Bookes concerning Heraldry, Titles of Honour and
Armes, or otherwise concerning the Office of Earle Marshall, shall be licenced
by the Earle Marshall, or by his appointment ; And further, that all other
Books, whether of Diuinitie, Phisicke, Philosophie, Poetry, or whatsoeuer,
shall be allowed by the Lord Arch-Bishop of CANTERBURY, or Bishop of
LONDON for the time being, or by their appointment, or the Chancellours, or

Vice Chancellors of either of the Vniuersities of this Realme for the time being.

Always prouided, that the Chancellour or Vice-Chancellour, of either of the Vniuersities, shall Licence onely such Booke or Bookes that are to be Printed within the limits of the Vniuersities respectiuely, but not in *London*, or elsewhere, not medling either with Bookes of the common Law, or matters of State.

IV. *Item*, That euery person and persons, which by any Decree of this Court are, or shall be appointed or authorized to Licence Bookes, or giue Warrant for imprinting thereof, as is aforesaid, shall haue two seuerall written Copies of the same Booke or Bookes with the Titles, Epistles, Prefaces, Proems, Preambles, Introductions, Tables, Dedications, and other things whatsoeuer thereunto annexed. One of which said Copies shall be kept in the publike Registries of the said Lord Arch-Bishop, and Bishop of LONDON respectively, or in the Office of the Chancellour, or Vice-Chancellour of either of the Vniuersities, or with the Earle Marshall, or principall Secretaries of State, or with the Lords chiefe Iustices, or chiefe Baron, of all such Bookes as shall be licensed by them respectiuely, to the end that he or they may be secure, that the Copy so licensed by him or them shall not bee altered without his or their priuitie, and the other shall remain with him whose Copy it is, and vpon both the said Copies, he or they that shall allow the said Booke, shall testifie vnder his or their hand or hands, that there is nothing in that Booke or Books contained, that is contrary to Christian Faith, and the Doctrine and Discipline of the Church of *England*, nor against the State or Gouernment, nor contrary to good life, or good manners, or otherwise, as the nature and subiect of the work shall require, which license or approbation shall be imprinted in the beginning of the same Booke, with the name, or names of him or them that shall authorize or license the same, for a testimonie of the allowance thereof.

V. *Item*, That euery Merchant of bookes, and person and persons whatsoeuer, which doth, or hereafter shall buy, import, or bring any booke or bookes into this Realme, from any parts beyond the Seas, shall before such time as the same book or books, or any of them be deliuered forth, or out of his, or their hand or hands, or exposed to sale, giue, and present a true Catalogue in writing of all and euery such booke and bookes vnto the Lord Arch-Bishop of CANTERBURY, or Lord Bishop of LONDON for the time being, vpon paine to haue and suffer such punishment for offending herein, as by this Court, or by the said high Commission Court respectively, as the seuerall causes shall require, shall be thought fitting.

VI. *Item*, That no Merchant, or other person or persons whatsoeuer, which shall import or bring any book or books into the kingdome, from any parts beyond the Seas, shall presume to open any Dry-fats, Bales, Packs, Maunds, or other Fardals of books, or wherein books are ; nor shall any Searcher, Wayter, or other Officer belonging to the Custome-house, vpon pain of loosing his or their place or places, suffer the same to passe, or to be deliuered out of their hands or custody, before such time as the Lord Arch-Bishop of CANTERBURY, or Lord Bishop of LONDON, or one of them for the time being, haue appointed one of their Chaplains, or some other learned man, with the Master and Wardens of the Company of Stationers, or one of them, and such others as they shall call to their assistance, to be present at the opening thereof, and to view the same : And if there shall happen to be found any seditious, schismaticall or offensiue booke or bookes, they shall forthwith be brought vnto the said Lord Arch-bishop of CANTERBURY, Lord Bishop of LONDON for the time being, or one of them, or to the High Commission Office, to the end that as well the offendor or offendors may be punished by the Court of Star Chamber, or the high Commission Court respectiuely, as the seuerall causes shall require, according to his or their demerit ; as also that such further course and order may be taken concerning the same booke or bookes, as shall bee thought fitting.

VII. *Item*, That no person or persons shall within this Kingdome, or else-where imprint, or cause to be imprinted, nor shall import or bring in, or cause to be imported or brought into this Kingdome, from, or out of any other His Maiesties Dominions, nor from other, or any parts beyond the Seas, any Copy, book or books, or parts of any booke or bookes, printed be-yond the seas, or elswhere, which the said Company of Stationers, or any other person or persons haue, or shall by any Letters Patents, Order, or Entrance in their Register book, or otherwise, haue the right, priuiledge, authoritie, or allowance soly to print, nor shall bind, stitch, or put to sale, any such booke or bookes, vpon paine of losse and forfeiture of all the said bookes, and of such Fine, or other punishment, for euery booke or part of a booke so imprinted or imported, bound, stitched, or put to sale, to be leuyed of the party so offending, as by the power of this Court, or the high Com-mission Court respectiuely, as the seuerall causes shall require, shall be thought fit.

VIII. *Item*, Euery person and persons that shall hereafter Print, or cause to be Printed, any Bookes, Ballads, Charts, Portraiture, or any other thing or things whatsoeuer, shall thereunto or thereon Print and set his and their owne name or names, as also the name or names of the Author or Authors, Maker or Makers of the same, and by, or for whom any such booke, or other thing is, or shall be printed, vpon pain of forfiture of all such Books, Ballads, Chartes, Portraitures, and other thing or things, printed contrary to this Article ; And the presses, Letters and other instruments for Printing, wherewith such Books, ballads, Chartes, Portraitures, and other thing or things shall be printed, to be defaced and made vnseruiceable, and the party and parties so offending, to be fined, imprisoned, and haue such other cor-porall punishment, or otherwise, as by this Honourable Court, or the said high Commission respectiuely, as the seuerall causes shall require, shall be thought fit.

IX. *Item*, That no person or persons whatsoeuer, shall hereafter print, or cause to be printed, or shall forge, put, or counterfeit in, or vpon any booke or books, the name, title, marke or vinnet of the Company or Society of Stationers, or of any particular person or persons, which hath or shall haue lawfull priuiledge, authoritie, or allowance to print the same, without the consent of the said Company, or party or parties that are or shall be so priuiledged, authorized, or allowed to print the same booke or books, thing or things, first had and obtained, vpon paine that euery person or persons so offending, shall not onely loose all such books and other things, but shall also haue, and suffer such punishment, by imprisonment of his body, fine, or otherwise, as by this Honourable Court, or high Commission Court respectiuely, as the seuerall causes shall require, it shall be to him or them limited or adiudged.

X. *Item*, that no Haberdasher of small wares, Ironmonger, Chandler, Shopkeeper, or any other person or persons whatsoeuer, not hauing beene seuen yeeres apprentice to the trade of a Book-seller, Printer, or Book-binder, shall within the citie or suburbs of London, or in any other Corporation, Markettowne, or elswhere, receive, take or buy, to barter, sell againe, change or do away any Bibles, Testaments, Psalm-books, Primers, Abcees, Almanackes, or other booke or books whatsoeuer, vpon pain of forfeiture of all such books so receiued, bought or taken as aforesaid, and such other punishment of the parties so offending, as by this Court, or the said high Commission Court respectiuely, as the severall causes shall require, shall be thought meet.

XI. *Item*, for that Printing is, and for many yeers hath been an Art and manufacture of this kingdome, for the better incouraging of Printers in their honest, and iust endeauours in their profession, and preuention of diuers libels, pamphlets, and seditious books printed beyond the seas in English, and thence transported hither ;

It is further Ordered and Decreed, that no Merchant, Bookseller, or other person or persons whatsoeuer, shall imprint, or cause to be imprinted, in the parts beyond the seas or elswhere, nor shall import or bring, nor willingly assist or consent to the importation or bringing from beyond the seas into this Realme, any English bookes, or part of bookes, or bookes whatsoeuer, which are or shall be, or the greater, or more part whereof is or shall be English, or of the English tongue, whether the same book or bookes haue been here formerly printed or not, vpon pain of the forfeiture of all such English bookes so imprinted or imported, and such further censure and punishment, as by this Court, or the said high Commission Court respectiuely, as the seuerall causes shall require, shall be thought meet.

XII. *Item*, That no stranger or forreigner whatsoeuer, be suffered to bring in, or vent here, any booke or bookes printed beyond the seas, in any language whatsoeuer, either by themselues, or their secret Factors, except such onely as bee free Stationers of London, and such as haue beene brought vp in that profession, and haue their whole meanes of subsistance, and liuelihood depending thereupon, vpon paine of confiscation of all such Books so imported, and such further penalties, as by this Court, or the high Commission Court respectiuely, as the seuerall causes shall require, shall be thought fit to be imposed.

XIII. *Item*, That no person or persons within the Citie of London, or the liberties thereof, or elsewhere, shall erect or cause to be erected any Presse or Printing-house, nor shall demise, or let, or suffer to be held or vsed, any house, vault, seller, or other roome whatsoeuer, to, or by any person or persons, for a Printing-house, or place to print in, vnlesse he or they which shall so demise or let the same, or suffer the same to be so vsed, shall first giue notice to the said Master and Wardens of the Company of Stationers for the time being, of such demise, or suffering to worke or print there, vpon paine of imprisonment, and such other punishment, as by this Court, or the said high Commission Court respectiuely, as the seuerall Causes shall require, shall bee thought fit.

XIV. *Item*, That no Ioyner, or Carpenter, or other person, shall make any printing-Presse, no Smith shall forge any Iron-worke for a printing-Presse, and no Founder shall cast any Letters for any person or persons whatsoeuer, neither shall any person or persons bring, or cause to be brought in from any parts beyond the Seas, any Letters Founded or Cast, nor buy any such Letters for Printing ; Vnlesse he or they respectiuely shall first acquaint the said Master and VVardens, or some of them, for whom the same Presse, Iron-works, or Letters, are to be made, forged, or cast, vpon paine of such fine and punishment, as this Court, or the high Commission Court respectiuely, as the seuerall causes shall require, shall thinke fit.

XV. *Item*, The Court doth declare, that as formerly, so now, there shall be but Twentie Master Printers allowed to haue the vse of one Presse or more, as is after specified, and doth hereby nominate, allow, and admit these persons whose names hereafter follow, to the number of Twentie, to haue the vse of a Presse, or Presses and Printing-house, for the time being, *viz*. Felix Kingstone, Adam Islip, Thomas Purfoot, Miles Flesher, Thomas Harper, Iohn Beale, Iohn Legat, Robert Young, Iohn Haviland, George Miller, Richard Badger, Thomas Cotes, Bernard Alsop, Richard Bishop, Edward Griffin, Thomas Purslow, Richard Hodgkinsonne, Iohn Dawson, Iohn Raworth, Marmaduke Parsons. And further, the Court doth order and decree, That it shall be lawfull for the Lord Arch-Bishop of CANTERBURY, or the Lord Bishop of LONDON, for the time being, taking to him or them six other high Commissioners, to supply the place or places of those which are now already Printers by this Court, as they shall fall void by death, or Censure, or otherwise: Prouided that they exceed not the number of Twentie, besides His Maiesties Printers, and the Printers allowed for the Vniuersities.

XVI. *Item*, That euery person or persons, now allowed or admitted to have the vse of a Presse, and Printing-house, shall within Ten dayes after the date hereof, become bound with sureties to His Maiestie in the high Commission Court, in the sum of three hundred pounds, not to print, or suffer to be printed in his house or Presse, any booke, or bookes whatsoeuer, but such as shall from time to time be lawfully licensed, and that the like Bond shall be entred into by all, and euery person and persons, that hereafter shall be admitted, or allowed to print, before he or they be suffered to haue the vse of a Presse.

XVII. *Item*, That no allowed Printer shall keep aboue two Presses, vnlesse he hath been Master or vpper Warden of his Company, who are thereby allowed to keep three Presses and no more, vnder paine of being disabled for euer after to keepe or vse any Presse at all, vnlesse for some great and speciall occasion for the publique, he or they haue for a time leaue of the Lord Arch-Bishop of Canterbury, or Lord Bishop of London for the time being, to have or vse one, or more aboue the foresaid number, as their Lordships, or either of them shall thinke fit. And whereas there are some Master Printers that haue at this present one, or more Presses [than] allowed them by this Decree, the Court doth further order and declare, That the Master and Wardens of the Company of Stationers, doe foorthwith certifie the Lord Arch-Bishop of Canterbury, or the Lord Bishop of London, what number of Presses each Master Printer hath, that their Lordships or either of them, taking vnto them six other high Commissioners, may take such present order for the suppressing of the supernumerarie Presses, as to their Lordships, or to either of them shall seem best.

XVIII. *Item*, That no person or persons, do hereafter reprint, or cause to be reprinted, any booke or bookes whatsoeuer (though formerly printed with licence) without being reuiewed, and a new Licence obtained for the reprinting thereof. Always provided, that the Stationer or Printer bee put to no other charge hereby, but the bringing and leauing of two printed copies of the book to be printed, as is before expressed of written Copies, with all such additions as the Author hath made.

XIX. *Item*, The Court doth declare, as formerly, so now, That no Apprentices be taken into any printing-house, otherwise then according to this proportion following, (*viz.*) euery Master-Printer that is, or hath beene Master or vpper Warden of his Company, may haue three Apprentices at one time and no more, and euery Master-printer that is of the Liuerie of his Company, may have two Apprentices at one time and no more, and euery Master-printer of the Yeomanry of the Company may haue one Apprentice at one time and no more, neither by Copartnership, binding at the Scriueners, nor any other way whatsoeuer ; neither shall it be lawfull for any Master-Printer when any Apprentice or Apprentices, shall run or be put away, to take another Apprentice, or other Apprentices in his or their place or places, vnlesse the name or names of him or them so gone away, be raced out of the Hall-booke, and never admitted again, vpon paine of being for euer disabled of the vse of a Presse or printing-house, and of such further punishment, as by this Court, or the high Commission Court respectiuely, as the seuerall causes shall require, shall be thought fit to be imposed.

XX. *Item*, The Court doth likewise declare, that because a great part of the secret printing in corners hath been caused for want of orderly imployment for Iourneymen printers, Therefore the Court doth hereby require the Master and Wardens of the Company of Stationers, to take especiall care that all Iourneymen-printers, who are free of the Company of Stationers, shall be set to worke, and imployed within their owne Company of Stationers ; for which purpose the Court doth also order and declare, that if any Iourneyman-Printer, and free of the Company of Stationers, who is of honest, and good behauiour, and able in his trade, do want imployment, he shall repaire to the Master and Wardens of the Companie of Stationers, and they or one of them, taking with him or them one or two of the Master Printers, shall go along with the said Iourneyman-Printer, and shall offer his seruice in the first place to the Master Printer vnder whom he serued his Apprentiship, if he be liuing, and do continue an allowed Printer, or otherwise to any other Master Printer, whom the Master and Wardens of the said Company shall thinke fit. And euery Master Printer shall bee bound to imploy one Iourney-man, being so offered to him, and more, if need shall so require, and it shall be so adiudged to come to his share, according to the proportion of his Apprentices and imployments, by the Master and Wardens of the Company of Stationers, although he the said Master Printer with his Apprentice or Apprentices be able without the helpe of the said Iourneyman or Iourneymen to discharge his owne worke, vpon paine of such punishment, as by this Court, or the high Commission Court respectiuely, as the seuerall causes shall require, shall be thought fit.

XXI. *Item*, The Court doth declare, That if the Master and VVardens of the Companie of Stationers, or any of them, shall refuse or neglect to go along with any honest and sufficient Iourney-man Printer, so desiring their assistance, to finde him imployment, vpon complaint and proofe made thereof, he, or they so offending, shall suffer imprisonment, and such other punishment, as by this court, or the high Commission Court respectiuely, as the seuerall causes shall require, shall bee thought fit to be imposed. But in case any Master Printer hath more imployment then he is able to discharge with helpe of his Apprentice or Apprentices, it shall be lawfull for him to require the helpe of any Iourney-man or Iourney-men-Printers, who are not imployed, and if the said Iourneyman, or Iourneymen-Printers so required, shall refuse imployment, or neglect it when hee or they haue vndertaken it, he, or they shall suffer imprisonment, and vndergo such punishment, as this Court shall thinke fit.

XXII. *Item*, The Court doth hereby declare, that it doth not hereby restraine the Printers of either of the Vniuersities from taking what number of Apprentices for their seruice in printing there, they themselues shall thinke fit. Prouided alwayes, that the said Printers in the Vniuersities shall imploy all their owne Iourney-men within themselues, and not suffer any of their said Iourney-men to go abroad for imployment to the Printers of *London* (vnlesse vpon occasion some Printers of London desire to imploy some extraordinary Workman or Workmen amongst them, with preiudice to their owne Iourneymen, who are Freemen) vpon such penalty as the Chancellor of either of the Vniuersities for the time being, shall thinke fit to inflict vpon the delinquents herein.

XXIII. *Item*, That no Master-printer shall imploy either to worke at the Case, or the Presse, or otherwise about his printing, any other person or persons, then such onely as are Free-men, or Apprentices to the Trade or mystery of Printing, vnder paine of being disabled for euer after to keep or vse any Presse or Printing-house, and such further punishment as by this court, or the high Commission Court respectiuely, as the seuerall causes shall require, shall bee thought fit to be imposed.

XXIV. *Item*, The Court doth hereby declare their firme resolution, that if any person or persons, that is not allowed Printer, shall hereafter presume to set vp any Presse for printing, or shall worke at any such Presse, or Set, or Compose any Letters to bee wrought by any such Presse ; hee, or they so offending, shall from time to time, by the Order of this Court, bee set in the Pillorie, and VVhipt through the Citie of *London*, and suffer such other punishment, as this Court shall Order or thinke fit to inflict vpon them, vpon Complaint or proofe of such offence or offences, or shalbe otherwise punished, as the Court of high Commission shall thinke fit, and is agreeable to their Commission.

XXV. *Item*, That for the better discouery of printing in Corners without licence; The Master and VVardens of the Company of Stationers for the time being, or any two licensed Master-Printers, which shall be appointed by the Lord Arch-Bishop of CANTERBURY, or Lord B. of LONDON for the time being, shall haue power and authority, to take vnto themselues such assistance as they shall think needfull, and to search what houses and shops (and at what time they shall think fit) especially Printing-houses, and to view what is in printing, and to call for the licence to see whether it be licensed or no, and if not, to seize vpon so much as is printed, together with the seuerall offenders, and to bring them before the Lord Arch-Bishop of CANTERBURY, or the Lord Bishop of LONDON for the time being, that they or either of them may take such further order therein as shall appertaine to Iustice.

XXVI. *Item*, The Court doth declare, that it shall be lawfull also for the said Searchers, if vpon search they find any book or bookes, or part of booke or books which they suspect to containe matter in it or them, contrary to the doctrine and discipline of the Church of *England*, or against the State and

Gouernment, vpon such suspition to seize upon such book or books, or part of booke or books, and to bring it, or them, to the Lord Arch-Bishop of CANTERBURY, or the Lord Bishop of LONDON for the time being, who shall take such further course therein, as to their Lordships, or either of them shall seeme fit.

XXVII. *Item*, The Court doth order and declare, that there shall be foure Founders of letters for printing allowed, and no more, and doth hereby nominate, allow, and admit these persons, whose names hereafter follow, to the number of foure, to be letter-Founders for the time being, (viz) John Grismand, Thomas Wright, Arthur Nichols, Alexander Fifeild. And further, the Court doth Order and Decree, that it shall be lawfull for the Lord Archbishop of CANTERBURY, or the Lord Bishop of LONDON for the time being, taking unto him or them, six other high Commissioners, to supply the place or places of these who are now allowed Founders of letters by this Court, as they shall fall void by death, censure, or otherwise.

PROUIDED, that they exceede not the number of foure, set downe by this Court. And if any person or persons, not being an allowed Founder, shall notwithstanding take vpon him, or them, to Found, or cast letters for printing, vpon complaint and proofe made of such offence, or offences, he, or they so offending, shal suffer such punishment, as this Court, or the high Commission court respectiuely, or the seuerall causes shall require, shall think fit to inflict vpon them.

XXVIII. *Item*, That no Master-Founder whatsoeuer shall keepe aboue two Apprentices at one time, neither by Copartnership, binding at the Scriueners, nor any other way whatsoeuer, neither shall it be lawfull for any Master-Founder, when any Apprentice, or Apprentices shall run, or be put away, to take another Apprentice, or other Apprentices in his, or their place or places, vnlesse the name or names of him, or them so gone away, be rased out of the Hall-booke of the Company, whereof the Master-Founder is free, and neuer admitted again, vpon pain of such punishment, as by this Court, or the high Commission respectiuely, as the seuerall causes shall require, shall be thought fit to bee imposed.

XXIX. *Item*, That all Iourney-men-Founders be imployed by the Master-Founders of the said trade, and that idle Iourney-men be compelled to worke after the same manner, and vpon the same penalties, as in case of the Iourneymen-Printers is before specified.

XXX. *Item*, That no Master-Founder of letters, shall imploy any other person or persons in any worke belonging to the casting or founding of letters, then such only as are freemen or apprentices to the trade of founding letters, saue only in the pulling off the knots of mettle hanging at the ends of letters when they are first cast, in which work it shall be lawfull for euery Master-Founder, to imploy one boy only that is not, nor hath beene bound to the trade of Founding letters, but not otherwise, upon pain of being for euer disabled to vse or exercise that art, and such further punishment, as by this Court, or the high Commission Court respectiuely, as the seuerall causes shall require, be thought fit to be imposed.

XXXI. *Item*, That euery person or persons whatsoeuer, which shall at any time or times hereafter, by his or their confession, or otherwise by proof be conuicted of any of the offences, by this, or any other Decree of this Court made, shall before such time as he or they shall be discharged, and ouer and aboue their fine and punishment, as aforesaid, be bound with good sureties, never after to transgresse, or offend in that or the like kinde, for which he, or they shalbe so conuicted and punished, as aforesaid ; And that all and euery the forfeitures aforesaid (excepting all seditious schismaticall Bookes, or Pamphlets, which this Court doth hereby Order to bee presently burnt) And except such Bookes, as the forfeitures are already granted by Letters Patents, shall be diuided and disposed of, as the high Commission Court shall find fit. Alwaies prouiding that one moitie be to the King.

XXXII. *Item*, That no Merchant, Master, or Owner of any Ship or Vessell, or any other person or persons whatsoeuer shall hereafter presume to land, or put on shore any Booke or Bookes, or the part of any Booke or Books, to be imported from beyond the seas, in any Port, Hauen, Creek, or other place whatsoeuer within the Realme of England, but only in the Port of the City of London, to the end the said Bookes may there be viewed, as aforesaid : And the seuerall Officers of His Maiesties Ports are hereby required to take notice thereof.

XXXIII. *Item*, That whereas there is an agreement betwixt Sir THOMAS BODLEY Knight, Founder of the Vniuersity Library at *Oxford*, and the Master, VVardens, and Assistants of the Company of Stationers (*viz.*) That one Booke of euery sort that is new printed, or reprinted with additions, be sent to the Vniuersitie of *Oxford* for the vse of the publique Librarie there ; The Court doth hereby Order, and declare, That euery Printer shall reserue one Book new printed, or reprinted by him, with additions, and shall before any publique venting of the said book, bring it to the Common Hall of the Companie of Stationers, and deliuer it to the Officer thereof to be sent to the Librarie at *Oxford* accordingly, vpon paine of imprisonment, and such further Order and Direction therein, as to this Court, or the high Commission Court respectiuely, as the seuerall causes shall require, shall be thought fit.

FINIS.

Table of Cases Cited

Selected Bibliography

Records in Print

A. Arber, Edward, editor. *A Transcript of the Registers of the Company of Stationers of London 1554–1640 A.D.* 5 vols. London and Birmingham: Privately Printed, 1875–94.
   These volumes contain:
   The Charter of 1557.
   Wardens' Accounts, 1554–96 (from 1571 in summary only).
   Entries of Copies, 1554–1640 (except 1571–76).
   Enrollment of Apprentices, 1554–1605 (except 1571–76).
   Admission of Freemen, 1554–1605 (except 1571–76) in full, and listed to 1640.
   Calls to the Livery, 1560–1604.
   Fines, 1554–1605.
   Star Chamber Decrees of 1566, 1586 and 1637.
   Balances of Renter Wardens' Accounts, 1600–27.
   Letters Patent of 1603 and 1616 to the Company by James I.
   Ordinances of 1678, 1681 and 1683.
   Various contemporary letters, petitions, reports, proclamations, licenses, notes on printers, and other manuscript and printed material bearing on the book trade up to 1645.
B. *A Transcript of the Registers of the Worshipful Company of Stationers; from 1640–1708 A.D.* 3 vols., London: Privately Printed, 1913–14. (No editor named; cited in this study as Eyre & Rivington.)
C. Greg, W. W. and E. Boswell, editors. *Records of the Court of the Stationers' Company, 1576 to 1602.* London: The Bibliographical Society, 1930.
D. Jackson, William A., editor. *Records of the Court of the Stationers' Company 1602 to 1640.* London: The Bibliographical Society, 1957.

Legislative Materials

A. *England*

Cobbett, William. *Parliamentary History from the Norman Conquest, in 1066, to the year 1803.* 44 vols. London: T. Hansard. Vol. 17, 1813.

Firth, C. H. and R. S. Rait. *Acts and Ordinances of the Interregnum, 1642–1660.* 3 vols. London: H. M. Stationery Office, 1911.

Great Britain. *House of Commons Journals, 1660–1745.* vols. VIII, XI, XII, XIV, XV, XVI, XXI, XXIII, XXXIV. London: H. M. Stationery Office.

Great Britain. *House of Lords Manuscripts,* n.s., 1693–1695. vol. 1. London: H. M. Stationery Office, 1900.

Great Britain. *House of Lords Manuscripts,* n.s., 1697–1699. vol. 3. London: H. M. Stationery Office, 1905.

The Parliamentary or Constitutional History of England; being a faithful account of all the most remarkable transactions in Parliament, from the earliest times, to the restoration of King Charles II. By several Hands. 24 vols. London: Printed and Sold by T. Osborne and W. Sandby, 1751–1762.

B. *United States*

United States Copyright Office. *Copyright Laws of the United States of America, 1783–1962.* Washington: Government Printing Office, 1962.

Elliot, Jonathan. *The Debates in the Several State Conventions on the Adoption of the Federal Constitution. As Recommended by the General Convention at Philadelphia, in 1787. Together with the Journals of the Federal Convention.* 5 vols. 2d ed. Philadelphia: J. B. Lippincott Co., 1836.

General Works

Adams, George Burton. *Constitutional History of England.* New York: Henry Holt & Co., 1921.

Baker, Elizabeth Feaster. *Henry Wheaton.* Philadelphia: University of Pennsylvania Press, 1937.

Blagden, Cyprian. *The Stationers' Company.* Cambridge, Massachusetts: Harvard University Press, 1960.

Carr, Cecil T., editor. *Select Charters of Trading Companies.* vol. 28. Selden Society Publications. London: Bernard Quaritch, 1913.

Clyde, William M. *The Struggle for the Freedom of the Press from Caxton to Cromwell.* Oxford, England: Oxford University Press, 1934.

Collins, A. S. *Authorship in the Days of Johnson*. London: R. Holden & Co., Ltd., 1927.

Crosse, Gordon. *A Short History of the English Reformation*. New York: Morehouse-Gorham, 1950.

Dunton, John. *The Life and Errors of John Dunton*. 2 vols. London: J. Nichols, Son & Bentley, 1818.

Elton, Geoffrey Rudolph. *The Tudor Constitution*. Cambridge, England: Cambridge University Press, 1960.

Fox, Harold George. *Monopolies and Patents*. Toronto: University of Toronto Press, 1947.

Frank, Joseph. *The Beginnings of the English Newspaper, 1620–1660*. Cambridge, Massachusetts: Harvard University Press, 1961.

Greg, W. W. *London Publishing Between 1550 and 1650*. Oxford: The Clarendon Press, 1956.

Hazlitt, W. Carew. *The Livery Companies of the City of London*. New York: MacMillan & Co., 1892.

Hicks, Frederick C. *Men and Books Famous in the Law*. Rochester, New York: The Lawyers Co-operative Publishing Co., 1921.

Judge, Cyril Bathurst. *Elizabethan Book-Pirates*. Cambridge, Massachusetts: Harvard University Press, 1934.

Kirschbaum, Leo. *Shakespeare and the Stationers*. Columbus, Ohio: The Ohio State University Press, 1955.

Kitchin, George. *Sir Roger L'Estrange*. London: Kegan Paul, French, Trübner & Co., Ltd., 1913.

Leadam, I. S., editor. *Select Cases before the King's Council in the Star Chamber*. vol. 16. Selden Society Publications. London: Bernard Quaritch, 1903.

McKillop, Alan Dugald. *Samuel Richardson*. Chapel Hill, North Carolina: University of North Carolina Press, 1936.

Miller, Edwin Haviland. *The Professional Writer in Elizabethan England*. Cambridge, Massachusetts: Harvard University Press, 1959.

Mumby, Frank Arthur. *Publishing and Bookselling*. London: Jonathan Cape, 1931.

Ogg, David. *England in the Reign of James II and William III*. Oxford: The Clarendon Press, 1955.

Plant, Marjorie. *The English Book Trade*. New York: R. R. Bowker Co., 1939.

Pollard, A. W. *Shakespeare's Fight with the Pirates and the Problems of the Transmission of his Text*. Cambridge, England: Cambridge University Press, 1920.

Prothero, George Walter. *Statutes and Constitutional Documents, 1558–1625*. Oxford: The Clarendon Press, 1913.

Steele, Robert. *Tudor and Stuart Proclamations, 1485–1714*. 2 vols. Oxford: The Clarendon Press, 1910.

Thomas, Isaiah. *The History of Printing in America.* 2d ed. 2 vols. Albany, New York: J. Munsell, 1874.

Unwin, George. *The Gilds and Companies of London.* London: George Allen & Unwin Ltd., 1938.

Warren, Charles. *The Supreme Court in United States History.* 2 vols. Boston: Little, Brown & Co., 1926.

Articles

Aldis, H. G. "The Book Trade, 1557–1625," *Cambridge History of English Literature.* IV, 458.

Anders, H. "The Elizabethan ABC with the Catechism," *The Library,* 4th ser., XVI (1936), 32.

Blagden, Cyprian. "The English Stock of the Stationers' Company," *The Library,* 5th ser., X (1955), 163.

———. "Book Trade Control in 1566," *The Library,* 5th ser., XIII (1956), 290.

———. "The Stationers' Company in the Civil War Period," *The Library,* 5th ser., XIII (1958), 1.

Friendly, Henry J. "In Praise of Erie and of the New Federal Common Law," 19 *The Record of the Association of the Bar of the City of New York* 64 (1964).

Gray, W. Forbes. "Alexander Donaldson and the Fight for Cheap Books," 38 *Juridicial Rev.* 180 (1926).

Greg, W. W. "Entrance, License and Publication," *The Library,* 4th ser., XXV (1944), 1.

Hulme, E. Wyndham. "The History of the Patent System under the Prerogative and at Common Law," *L. Q. Rev.,* XII (April 1896), 141.

———. "The History of the Patent System under the Prerogative and at Common Law. A Sequel," *L. Q. Rev.,* XVI, (January 1900), 44.

McKerrow, R. B. "A Publishing Agreement of the Late Seventeenth Century," *The Library,* 4th ser., XIII (1932), 184.

Pollard, Graham. "The Early Constitution of the Stationers' Company," *The Library,* 4th ser., XVIII (1937), 235.

Shaaber, M. A. "The Meaning of the Imprint in Early Printed Books," *The Library,* 4th ser., XXIV (1944), 120.

Sisson, C. J. "The Laws of Elizabethan Copyright: The Stationers' View," *The Library,* 5th ser., XV (1960), 8.

Walker, J. "The Censorship of the Press During the Reign of Charles II." 35 *History,* n.s., 219 (1950).

Index

ABC, The: identified, 5; controversy over patent for, 103–104; 90

Act of 1653, 134

Actors, Peter: appointed royal printer by Henry VII, 81

Appeal of William Seres the Younger to Lord Burghley, 42–43, 64

Aston, Justice: opinion in *Miller* v. *Taylor* discussed, 170–171, 177

Author: rights of, discussed, 64–77; agreement with bookseller, 66–67; nature of conveyance to stationer, 73, 75, 76; copy returned to, 69; creative rights, 71, 77; relationship to stationers, 65, 66; right to payment from stationers, 68; right to stationer's copyright, 64–65. *See also* Statute of Anne

Baldwin, Justice Henry: opinion in *Wheaton* v. *Peters* discussed, 210–211

Barker, Christopher: notes on behavior of John Wolfe, 97–99; 36, 98. *See also* Printing patent

Barkstead, John, 134

Battle of the Booksellers. *See* Booksellers

Beckett, Thomas, 172

Bill, John: *History of Doctor Fulke's Answer to the Rhemish Testament*, 63, 68, 78; 73

Birkenhead, Sir John: Surveyor of the Press, 134

Bodley, Sir John, 138n

Bookbinders, 35, 44

Booksellers: monopoly of resented, 7, 13, 17; Statute of Anne designed to destroy monopoly, 14; Battle of the Booksellers, 15, 151–179; growing power of in sixteenth century, 45; and efforts to secure legislation, 154–158; litigation of, 158–179

Brotherhood of Stationers. *See* Stationers' Company

Burghley, Lord: Petitioned in 1582, 99; 100

Camden, Lord, 178

Caxton, William, 4, 20, 21, 22

Censorship: governmental policy, 6, 20; relationship to development of copyright, 21, 114–115, 143; arguments of Stationers in favor of, 128–130; efforts to secure new legislation, 138–143; objections to renewal of Licensing Act, 139–142

Censorship acts. *See* Star Chamber Decrees; Ordinances of 1643, 1647, 1649; Act of 1653; Orders of Lord Protector; Licensing Act of 1662

Charles II, 125

Charter: granted to Stationers' Company, 4, 27; reasons for grant, 29; confirmed by Elizabeth, 36

Commissioners concerning the Printers of London: appointed, 41

Common-law copyright: sought by booksellers, 15; author's common-law copyright promoted by booksellers, 153; recognized in *Millar* v. *Taylor*, 168–172; limited in *Donaldson* v. *Beckett*, 172–179

Conger, The, 151–152

Connecticut: copyright statute, 183, 186, 189

Printed in the United States
92705LV00003B/255/A